Just Wages for Church Employees

American University Studies

Series VII
Theology and Religion
Vol. 153

PETER LANG
New York • San Francisco • Bern • Baltimore
Frankfurt am Main • Berlin • Wien • Paris

Frank D. Almade

Just Wages for Church Employees

PETER LANG
New York • San Francisco • Bern • Baltimore
Frankfurt am Main • Berlin • Wien • Paris

Library of Congress Cataloging-in-Publication Data

Almade, Frank D.
  Just wages for church employees / Frank D. Almade.
      p.   cm. — (American university studies. Series VII, Theology and religion; vol. 153).
  Includes bibliographical references.
  1. Catholic Church—Employees.   2. Wages—Church employees.
  3. Wages—Religious aspects—Catholic Church.   4. Catholic Church—Doctrines.   5. Catholic Church—Doctrines—History.   I. Title.   II. Series.
  BX1919.A45   1993   241'.64—dc20   93-17331
  ISBN 0-8204-2126-X   CIP
  ISSN 0740-0446

Die Deutsche Bibliothek-CIP-Einheitsaufnahme

Almade, Frank D.:
Just wages for church employees / Frank D. Almade. - New York; Berlin;
Bern; Frankfurt/M.; Paris; Wien: Lang, 1993
  (American university studies: Ser. 7, Theology and religion; Vol. 153)
  ISBN 0-8204-2126-X
NE: American university studies / 07

BX 1919
.A45
1993

The paper in this book meets the guidelines for permanence and durability of the Committee on Production Guidelines for Book Longevity of the Council on Library Resources.

© Peter Lang Publishing, Inc., New York 1993

Printed in the United States of America.

TABLE OF CONTENTS

ACKNOWLEDGMENTS

"As each one has received a gift, use it to serve one another as good stewards of God's varied grace." (1 Peter 4:10)

Many, many people have helped me bring this book to completion. I am grateful to the teachers and administrators of the Bishop's Latin School and Duquesne University in Pittsburgh, and St. Mary's Seminary and University in Baltimore, who played such an important role in my intellectual and spiritual formation. In particular, I thank the faculty of the Department of Theology at Duquesne for the example of their excellent teaching and scholarship. My dissertation director, James P. Hanigan, guided me as a wise mentor with a critical eye and supportive hand.

I am grateful for the loving support I received from the staff of St. Mary of Mercy Parish, Pittsburgh, where I lived and worked while I did the research and writing for this book. They are church where it is difficult to be Christian: in the midst of a hectic downtown business district. They were tolerant of my absences, when I put on my play clothes to walk up the hill to the Bluff to do research, read and write. My companions in the rectory, John Kozar, Charlie Bober, Frank Glenn, Ron Lengwin, Frank Siler, and Frank Sokol, exemplified for me priestly service, hospitality, and humor.

Many people have gifted me with their skill and expertise. Evelyn Farnsworth, R.S.M., converted the 458 sheets of raw responses into manageable and intelligible data. David Wiehagen produced the tables and pie charts, and guided me through the jungles of Multimate Advantage and WordPerfect. The staff of the Duquesne University Library provided a congenial, disciplining cell in which to work, and assistance in abundance. John Flaherty gave solid advice in planning the workers' survey. Tom Tobin lent support with a "good housekeeping seal of approval" letter from the chancery. Jim Garvey was a wonderful listener and sounding board for my crazy ideas. Cathy Kroepil pointed out many errors with sharp proofreading. (Any errors, of course, that remain are mine.)

There have been many families who have sheltered and affirmed me during my pursuit of a doctorate. Elaine and David Wiehagen, Patty and Dick Flaherty, Cookie and Jim Thomas, Betty and John Reed, Elsie and John Florian, and Mary Ann and Jim Budd opened their homes and hearts to me along the way.

My Mafee friends are a wonderous gift from God: Maryjane Klein, O.S.F., Alice M. Kulikowski, Edward M. Reppa, and Eugene Bonacci, C.P. I love you with all my heart.

Finally, I dedicate this book to three workers who are its patron saints. My father, Frank Almade, steel mill clerk, and my mother, Mary Habjan

Almade, telephone operator and later janitress, have been quiet, steady, and loving examples of self-sacrifice in working for their sons' growth, education, faith, and future. They have shown me how commitment and generosity are synonyms of love. Joseph, husband of Mary and carpenter of Nazareth, has also been a patron of this project. His rough hands and just presence guided Jesus in learning the meanings of work, family, sacrifice, and love.

"Without cost you have received; without cost you are to give." (Matthew 10:8)

Permission to quote from David Hollenbach, *Claims in Conflict* (1979), and *Justice, Peace and Human Rights* (1988), is given by Paulist Press, 997 Macarthur Blvd., Mahwah, NY 07430. All rights reserved.

Frank D. Almade
Palm Sunday 1993
Incarnation Parish
Pittsburgh

INTRODUCTION

The right to a just wage is one of those issues in Catholic moral teaching which has been taught for a long time, but which few people today know or discuss. There has not been any substantial theological writing on this issue in over a generation. The need to discuss from an ethical perspective what employers pay workers for their labor is as acute as ever. However, the desire to ask this hard question is lacking today. John C. Haughey views it this way. "In our American culture money talks all the day long and faith is virtually silent. It's not like faith to be silent, but in the presence of money it has learned to accept a monologue."[1] As the first chapter tries to demonstrate, discussion of a just wage reaches deep into Christian tradition. It is a perennial question: what is fair when one person engages another to work for hire? The first two chapters of this dissertation attempt to recover the teaching on a just wage. There is a retrieval of what major moralists said on this subject up to 1891, and after the promulgation of *Rerum Novarum* that year, the teaching on the just wage in the papal, conciliar, and synodal documents of this century. The next chapter presents the theological roots of the right to a just wage. The dignity of the human person is fundamental to understanding human beings and their relationships in community. The right to a just wage is one among the constellation of all human rights, which identify the conditions of human dignity, as it is lived out in families, nation-states, and societies. The just wage always takes into consideration how compensation for work supports family life.

Chapter Three marks new ground. It uses the church's own words to turn its own valuable teaching in on itself. What is fair when *the church* engages workers for hire? This chapter examines in detail the few explicit texts from Catholic social teaching which discuss how the church should employ when it is an economic actor. The right to a just wage applies as well to men and women employed by the church. If the church is to teach justice, it must practice it as an employer.

In order to get a realistic picture of what church workers receive in cash compensation and in benefits, and under what conditions they work, the writer conducted a survey of certain parish workers in Allegheny County, in the Diocese of Pittsburgh. Chapter Four offers the results of the survey. It presents the data from the respondents in relation to government figures on workers in Allegheny County, in the Commonwealth of Pennsylvania, and in the United States. The wage figures are also compared to two different benchmarks for a reasonable standard of living. Comments volunteered by the respondents give expression to their feelings and some of the intangibles of working for the church.

The final chapter tries to use the history of the just wage, the magisterial teaching, critical commentaries, and survey data to present criteria for a just wage, for all workers, and in particular, for church employees. The criteria are expressed in twelve axioms. Two general themes run through the twelve axioms. Attempting to implement a just wage is both complex and a process.

Setting just wages involves juggling and judging many factors: the needs of the workers, the principles of church teaching, area standards of living, the local labor market, the church's financial ability to pay, and concern for the common good. A just wage is never about wages alone. At all times this complexity has to be acknowledged and faced. But one is not without resources. This is where process comes in. Justice demands a public system for the setting of wage scales, benefits packages, conditions of employment, steps for possible promotion, and grievance procedures. Justice also says that the process of setting a just wage includes the participation of the workers. A process without consultation and worker participation cannot claim to be just.

If the church is to retain its integrity as a voice for justice in economic affairs, it is essential to act in a just manner as an employer. The road to a just wage is a process of employment administration which is aware of the complexities of enacting social doctrine, marked by the participation of all who are affected, and committed to its implementation.

During the research for this volume it was not hard to notice the sexist language, both in the Latin and in translations of scholastic and magisterial documents. The translations as quoted have not been changed, for the purposes of historical accuracy. However, every attempt has been made to avoid sexist language in the text, and to be sensitive to gender issues in applying the right to a just wage.

NOTES

1. John C. Haughey, *The Holy Use of Money: Personal Finances in the Light of Christian Faith* (Garden City, NY: Doubleday, 1986), 1.

ABBREVIATIONS

AA	*Apostolicam Actuositatem*: Vatican II, Decree on the Apostolate of the Laity (1965)
AG	*Ad Gentes*: Vatican II, Decree on the Church's Missionary Activity (1965)
CA	*Centesimus Annus*: John Paul II, On the One Hundredth Anniversary of *Rerum Novarum* (1991)
CC	*Casti Connubii*: Pius XI, On Christian Marriage (1930)
CF	*Charter of the Rights of the Family*: Holy See (1983)
CIC/17	*Codex Iuris Canonici*: The Code of Canon Law (1917)
CIC/83	*Codex Iuris Canonici*: The Code of Canon Law (1983)
CP	*The Challenge of Peace: God's Promise and our Response*: U.S. Catholic Bishops (1983)
DH	*Dignitatis Humanae*: Vatican II, Declaration on Religious Liberty (1965)
DI	*De Iustitia in Mundo*: Synod of Bishops, On Justice in the World (1971)
DR	*Divini Redemptoris*: Pius XI, On Atheistic Communism (1937)
DSM	*De Sacerdotio Ministeriali*: Synod of Bishops, On the Ministerial Priesthood (1971)
EJA	*Economic Justice for All: Pastoral Letter on Catholic Social Teaching and the U.S. Economy*: U.S. Catholic Bishops (1986)
FC	*Familiaris Consortio*: John Paul II, On the Family (1981)

GS   *Gaudium et Spes*: Vatican II, Pastoral Constitution on the Church in the Modern World (1965)

LE   *Laborem Exercens*: John Paul II, On Human Work (1981)

MM   *Mater et Magistra*: John XXIII, Christianity and Social Progress (1961)

OA   *Octogesima Adveniens*: Paul VI, On the Eightieth Anniversary of *Rerum Novarum* (1971)

PC   *Perfectae Caritatis*: Vatican II, Decree on the Appropriate Renewal of Religious Life (1965)

PP   *Populorum Progressio*: Paul VI, On the Development of Peoples (1967)

PT   *Pacem in Terris*: John XXIII, Peace on Earth (1963)

QA   *Quadragesimo Anno*: Pius IX, On the Reconstruction of the Social Order (1931)

QAM   *Quod Apostolici Muneris*: Leo XIII, On the Evils of Socialism (1878)

QP   *Quamquam Pluries*: Leo XIII, On Devotion to St. Joseph (1889)

RH   *Redemptor Hominis*: John Paul II, On Human Redemption (1979)

RN   *Rerum Novarum*: Leo XIII, On the Condition of Workers (1891)

SL   *Sertum Laetitiae*: Pius XI, On the Anniversary of the American Hierarchy (1939)

SRS   *Sollicitudo Rei Socialis*: John Paul II, The Social Concerns of the Church (1987)

CHAPTER ONE

CHURCH TEACHING ON THE JUST WAGE

The question of a just wage for the church employee must begin with the wider issue of a just wage for every worker. This chapter is intended to examine what the church has traditionally taught about the just wage. It begins with general comments on work by selected Fathers of the church. During the medieval period Thomas Aquinas gave a foundation for theological analysis of the virtue of justice, which was used and applied by his scholastic successors. Three scholastic moralists who questioned the complacent acceptance of the common wage as a just price will be examined. The writings of two pioneers of the social movement within the Catholic Church, Cardinal Manning of England and Bishop von Ketteler of Germany, are next reviewed. Then there follows a review of the papal teachings and pronouncements on the just wage, beginning with Pope Leo XIII, through the Second Vatican Council, up to Pope John Paul II.

Through this chapter's review two dominant themes emerge. Remuneration for work should supply the basic and fundamental needs of the workers and their families, and the dignity of the human person grounds the right to a fulfilling human life.

The Fathers of the Church

The Fathers of the church were not directly concerned with the economy, any more than they directly addressed politics, class structure, or the arts. They did not directly address the justice of wages or remuneration for work, either. But in their eyes all human activities had a moral dimension, and therefore to the Fathers what *homo economicus* does was worthy of Christian reflection.

Tertullian wrote that the daily activities of the Christians are the same as those of the pagans.

> We do not fail to frequent the forum, the marketplace, the baths, the shops, the workshops, the inns, and your fairs, and to have all other relations in which our life with you in this world finds expression. With you we sail the sea, enter military service, work the land and trade in its fruits, just as we publicly sell for your use the products of our trades and labors.[1]

The ordinary work life of the Christians was criticized by the pagans. Patristic writers were constantly defending themselves against the charge of laziness. This was not a new charge. Tacitus criticized the Jews for idleness, citing their rest on the Sabbath and their fallow fields every seventh year.[2] Tertullian was much distressed when he heard pagans complain that Christians, too, were idle. The church order *Didascalia Apostolorum* said, "Be occupied in the things of the Lord or engaged upon your work, and never be idle," and "teach your children crafts that are agreeable and befitting to religion, lest through idleness they give themselves to wantonness."[3] In the fourth century *Apostolic Constitution*, one chapter was entitled, "The Idle Believers Must Not Eat." Several apostolic references are cited: fisherman Peter, leather workers Paul and Aquila, and farmers, who are the descendants of Judas, son of James.[4] Epiphanius said Christians must not be idle or sluggish, but work with their own hands, as Paul said, and if not, eat not. He cited Hebrew Scripture models: herdsman Abraham, Elijah, who provided for a poor widow and her son, the rich Job who worked constantly, and the proverb which warned against idleness.[5]

The reason why Christians were criticized for their seeming idleness was their understanding of the purpose of work. For the pagan, work was the path to wealth, and wealth was the path to luxurious (and sinful) idleness. For the Christian, work was to provide for the necessities of life. It was a human obligation. Several patristic texts repeated approvingly Paul's words, "If anyone was unwilling to work, neither should that one eat."[6]

In this regard, what was necessary was also seen as a virtue. Origen viewed labor as born from the will of God, who made human beings exercise their inventiveness and creativity by working in the world. People worked for their food, clothing, and shelter.[7]

What a laborer must do, in any occupation, was obey the religious and moral law. Even if in principle trades and professions are worthwhile in themselves, some were to be avoided because of the vice or illicit activities inherent in them. Ignatius said simply, "Flee evil acts." The Christian was to bring his faith to his work "by freeing them of dishonesty and the hateful fever for gain."[8] This was not easy, as commerce and trade were generally considered to be full of lying and cheating in negotiations. But it was considered to be possible. Clement of Alexandria stated:

> Because it is possible to hear divine wisdom, because it is possible to live, it is not impossible to conduct the affairs of the world in a fitting way in keeping with the laws of God. Then when buying or selling, let no one name two prices for the things he is purchasing or selling, but speak plainly and

honestly. If he loses something, he will at least gain in truth, and be the richer by an upright disposition.[9]

The fruit of one's work was that one avoided idleness, and therefore temptations to luxuries and frivolities.   In his homily on Hanna, John Chrysostom condemned the rich, not because they were rich, but because they were idle. There must be a moral purpose for the wealth and time at their disposal. In another homily, he attacked not the rich but those who use wealth badly. Unlike the rich, who are idle, he says, the poor keep busy. They lack leisure, and of necessity they are concerned with daily labor. They work and make a living so as to bring up a family. "I say this not to provide a defense for them but to show how much greater an accusation the rich deserve."[10]

In general, the Fathers condemned the unrestrained pursuit of wealth and the failure of the rich to contain their greed. Christians were to work for their daily bread. Excess wealth was to be shared with the poor in charity. Yet the Fathers never demanded unconditionally that rich Christians distribute everything that they possessed to the poor. Wealth itself was not condemned outright, only the failure to share wealth with the poor was condemned.[11] Ambrose expressed an extreme position when he concluded that since poverty and wealth are completely fortuitous, wealth cannot be seen as a reward for virtue nor poverty as a punishment for sins.[12] However, Ambrose's overall concern was that Christians avoid the temptation to avarice that came with being wealthy. What the Fathers in general counselled was virtuous labor and the just use of time and talent, which leads to holiness and true wealth in eternal life.[13]

Thomas and the Scholastics

Like the Fathers, Thomas Aquinas (1224-1274) did not deal directly with the just wage. But he was responsible for the classical breakdown of the divisions of justice: commutative, which regulates actions between private persons; distributive, which regulates actions by the social whole toward parts of the whole; and legal, which regulates actions by the parts of the whole toward the common good.[14] In the last one hundred years it has generally come to be recognized that the term "social justice" has a very close resemblance to the Thomistic term legal justice, and can be used synonymously.[15] For Thomas and for the scholastics, the question of the laborer's wage was contained in the doctrine of just price. The amount a farmer or merchant received for a product had to cover the cost of his labor and materials, as well as provide for his living expenses and that of his family. Thomas, unlike Aristotle, judged that profit, which is the reason for commerce, was not an evil thing in itself. Profit could be justified when directed to the needs of families and the public good, or given to help the poor.[16]

In his treatment of justice in buying and selling, Thomas followed Aristotle closely, as well as his contemporary, Albert the Great. Albert's basic principle was: justice demands that equality should reign in contracts of exchange.[17] Thomas pointed out that there are two methods of determining equivalence in the exchange, an equality of quantity or of work, and an equality of need satisfied, or utility.[18] In the first exchange, the determination of justice seems relatively simple. The price should be neither greater nor less than the value of a thing. But in the second exchange, the buyer has great need of an object and the seller places a price on the object which attempts to correspond with what the object was worth to him. The temptation of greed may move the seller to raise the price far above its customary value. Flynn says, "Obviously, the extra charge for loss must be proportionate to the seller's loss and not to the buyer's need. That the recompense cannot be mathematically determined any more than can the price of the thing itself is obvious."[19]

Thomas did not offer a precise formula to determine the just price. He warned us, "We cannot always fix the just price precisely; we sometimes have to make the best estimate we can, with the result that giving or taking a little here or there does not upset the balance of justice."[20]

Where is the "best estimate" to be found? Thomas, and most of the moralists who followed him, sought it not in an individual and arbitrary judgment (such as that of a prince, or other "objective" authority), but in a communal estimate. Determining this common estimate became one of the difficult, and key, elements in assessing a just price.

In the post-Thomistic development of the scholastic teaching on just price and just wage, several themes are prominent. They are equal pay for equal working capacity, to each according to his status, and concern for the common good.[21]

In analyzing the equality of the just price, scholastic writers looked at the contract between laborer and purchaser. This contract involved all three traditional divisions of justice. (Although a few scholastics add qualifications,[22] most saw no difference in the contract for a person's labor and the contract for the lease of a farm or farm animal.) Only later would there be emphasis on the principle that labor cannot be bought and sold like any piece of merchandise.[23] Commutative justice would apply in the simple sale, or contract, between two parties. The normal presumption was that the laborer was free to enter into the contract "in full ownership of his own abilities, entitled either to sell his labour power or (as when he enters religion) to give it away."[24] The worker must do an honest job to earn his or her pay.[25] Similarly, the employer is bound to manage competently, honestly and without coercion. The employer is not to engage in monopolistic practices, but manage his work and funds in order that workers have steady employment.

An important point is that the usefulness of one's labor is not judged against a particular job, but against the labor market as a whole.

> The right principle is equal pay for equal working capacity, not simply equal pay for equal work. Pay is to be related to the social value of the labour employed, not to its value to the individual employer, and the employer who underuses his labour force must pay its full price all the same.[26]

Why a social, not an individual, interpretation? Bernadino of Siena (1389-1449) explained:

> Equity was and is to be measured by reference to the common good, and as is expedient for the common good, for nothing is worse than to prejudice the common and universal good for the sake of particular and private advantage.[27]

This social perspective of an individual transaction was to be applied throughout the economy. The scholastics insisted on a framework of legal or social justice. If equity is observed, employer and employees will have created conditions so that the economy is robust and stable, with little unemployment.

> In the current terminology of economics, scholastic tradition asks that employees of any given trade should be paid at a rate equivalent to the true value of the marginal product of workers of that grade in their particular labour market, assuming that social as well as individual management is efficient and therefore that the market is free from monopoly, fraud, or other disorganization.[28]

A second aspect to the scholastic tradition was the understanding of stability (if not outright limitations on freedom) of particular classes of workers, which gives the opportunity "to earn enough to keep himself and his wife and children at the standard customary in his social class: also to meet any costs he incurs as a producer."[29] Earlier authors such as Henry of Langenstein (1340-1397) felt that any accumulation of surplus by a worker, beyond what was needed for present and future needs, was an expression of "damnable greed, desire for pleasure, and pride."[30] Later writers[31] were more open to upward mobility because of ability. They cautioned that there is no right to such a social move, and that all must be aware of human limitation and practice humility throughout.

Within this context of social stability, the worker was to fix his price, "that he may be able to manage and provide for himself and others according to his status."[32] This wage was "the expression of employees' status in the social order as a whole and a--indeed *the*--chief way of giving them the means to keep it up, and its rightness may be judged from this point of view as well."[33]

Here is an explicit link between upholding the social status of the worker, and the means to do so. To hold his status, the worker had to charge a wage sufficient for his natural needs, such as food, drink, clothing, housing, and upkeep of tools.[34] Implicit in the status quo for the worker is the worker's care for his family. The scholastic writers seemed to have presumed the context, and so the care, of the family for the worker. Yet Fogarty cautions that "it is only by a drastic forcing of texts that a specific doctrine of a family living wage can be read."[35]

The third concern of scholastic teaching on just wage was the common good. All individual contracts or issues of personal fulfillment were set within a social context, and placed within a societal effort. The worker has social obligations: to his family, to the poor, to the church, for taxes, and for community assistance.

Within this context, "justice resides in the price or wage structure more than in any individual rate."[36] Consumers are to restrain demands, so as to enjoy a lower and steadier cost of living. Those who are granted privileges, such as nobility or clergy, are also bound to serve the common good. The moralists are clear, too, that the economy is to be governed so as to offer its participants the best chance of high and secure real wages.

An exhaustive review[37] of 150 moralists in the century and a half prior to *Rerum Novarum* shows that only three offer wage doctrine which could support Leo's teaching: Benedict Stattler (1728-1797) of Germany, Augustine Lehmkuhl (1834-1918) of Germany, and Joseph Aertnys (1828-1915) of Holland. Each supports the idea of a living wage for the worker, and for his family.

For the most part, other moralists writing before *Rerum Novarum* only imply that a "family wage," or one sufficient for the support of worker and the worker's family, is necessary for justice. However, in many cases, the moralists have an outdated notion of the worker being a hired hand for a master who supplies the necessities of life. Often the moralists totally ignore the factory or industrial worker. They fail to define "wage," and give a brief rule of thumb such as "the just wage is whatever is commonly given," which is ambiguous and fails to deal critically with the morality of current practice. It often allows what is practice to be equated with what is morally right.

Let us look at the three moralists who were most explicit about a wage doctrine. Benedict Stattler wrote his *Ethica Christiana Communis* about

1790, after a career as a seminary and university professor. He established the obligation of a person to work as a social duty for the common good. Alone among nineteenth century moralists, he also held that the doctrine of work includes a right to employment. He proceeded to spell out how to measure the value of wages, the relationship of price to value, and how prices of goods and labor are interdependent and must be in conformity with the purpose of private property. Within the institution of private property, he said, there is the necessity that the exchange of goods and labor enable all to obtain "the necessaries and conveniences" of life. From this follows his General Rule:

> When the world's goods have all been privately appropriated, the first necessary precaution, in establishing prices of any goods and labor, is to prevent the necessaries of life and even the conveniences from being put beyond the reach of anyone willing to work conscientiously and usefully as far as his strength allows.[38]

Each person who wants to work should have the opportunity to do so. Prices are just when there is enough work available for those who seek it, and when goods can be purchased with the remuneration from work for one's basic needs.

A corollary follows: that private property stimulate the desire for people to perform skillful work in society. Those who sell things (the owners of private property) are not to set their prices so high that people are deprived of what is necessary for life. Also, prices are to be set in order to encourage people to pursue "the chief means of happiness: universal desire to work, prudent division of all necessary and useful labour, the perfection of each one's labours, and finally a balanced frugality in the use of good."[39]

In this argument Stattler did not refer to scripture or other theologians. It is an appeal to natural law. One cannot deprive laborers of the necessities of life. A wage that is just could ideally encourage more people to look for work. The operation of his chief moral rule required a balance between the cost of living and the buying power of the smallest wage. He tries to promote a difficult, yet possible equity--what would later be termed a just wage.

Augustine Lehmkuhl wrote in the mid 1880s, after a career as a teacher. His first edition of *Theologica Moralis* reviewed the obligation of most people to learn a trade (the rich are merely obliged to avoid idleness!); said that what was the norm of payment for work, by law or custom, would be considered as just; but also said, when calling for wage contracts to be free, that an employer is obliged to give a minimum just price always, even in a crowded labor market. In this last statement the moralist explicitly affirmed a "living wage" is justly due a worker, whatever the condition of supply of labor.[40]

In his third edition, published in 1886, Lehmkuhl added a section on workers in factories and their just wage. He was the first moralist to treat industrial wages. Healy outlines Lehmkuhl's conclusions in five points.

> I. Profit sharing is not the necessary solution; fixed wages, independent of the firm's profit and loss are admissible.
>
> II. The proximate norm of justice is the really free agreement between worker and master.
>
> III. The remote determination of the just payment is composed of many causes--wages and commodity prices are interdependent. Now the just price of goods depends on 1) the price of raw materials, 2) production expenses, 3) the master's income, corresponding to his industry and risk, 4) the wage of factory workers which *per se* should be such that (the total income permitting) an able bodied worker can fittingly support himself and his family according to his condition, or even be able to make a little savings from his wages. *Per accidens* it not infrequently happens that these amounts can without injustice fall below the *per se* just norm.
>
> IV. To secure the high profit to which they are accustomed and to offset unusual expenditure, wages may not be lowered below the otherwise minimum of justice.
>
> V. Since private competition is not able to preserve justice and charity, in the actual circumstances of today wages and prices must be regulated, if they cannot be wholly determined, by public authority.[41]

It is clear that Lehmkuhl's norm for a proper wage is a family wage. He also recognized that actual prices, profits and wages can without injustice stand at less than just levels. He offered no solutions to this paradox. Yet in this teaching he anticipated the thrust of *Rerum Novarum*.

The third moralist who offered new insights into wage doctrine was Joseph Aertnys. This Redemptorist taught moral theology for forty years, and near the end of his career published his *Theologia Moralis*. The first edition appeared in 1886, the second and revised edition in 1890. His first edition only repeated standard teaching of moralists of the day on wage norms: the employer has a duty to make full payment to a worker; the agreed to or customary salary is that which reaches at least the minimum payment usually given. This ambiguous phrase seemed to support a subsistence wage, and led to the conclusion that whatever happens in labor agreements is just.

But in his second edition he added one question, which almost every other moralist of his century failed to deal with. He asked, what are the obligations of masters to their workers, especially in factories? It was with this inquiry that the social question of the nineteenth century breaks into his teaching.[42] He replied to his question that the master has a duty to make a just payment. This is not one "on which the workers do not starve to death, rather it should be big enough so that they can live properly according to their condition."[43] Part of the worker's "condition" is his family. For support, Aertnys reached back to a fifteenth century writer, St. Antoninus of Florence, for support.

> The purpose of his payment [St. Antoninus wrote] should be that by it he can manage and provide for himself and his family according to his state; the purpose of supporting himself and his family should be that he can live virtuously; the purpose of living virtuously is the attainment of glory; as St. Augustine says, "the reason why everyone should pursue the good life is in order that he may be granted eternal life."[44]

This addition is significant for several reasons. In turning his attention to some practical applications in the second edition of his textbook, Aertnys showed that his thinking developed on this topic. He began to look at wages from the perspective of the moral obligation of the employer. Healy comments how unusual it was for moralists of that time to be influenced by the world around them. Secondly, he did not cite his fellow Redemptorist, St. Alphonsus Liguori, in this additional question. He rather justified his "new" teaching with another, much older, authority. Thirdly, he rejected a mere subsistence wage for workers, which by implication he understood was often being paid. Finally, in this case the virtue of justice was to be exercised not only toward the worker, but toward his family as well.

Manning and von Ketteler

Before plunging into the waters of papal pronouncements, it is necessary to take note of two men, prominent members of the hierarchy, who raised the attention of the teaching church to the concerns of the working classes, and, indirectly, to a living wage. They were Edward Cardinal Manning of Westminster and Bishop Wilhelm Emmanuel von Ketteler of Mainz.

Manning (1802-1892) had expressed concern for the poor and for workers earlier in life,[45] but it was only when he spoke as the highly respected Cardinal Archbishop of Westminster that his words became authoritative--and controversial.

In December 1872 he appeared in Exeter Hall in London on behalf of the Agricultural Labourer's Union, and by his appearance showed where his sympathies lay. In 1874 he spoke at the Leeds Mechanics Institute, on "The Dignity and Rights of Labour." This speech is an important guide to his thoughts, and worth examining.

In this address he defined labor as "the honest exertion of the powers of our mind and of our body for our own good and for the good of our neighbour."[46] In this labor "there is a true dignity," and the laborers "are entitled to all respect for the dignity of their state and of their work." The labor of mind and body with the created instincts of human beings advances society.

Furthermore, labor has all the rights of property. "There is no personal property so strictly one's own." Part of this is the freedom of workers to determine for whom they will work, and the right to say whether they can subsist on certain wages. Part of this is the right of labor to protect itself, especially through associations of those with common interest. Cardinal Manning traced the free association of workers back to the Greek and Roman civilizations, and found such unions "sound and legitimate" and "entirely in accordance with natural right and with the highest jurisprudence."[47]

Finally, Manning saw that the free exchange of capital is limited by the moral law. If family life is destroyed and the laborer reduced to a creature of burden by the oppressive hours or lowest wages, Parliament must step in to regulate for the common good. It has already done so, he said, in forbidding the employment of children before a certain age.

As had happened to others who argued for the rights of workers, Cardinal Manning was labeled a "socialist." In 1885, during an unemployment crisis, Manning denounced *The Times* of London for advocating that workers produce as much profit as possible so that employers would have enough money to engage more labor. He said at this time, "Every man has a right to work or to bread."[48] In 1888, the Cardinal stressed the fundamental right to life.

> A starving man has the natural right to his neighbor's bread. .
> . . The law of natural charity recognizes in each the same right
> to live and imposes on us all according to our power the
> obligation to sustain the life of others as we sustain our own.[49]

His argument was that providing work and food for the unemployed was not a whim of kindness. It was a right due in strict justice to the unemployed poor.

Cardinal Mannings's work was not confined to speeches. One year later, at age 82, he worked for over a month for reconciliation of the London dockers' strike. Two hundred thousand people were affected, including fifty thousand workers. Yet his success in resolving the strike before violence broke out only intensified his vision of growing numbers of the unemployed "starving in the midst of wealth and prosperity from which they are excluded."[50] His insight in 1874 that the worker's skills and efforts were "live money" or "the first capital" was captured in his maxim, "The living capital must eat; the dead capital can sleep."[51]

Bishop Wilhelm Emmanuel von Ketteler's place in the history of the social teachings of the Catholic Church was assured when, in a quotation often repeated, Pope Leo XIII said of him, "He was my great precursor in the labor field."[52] Ketteler (1811-1877) received that deserved accolade because of almost thirty years of work defending the poor and advancing the Catholic Church's concern for the worker.[53] Like Cardinal Manning, he urged a just wage for the worker, and through his writings set a context and attitude of concern which was to lead directly to Pope Leo's pronouncements on social reform.

Two issues from his formative years provide a backdrop to his social concern. The well known charity of his parents tempered his status as a member of the nobility. Later in life, at his consecration as bishop, he took a vow of poverty, and by all accounts lived it out in exemplary Christian charity. Secondly, during the time of decision after he had resigned his position as a government lawyer and before he was ordained a priest in 1844, he became associated with a circle of progressive Catholic thinkers. Led by writer Joseph Gorres and lawyer George Phillips, the intellectuals of Munich in their discussions opened von Ketteler to the possibilities of the church supporting social reform in the midst of an un-Christian state. Von Ketteler read church history through the works of Dollinger and Mohler, and recognized the church as a power in her own right, a power which was being cleverly neutralized by unfriendly forces in Germany. From this point von Ketteler grew convinced of the need forcefully to assert the rights and wisdom of the church, such that he later earned the sobriquet, "The Fighting Bishop."

Von Ketteler first received public attention when he preached at the funeral of two deputies to the Frankfort Assembly in 1848. He spoke of the need for social reform. It was not to come from the law or from a mob murdering public servants. It would come from hearing the cries of the poor and helpless, and seeing that "the Church alone possessed the key to the solution of the social question."[54] In von Ketteler's own words,

> here is only one means to put into actuality these great ideas and that is that we again turn to Him who gave the world such ideas, to the Son of God, Jesus Christ . . .[55]

Throughout his life he was to preach that the social question was first of all a matter of ethics. Only when the heart and soul were in the right place could right relations exist in society.

In six sermons given in Berlin later that same year, quickly published, and in a speech to the First General Conference of Catholics in Mainz, von Ketteler pursued the social question. He became a prophet and inspirer of the social movement among German Catholics. Two years later von Ketteler was named bishop of Mainz.

It was only years later that he addressed the economic and labor issues of the social question in a sustained way. In 1864 von Ketteler published *The Labor Question and Christianity*.

The bishop began by acknowledging the sad state of the worker and the worker's wage.

> The so-called labor problem is essentially a question of the worker's livelihood. Therefore it is first of all a question of providing for the basic needs: food, clothing, and shelter.[56]

He described the problems of the laborer in his industrialized country, and saw them growing worse. The economic problems were more important that the political ones, he said, because more people were involved. It was a matter of seeing clearly.

> The satisfaction of the material needs of the working class, the provision of all of the necessities of life for the worker and his family rests, with so few exceptions that it only proves the rule, on the working wage. . . . The truth of this proposition has been so well established . . . On the one hand, it reflects the plight of the worker; and on the other, it provides the keystone for evaluating all of the proposals for improving the condition of labor.[57]

Von Ketteler rejected "liberal" responses (unconditional freedom of trade and enterprise, cultural formation of the working class, certain worker organizations) and radical, socialist ones (state-funded capital, distribution of profits to workers). He found the causes of subsistence wages in unrestrained free trade and the dominance of capital, and rejected both as detrimental to the workers.

The trajectory of his analysis (for he proposed no practical solutions) can be seen in his understanding of private property. Again he rejected the extremes: on the one hand, the liberal position of unhampered right to gather and possess as much property as possible, with no communal responsibility, and on the other, the radical scheme of holding all goods in common, with no private property. He contended that the things of the world were made for the sustenance of all. Ownership is good, and indeed for some, essential to productive work. However, no property is without its responsibility. All property is to be held and used in light of God's purpose to sustain human beings through the goods of the earth. "When we speak of a natural right of ownership, there can be no question of time and complete proprietorship, but only of a usufructuary right."[58] He embraced the argument of Thomas Aquinas and claimed the ultimate reason for private property, understood in this way, is to build and preserve peace on earth.

Obviously this is a religious argument ("Property, like authority, has its deep and abiding roots in religion, in the living God, and in Christianity."[59]), but it is also one that speaks from natural law to common sense. The bishop asserted his right and responsibility to speak as a Christian leader to the terrible conditions of labor. He spoke for people in need.

Though strong in raising his voice in outrage with Christian principles, von Ketteler was weak in practical remedies. "I am satisfied to be able to contribute to awakening Christian charity toward a solution" to the labor question.[60] He called for experts in science, economics, and politics to propose the details. He did support some vaguely sketched versions of worker associations, unions, and cooperatives. He was uncertain on the role of the state. But the bishop also seemed to say that only committed Christians can bring about justice in the economic order.

> It is the spirit of self-denial and humility which Christianity alone engenders in men which can bring about in the working class the diligence, thrift, and contentment that are necessary for the genuine well-being of both workers and their employers; . . . Make no mistake about it, truly successful associations, . . . will only be possible among workers who are motivated by a living Christianity.[61]

In later years Bishop von Ketteler would modify his views on the state, encourage the use of credit unions for workers to raise capital, reject the exclusive role of the Catholic Church in solving the labor problem, and make specific proposals for workers. He was the prime motivator behind a national gathering of bishops for discussion of common interests, including the labor issues. The bishops of Germany met for the first time on September 1, 1869, at Fulda, to discuss the upcoming general council. Point eight on the agenda was, "The efforts of the Church to care for the factory workers, the journeymen, the apprentices and unemployed domestic servant women."[62] He came to believe in the need for parliamentary representation of Catholics, and his support was important to the founding of the German

Center Party, which over time enacted legislation which von Ketteler had proposed.[63]

Bishop von Ketteler stirred up historic awareness of human injustice to workers and a desire for change. Hogan summarizes his impact.

> If Ketteler deserves any credit at all for the social reform and the revised spirit in the Church of his day, it was because he was the person who, though he did not initiate the program, succeeded by perseverance to bring the German clergy [and Catholic people] back to a lively interest in the needs of the common laborer.[64]

Pope Leo XIII

The history of the church's social teaching, and its doctrine on just wages, shifts into a new gear with the writings of Pope Leo XIII. This former bishop of Perugia and papal diplomat was known as well-read and scholarly. His twenty-five year pontificate saw him issue 86 encyclicals, as well as many significant apostolic letters and *motu proprios*. His interest in social, economic, and political questions probably was aroused by his three years as nuncio to Brussels, 1843-46, where he encountered the advances in trade, technology, finance, and marketing that were to mark modern capitalism. Also

> the future Pope was able to see at first hand the problems of a new social disorder: wide unemployment, poverty, and general distress of the working class, squalid slums, and a feeling of hopelessness in the hearts of the propertyless workers.[65]

Camp's interpretation of Leo's pontificate is that Leo became convinced "that the previous Vatican policy [under Pope Pius IX] of unadorned opposition to modern society was no longer satisfactory."[66]

Pope Leo's concern for workers can be seen from the very beginning of his pontificate. In his second encyclical, *Quod Apostolici Muneris*, issued only ten months after his election, he addressed the bishops of the Catholic Church on the evils of socialism. He condemned those who reject obedience to God, marriage and the family, rightful ownership of private property, and the sovereignty of lawful rulers (QAM, 1).[67] At the same time he affirmed the responsibility of the church to speak on economic and political issues.

> But Catholic wisdom, sustained by the precepts of natural and divine law, provides with especial care for public and private tranquility in its doctrines and teachings regarding the duty of

government and the distribution of the goods which are necessary for life and use. (QAM, 9)

He urged the bishops to work with "artisans and workmen," who are easily lured by the specious hope of riches, so that they understand Catholic teaching and their place in divine and civil order. He even asked the bishops to encourage societies of workers "under the guardianship of religion." (QAM, 11)

This note of practical concern for workers would grow in later writings. For example, in a brief encyclical on devotion to St. Joseph, *Quamquam Pluries*, Pope Leo praised Joseph because "regularly by his work he earned what was necessary for nourishment and clothing [for Mary and Jesus]." (3) The work of the carpenter Joseph is an example of the dignity of work.

> It is, then, true that the condition of the lowly has nothing shameful in it, and the work of the laborer is not only not dishonoring, but can, if virtue be joined to it, be singularly ennobled. (QP, 4)

Human work, at whatever social level, has dignity.

But it is in his encyclical *Rerum Novarum* that Pope Leo XIII clearly expressed his teaching on the dignity of labor and the moral necessity for a just wage.

Leo began by acknowledging the need for addressing the terrible conditions of working people.

> We clearly see, and on this there is general agreement, that some opportune remedy must be found quickly for the misery and wretchedness pressing so unjustly on the majority of the working class . . . Hence, by degrees it has come to pass that working men have been surrendered, isolated and helpless, to the hardheartedness of employers and the greed of unchecked competition. (RN, 3)

He went so far as to say that these "covetous and grasping" and "very rich men . . . lay upon the teeming masses of the laboring poor a yoke little better than slavery itself." (RN, 3) What first must be done is "to save unfortunate working people from the cruelty of men of greed, who use human beings as mere instruments for money-making." (RN, 42) Human beings are not to be used. They are imbued with dignity that cannot be taken away, nor even given away. Human dignity demands that workers be treated justly (RN, 40).

Leo rejected the socialist response to the workers' "misery and wretchedness"--class warfare. Using the analogy of the body, he stated that

> in a State it is ordained by nature that these two classes should
> dwell in harmony and agreement, so as to maintain the balance
> of the body politic. Each needs the other: capital cannot do
> without labor, nor labor without capital. (RN, 19)

All have equal claim to the products of their labor. "In this respect all men are equal; there is no difference between rich and poor, master and servant, ruled and ruler."[68]

To clarify the foundation of the just wage, Leo stated two essential qualities of human labor. It is both personal and necessary. What the laborer does is his "exclusive property." (RN, 44) What the laborer does is also for self-
preservation. The exertion of strength and energy allows the laborer to obtain what is needed to support and preserve life. "If one man hires out to another his strength or skill, he does so for the purpose of receiving in return what is necessary for the satisfaction of his needs." (RN, 5) The pope is referring to a laborer who does not have any other resources, such as income-producing property or an inheritance, to provide for his basic needs other than the wages paid for the work done. Wages are what is given for him to live on. The laborer would be treated unjustly if forced to work for a wage insufficient for his needs. This is directly contrary to the purpose of work.

> It necessarily follows that each one has a natural right to
> procure what is required in order to live, and the poor can
> procure that in no other way than by what they can earn
> through their work. (RN, 44)

But Leo took the necessity of work further. He rejected the so-called Iron Law of Wages,[69] which said that wages, like prices, are determined in a free market by the random interaction of the buyer and seller, and the availability of goods. Leo said that if a worker has freely entered into an agreement to work, and the wages agreed upon are inadequate for the necessities of life, the employer is still obliged to pay a just wage. Strict contractual justice may be satisfied by the contract, but not the fuller justice that flows from human dignity. The pope stated that there is

> a dictate of natural justice more imperious and ancient than any
> bargain between man and man, namely, that wages ought not to
> be insufficient to support a frugal and well-behaved

wage-earner. (RN, 45)

For the employer to carry out the contract is not enough; the employee has a right to meet the needs of life, and he or she cannot sign away that right to life.[70]

When Pope Leo spoke of the sufficient remuneration for one's labor, he had in mind enough to support the worker in a reasonable and frugal manner.[71] This applied as well to the support of the worker's family. This support would permit the flourishing of the "society" of the family. Among the basic needs which Leo mentions are food, housing, clothing, physical well-being, provision for children and their rearing and education, opportunity to own property, and guarantees for the future.[72] These are not luxuries, but what human beings need in the practical order to express the innate dignity which is theirs. He could not put a specific monetary figure on these necessities, and he recognized that many (unnamed) factors were involved in the setting of full and just remuneration. (RN, 20) Nevertheless the rights of the family to basic needs were "at least equal" to the rights of the community, and were to be protected (RN, 20).

Justice in wages demanded both employees and employers own up to their responsibilities. The employee is to carry out fully the terms of his contract of hire, as was the employer. However, Leo was aware of the great abuses in shops and factories, and expressed his distrust of employers by treating the duties of employers in greater detail:

> The employer is bound to see that the worker has time for his religious duties; that he not be exposed to corrupting influences and dangerous occasions; and that he be not led away to neglect his home and family, or to squander his earnings. Furthermore, the employer must never tax his people beyond their strength, or employ them in work unsuited to their sex and age. His great and principal duty is to give every one what is just. (RN, 20)

The pope recognized that not always does the employer act in good faith. Workers have the right to form associations or unions to defend their just claims (RN, 49-51). Also, the state can and should protect the rights of working people. The poor and the powerless have a special claim to the state's protection (RN, 37-40).

In *Rerum Novarum* Pope Leo XIII built a solid foundation for the judgment of what constituted a just wage. It is the inherent dignity of the person that is the foundation of the worker's right to just remuneration for his or her labor. This dignity cannot be stolen or bargained away. The wage which a worker receives must meet minimum, practical, and basic needs, for the worker and the worker's family.

The two successors of Leo XIII, Pius X and Benedict XV, addressed the issue of the just wage in brief and minor texts.[73] They repeated Leo's words on a just wage. But they were leery of the radical claims of workers and the demands of Christian democrats. They felt the working class should be satisfied with the existing economic structure. They placed more importance on the role of charity, and passed over in silence the often deplorable conditions of industrial workers.

Pope Pius XI

In three important encyclicals, Pope Pius XI reiterated and developed the teaching of Leo XIII on the just wage. The first was in his encyclical on Christian marriage, *Casti Connubii*. He discussed the need for preparation for marriage, and for basic necessities for married couples. Then he said:

> And so, in the first place, every effort must be made to bring about that which Our predecessor Leo XIII, of happy memory, has already insisted upon, namely, that in the State such economic and social methods should be adopted as will enable every head of a family to earn as much as, according to his station in life, is necessary for himself, his wife, and for the rearing of his children . . . To deny this, or to make light of what is equitable, is a grave injustice . . .; nor is it lawful to fix such a scanty wage as will be insufficient for the upkeep of the family in the circumstances in which it is placed. (CC, 117)

Pius is explicitly calling upon the work of Leo to support his statement. He sees a just wage as that which supports both the head and members of the household. This is a practical necessity, essential to the human working out of God's plan in a couple's marriage.

Pius' most important contribution came in his encyclical *Quadragesimo Anno*. It was issued in the midst of the great worldwide Depression, and was an attempt at expressing a blueprint for action, a Christian program for the establishment of justice for the working class. The pope used the occasion of the fortieth anniversary of *Rerum Novarum* to issue the encyclical. In this way he enthusiastically acknowledged the importance of Leo's writings on social and economic questions. He called Leo's 1891 letter the "Magna Charta" of all Christian social activity (QA, 39). He reiterated the fundamental dignity of the human person. This is the foundation for the Church's understanding of how society is to be ordered (QA, 28; DR, 29).

On several issues, Pope Pius repeated the teachings of Leo: the right to own property; the twin characteristics of property, individual and social; the obligations of those with superfluous income; the mutual, supportive, and interlocking roles of capital and labor; the rejection of violence to resolve workers' injustices; and the principle of just distribution of goods (QA, 44-58). All of these are built on the dignity of the human person, who is always considered in society. One of the ways this dignity is expressed is in labor. In the words of an important commentary on Pope Pius XI, "Work is a constituent element of the human person in his economic activity."[74] When work is oriented toward the proper end or goal, namely God, we see its inherent dignity.

> Nor is it to be thought that gainful occupations are thereby belittled or judged less consonant with human dignity; on the contrary, we are taught to recognize in them with reverence the manifest will of the Divine Creator Who placed man upon the earth to work it and use it in a multitude of ways for his needs. (QA, 136)

Because of this human dignity, "the worker must be paid a wage sufficient to support him and his family." (QA, 71) When the dignity is ignored, or when the social and individual character of work is neglected, it will be very difficult, if not impossible, to pay a worker justly. Considering the needs of the worker and his family is the first factor in the payment of a just wage.

Pius saw two other factors involved in determining the just wage. The fiscal situation of the business must be considered. Workers cannot demand excessive wages, which may force a business to fail. However, mismanagement, lack of energy or initiative, or indifference to technical progress are not sufficient reasons to lower wages below what is just. Employees, employers, and public authorities need to work together. If outside forces cause a business to fail, or to make so little profit that managers cannot pay a just wage, "those who are thus the cause of the injury are guilty of grave wrong." (QA, 72)

The third factor to be considered in setting the just wage is the common good. The pope acknowledged how the lowering or raising of wages and salaries can affect the rate of unemployment. Part of the common good is that those who are able and want to work should be given the opportunity. Unemployment is an "evil," and has far ranging effects. Therefore it is "contrary to social justice" for wages to be raised or lowered for mere personal gain and without concern for the common good (QA, 74-75).

The concern for the common good is a special characteristic of this pope's teaching on the just wage.[75] He saw the wage in tension with the needs and demands of particular businesses, and with the competing interests and occupations of the whole social economy. His use of the term "social justice" presumed the possibility, even the necessity, of change at the level of both the individual and society.

> Still, in order that . . . what remains to be done may be accomplished, and that even more copious and richer benefits may accrue to the family of mankind, two things are especially necessary: reform of institutions and correction of morals. (QA, 77)

In Pius's worldview, society is not static, and change in economic affairs is possible, and necessary. This was true in a particular way at the level of social institutions. All change that happens must respect the "most weighty principle" of subsidiarity.

> Just as it is gravely wrong to take from individuals what they can accomplish by their own initiative and industry and give it to the community, so also is it an injustice and at the same time a grave evil and disturbance of right order to assign to a greater and higher association what lesser and subordinate organizations can do. (QA, 79)

Each level of society is to be respected for what it can contribute to the common good. All levels need to work together in harmony. These elements of the whole social fabric are to be guided by social justice. To promote cooperation among different industries and professions, Pius encouraged the formation of guilds and free associations.[76]

The pontiff also saw a positive role for the state. He supported Leo's understanding that civil authority is not merely to guard the law, but to encourage and support the welfare of all, with "chief consideration . . . to be given to the weak and the poor." In his encyclical on atheistic communism, *Divini Redemptoris*, he stated that

> Catholic doctrine vindicates to the state the dignity and authority of a vigilant and provident defender of those divine and human rights. (DR, 33)

Here again, the pope acknowledged the human rights of workers, including the right to a just and family wage, which flow from the dignity of the human person. The pope condemned all elements in the world economic system which reject "the human dignity of the workers, the social character of economic activity and social justice itself, and the common good." (QA, 101) Labor is not a commodity, nor can it be. Strict adherence to contracts, or the letter of commutative justice, is not enough.

> But social justice cannot be said to have been satisfied as long as workingmen are denied a salary that will enable them to secure proper sustenance for themselves and their families; as long as they are denied the opportunity of acquiring a modest fortune and forestalling the plague of universal pauperism; as long as they cannot make suitable provision through public or private insurance for old age, for periods of illness and unemployment. (DR, 52)

In his commentary on *Quadragesimo Anno*, Oswald von Nell-Breuning saw the call for a salary adequate to support both the worker and his family as absolute and a demand of social justice. He wrote:

> The public in such a community contradicts social justice until conditions have been changed so that a family wage can be paid . . . to every adult worker.[77]

Pope Pius XI recognized that several factors would have to be taken into consideration when judging what would be a just wage. But only when such a wage is paid was justice met.

It is important to note that throughout his writings on a just wage Pius distinguished between that due in justice and that given in charity. Social charity is a key principle of the economic life of society, and it is necessary for the fuller "union of minds and hearts." But "no . . . charity can substitute for justice which is due as an obligation and is wrongfully denied." (QA, 137) He stated in *Divini Redemptoris*:

> A "charity" which deprives the workingman of the salary to which he has a strict title in justice, is not charity at all, but only its empty name and hollow semblance. The wage-earner is not to receive as alms what is his due in justice. And let no one attempt with trifling charitable donations to exempt himself from the great duties imposed by justice. (DR, 49)

Pope Pius XII

In numerous talks and addresses, Pope Pius XII continued the teaching of his predecessors on the living wage. Although he never wrote a sustained and lengthy examination of the social question, he often raised particular issues in his speeches. He reasserted the foundational principle of the dignity of the human person. This dignity is concretely expressed through rights and duties, in a "community of morally responsible citizens."[78]

In his encyclical on the one hundred fiftieth anniversary of the establishment of the hierarchy in the United States, *Sertum Laetitiae*, Pope Pius spoke about the social question in America.

> Now if the rich and the prosperous are obliged out of ordinary motives of pity to act generously towards the poor their obligation is all the greater to do them justice. The salaries of the workers, as is just, are to be such that they are sufficient to maintain them and their families. (SL, 36)

He then repeated the words of Pius XI from *Quadragesimo Anno* on the need for a family wage from the teaching on social justice. He also called for reforms in circumstances when a just wage was not being guaranteed.

In his radio address on the feast of Pentecost, 1941, Pius celebrated the fiftieth anniversary of *Rerum Novarum*. He repeated Leo's instruction on the two characteristics of work, namely, that work is both personal and necessary. Labor is personal because a particular human being carries it out. Labor is necessary to secure what is indispensable for life. In this way "man has a natural, grave, individual obligation to maintain life." From these two attributes, and the profound obligation to sustain life, it follows that each individual has the right to use work to provide for oneself and one's children. For each person, as a living being with the gift of reason, can and must exercise "the fundamental right to make use of the material goods of the earth."[79]

In an important Christmas address, the Holy Father examined the basic principles of the internal order of nations, which he viewed as prerequisites for lasting international peace. He had heard the "agitation and bitter conflict" of the labor movement of the past one hundred years, and understood the desire for justice.

> What man, and especially what priest or Christian, could remain deaf to the cries that issue from the depths and call for justice ... in a world ruled by a just God?[80]

His foundation for justice was the dignity of the human person, and the right which flows from this natural foundation to make use of the goods of the earth. To prevent a worker from using such goods, or as the pope expressed it, to have "a worker . . . condemned to an economic dependence and slavery" is irreconcilable with his rights as a person.

What did Pius see as fundamental personal rights? They are: the right to grow and develop physically and spiritually; to worship in private and in public; to marry and carry out married life; to work, and so maintain a family; to choose one's state in life freely; to use material goods. Work stands out among these rights, as the "indispensable means toward gaining over the world that mastery which God wishes." Work has its own noble dignity. From its dignity is the practical conclusion for "a just wage which covers the needs of the worker and his family."[81] A social order which provides a just wage will also promote the opportunity for higher education for one's children, a spirit of good will in each neighborhood, and a sense of human solidarity with the various classes and peoples of a nation. In an address to Italian workers in 1943, Pope Pius spelled out clearly that a just salary makes it possible

> for the parents to fulfil their natural duty to rear healthily
> nourished and clothed children; a dwelling worthy of human
> persons; the possibility of securing for the children sufficient
> instruction and a becoming education; of foreseeing and
> forestalling times of stress, sickness and old age.

These rights which flow from human dignity must be seen in the context of society. Pope Pius XII was wary of the individualism of the age. He saw each worker within the national economy, with workers' rights supported by the laws of the state. He said, "The whole complex structure of society is in need of adjustment and improvement."[82] No individual worker would attempt to secure his or her own rights by destroying the rights of others. Every working person recognized his or her place in society by observing

> respect for the human person in all men, no matter what their
> social position; acknowledgment of the solidarity of all people
> in forming the human family; and the imperative demand on
> society to place the common good above personal gain, the
> service of each to all.[83]

The successors of Pius XII would offer further insights and guidelines for constructing the structures and relationships for work within society, and indeed, the world community of nations.

Pope John XXIII

Pope John XXIII contributed substantially to the development of Catholic social teaching with two important encyclicals, *Mater et Magistra* and *Pacem in Terris*. He continued to assert the dignity of the human person, while acknowledging and explicating the growing interdependence of individuals and nations, and complexity in their various relations. He used the language of human rights to determine the conditions for upholding human dignity. He supported the right to a just wage as an essential human and economic right.

Following the example of his predecessors, Pius XI and Pius XII, John celebrated the anniversary of *Rerum Novarum* in 1961 with a substantial text on the economic and social questions of the day. He praised Leo's work as "magnificent," "outstanding," and having "universal acclaim." (MM, 7-8) The first two sections of *Mater et Magistra* repeat and affirm basic elements of *Rerum Novarum*'s teaching. The fundamental principle of all Catholic social teaching is clearly stated.

> [Catholic social] teaching rests on one basic principle: individual human beings are the foundation, the cause and the end of every social institution. This is necessarily so, for men are by nature social beings. This fact must be recognized, as also the fact that they are raised in the plan of Providence to an order of reality which is above nature. On this basic principle, which guarantees the sacred dignity of the individual, the Church constructs her social teaching. (MM, 219-220)

In the reconstruction of the social order according to this principle, the first major question Pope John addressed is work. It is a human activity, and therefore it is not a commodity or property. Marketplace forces do not determine work's worth or remuneration; the laws of justice and equity do (MM, 18). Work is, in most cases, the sole means of livelihood for a worker and his family. This becomes important in judging the value of work.

Pope John takes this thought further when he says a human "right and duty to be primarily responsible for his own upkeep and that of his family" is an essential personal right (MM, 55). He recognizes with sadness the millions of workers around the globe who are "condemned through the inadequacy of their wages to live with their families in utterly sub-human conditions." (MM, 68) Also, he knows the disparities within so many countries, of a privileged few living in luxury next to the severe poverty of the majority. In some countries this condition was a result of industrialization in its infancy; in others it was because the desire for national prestige or more and greater weapons outstripped the desire for social justice.

In response to these conditions, John repeated the papal expression of the right to a just wage.

> We therefore consider it Our duty to reaffirm that the remuneration of work is not something that can be left to the laws of the marketplace; nor should it be a decision left to the will of the most powerful. It must be determined in accordance with justice and equity; which means that workers must be paid a wage which allows them to live a truly human life and to fulfill their family obligations in a worthy manner. (MM, 71)

In keeping with the greater sophistication of the economic thinking in *Mater et Magistra*, John recognized that the right to a just wage does not automatically or easily specify a particular amount of money. It must be determined in each locale, with due regard for the historical and social factors of each country. Several concerns are involved: the contribution of each individual worker to the economy; the financial state of the worker's company; the situation of the whole working force of the particular country; and "the requirements of the common good of the universal family of nations of every kind, both large and small." (MM, 71)

This respect for the historical and international socio-economic factors involved is characteristic of *Mater et Magistra*. John was well aware of the multiplication of social relationships in the world, "that is, a daily more complex interdependence of citizens." (MM, 59) Hollenbach paraphrases Pope John: "Society, in other words, is becoming more dense and interlocking. Human interrelations are governed by a highly complex and interrelated set of structures."[84]

One of these important and growing social structures is government. Government's role is to protect the rights which flow from human dignity.

> It is furthermore the duty of the State to ensure that terms of employment are regulated in accordance with justice and equity, and to safeguard the human dignity of workers by making sure that they are not required to work in an environment which may prove harmful to their material and spiritual interests. (MM, 21)

Where there is inequality in the standards of living, or working conditions, or rates of employment, governmental authorities are to work with other agencies and private enterprise to eliminate or reduce imbalances.

Workers are to participate as well in the businesses and industries in which they work. The pope did not want to give hard and fast rules. He did encourage cooperation, understanding, and good will, which can lead to "a true human community" of employers and employees.

The lengthy and specific economic focus of *Mater et Magistra* is given a strong theoretical structure in Pope John's final encyclical, *Pacem in Terris*. In this highly regarded systematic document, the pope articulates the understanding of human rights as the basis for international peace. Central to this theory is the most basic principle of Catholic social theory, the dignity of the human person.

> Any well-regulated and productive association of men in society demands the acceptance of one fundamental principle: that each individual man is truly a person. His is a nature, that is, endowed with intelligence and free will. As such he has rights and duties, which together flow as a direct consequence from his nature. These rights and duties are universal and inviolable, and therefore altogether inalienable. (PT, 9)

Human dignity, and the rights and duties which are expressions of it, is supported in a multitude of relationships: between persons, between individuals and public authorities, between states, and among nations within the world community.

Pope John then detailed the rights which are integral to human beings. It is the most comprehensive list of rights in Catholic social teaching. The list draws from all the major documents since Leo XIII. It expresses rights related to life and a human standard of living, moral and cultural values, religious activity, family life, assembly and association, freedom of movement, and economic and political rights (PT, 11-27). One of the specific economic rights is to a just wage.

> The worker is likewise entitled to a wage that is determined in accordance with the precepts of justice. This needs stressing. The amount a worker receives must be sufficient, in proportion to available funds, to allow him and his family a standard of living consistent with human dignity. (PT, 20)

Each human right also has its concomitant duty. To every human right there corresponds the duty that this right be respected by the subject of the right himself or herself, by other individual persons, and by society. Pope John expressed the need for mutual collaboration.

> Since men are social by nature, they must live together and consult each other's interests. That men should recognize and perform their respective rights and duties is imperative to a well ordered society. But the result will be that each individual will

make his whole-hearted contribution to the creation of a civic
order in which rights and duties are ever more diligently and
more effectively observed. (PT, 31)

Pacem in Terris notes as well that human beings must enjoy freedom
in thought and action in order to carry out rights and duties.

As in past papal documents, government is seen as a guarantor of the
rights of people. Civil authorities must make sure that rights "are
recognized, respected, coordinated, defended and promoted." (PT, 60)
Among the specific economic rights to be protected and encouraged is the
right to a just wage in useful work.

The government is also required to show no less energy and
efficiency in the matter of providing opportunities for suitable
employment, graded to the capacity of the workers. It must
make sure that working men are paid a just and equitable wage,
and are allowed a sense of responsibility in the industrial
concerns for which they work. (PT, 64)

The common good requires not just the mere expression of support for
rights, but also that government concretely take steps to promote these rights.
It is in the interest of the common good that wages be just, in accord with
human dignity, and that those who deserve work are able to find
employment.

Throughout Pope John's treatment of human rights there is the
insistent understanding of the interdependence of all persons, communities,
and nations. Respect for dignity can only happen in a "community of
morally responsible persons," to use Pius XII's phrase. Interdependence is
expressed both among persons and among nations. Hollenbach says,

the rights which protect human dignity, therefore, are the rights
of persons *in* community. They are neither exclusively the
rights of individuals against the community nor are they the
rights of the community against the individual.[85]

During his pontificate, Pope John XXIII continued to defend the right
to a just wage for the worker and the worker's family in both his major
social encyclicals. One sees the wealth of concern by the Pontiff for workers
and for justice in national and international economic systems in *Mater et
Magistra*. In *Pacem in Terris* the specific economic right to a just wage is
renewed within a systematic treatment of the rights and duties due to all
human beings. These are firmly rooted in basic human dignity. Further, the
interdependence of all people, including workers, is stressed. The demands

for just structures must always take into account the various relations of individuals, communities, and nations.

Pope John's optimism could see "a progressive improvement in the economic and social conditions of working men" as a characteristic of his day (PT, 40). Yet he also knew that the work of justice is a constant endeavor. "Daily is borne in on us the need to make the reality of social life conform better to the requirements of justice." (PT, 155) His social teaching would be continued by the ecumenical council he called, Vatican II, and by his successor, Pope Paul VI.

Vatican Council II

The teaching of Pope John XXIII and his predecessors on the dignity of the human person and the right to just remuneration can be seen in two documents of the Second Vatican Council.

In the Declaration on Religious Freedom, *Dignitatis Humanae*, the Fathers of the Council acknowledged the world's growing appreciation of human dignity and stated their intention to explain its relation to Christian doctrine.

> A sense of the dignity of the human person has been impressing itself more and more deeply on the consciousness of contemporary man.
> . . . This Vatican Synod takes careful note of these desires in the minds of men. It proposes to declare them to be greatly in accord with truth and justice. . . . In taking up the matter of religious freedom this sacred Synod intends to develop the doctrine of recent Popes on the inviolable rights of the human person and on the constitutional order of society. (DH, 1)

The Fathers of the Council want all men and women to see what is essential to each human being: God-given, inviolable dignity. This dignity is to be affirmed in the language of law and government, and in the language of Christian teaching. Human dignity must be upheld for the order within nations and society to be just and true.

The document develops its argument for religious liberty in Chapter II by building upon the social teachings of the popes, beginning with Leo XIII. The foundation for religious freedom, and for all human rights, "has its foundation in the very dignity of the human person, as this dignity is known through the revealed Word of God and by reason itself." (DH, 2) This concern for the dignity of the person marks and unites the entire document.[86]

Human dignity is also the core concern in the Pastoral Constitution on the Church in the Modern World. In *Gaudium et Spes* the Council Fathers were at pains to reach out to all people, especially those who oppose the church. They wrote, "The Church knows that her message is in harmony with the most secret desires of the human heart when she champions the dignity of the human vocation." (GS, 21) Certain basic rights and duties result from human dignity. In article 26 the document summarizes several of these rights. Among those things needed are food, clothing, shelter, education, and work. These human rights are due to all. They are to be respected by all governments, whatever their ideology. In a special way Christians must come to see that hard work is needed to make real the full human life these rights point to. "The ferment of the gospel, too, has aroused and continues to arouse in man's heart the irresistible requirements of his dignity."

In the section on socio-economic life, the Council affirmed past teaching that labor is personal, and superior to the capital or goods which are produced. Labor is the ordinary way by which one supports self and family. Labor allows human beings to participate in the work of God the Creator, to bring the world to perfection. Jesus himself worked with his hands as a carpenter at Nazareth, to support himself and his mother.

In an important assertion, the Council insisted that society is obliged to find suitable employment opportunities for its citizens. Society must "work" at finding jobs; in like manner, each worker must carry out his or her duties faithfully. Then the document states:

> Finally, payment for labor must be such as to furnish man with the means to cultivate his own material, social, cultural, and spiritual life worthily, and that of his dependents. What this payment should be will vary according to each man's assignment and productivity, the conditions of his place of employment, and the common good. (GS, 67)

With this statement the Vatican Council affirms past papal teaching on the just wage. Each person on the earth has a certain inviolable dignity. There are basic needs which are necessary to uphold human dignity. The primary way that individuals and families are provided with these basic human necessities is through the exertion of a worker. Each jobholder is to be faithful to the duties assigned him or her. In return, the Council says, each worker in justice is entitled to receive a wage which will allow him or her to provide the essential human needs for self and family.

In article 71, *Gaudium et Spes* acknowledged that in underdeveloped countries around the world there are large estates where workers are hired for a pittance. They are not given what is necessary to uphold their worth as human beings, or to give them an opportunity for personal initiative and advancement. Where there is such "personal servitude," reforms are to be initiated to increase wages, improve working conditions, provide job security and offer the opportunity for advancement. This call for reform shows the seriousness with which the Council Fathers upheld human dignity and the basic rights inherent to human beings. They call for Christians to use their skills in the socio-economic order for justice and for charity, to build up human prosperity and world peace. Indeed, Christians are to be exemplary in bringing justice and the right order of human values in the world to perfection.

Pope Paul VI

The pontificate of Pope Paul VI continued the work of the Second Vatican Council, begun by Pope John XXIII, and the development of Catholic social teaching. In his two major documents on social matters, the encyclical *Populorum Progressio* and the apostolic letter *Octogesima Adveniens*, he emphasized the interdependence of nations. He stressed the need for coordination by all nations in social and economic development. Rich nations had to be aware that "the hungry nations of the world cry out to the peoples blessed with abundance." (PP, 3)

The pope stood firmly on the shoulders of his predecessors in upholding the principle of human dignity. He was especially concerned that this principle be seen from the perspective of nations increasingly interconnected. He pointed out that dignity is not limited to economic development. To be authentic, development must foster the growth of the whole person (PP, 14). This includes the basic material needs of life: freedom from oppressive political structures and exploitation by employers; and the opportunity to pursue and "enjoy the higher values of love and friendship, of prayer and contemplation." (PP, 20) Hollenbach summarizes the pope.

> Material well-being is not simply instrumental in value. It is not a means of dignified life. It is, rather, *integral* to the standard of all moral value, human dignity. . . . It is thus that *Populorum Progressio* can draw a firm conclusion that the development of persons must simultaneously include progress on the material level and greater realization of the higher values of human existence.[87]

Within this understanding of "integral" development, Pope Paul breaks no new ground in labor issues. In *Octogesima Adveniens*, written to commemorate the eightieth anniversary of *Rerum Novarum,* he affirms the dignity of the worker, the worker's right to work, to a chance to develop his qualities and his personality in the exercise of his profession, to equitable remuneration which will enable him and his family "to lead a worthy life on the material, social, cultural and spiritual level" and to assistance in case of need arising from sickness or age. (OA, 14)

To the Holy Father, a just wage is more than the means to a minimum standard of living. For the worker and his family, it is a door to that integral development of body, mind, and spirit which includes the potential for such "higher values" as mentioned above. The creative effort of the worker is seen within community--local, national, and global. When work is done without selfish motives, it has the potential to complete the work of God the Creator. It can bring people together to share their common bonds of dignity and their common duty in carrying out love of neighbor. It can make people strive to promote living conditions which are worthy of the children of God (PP, 27-28 and 82).

The pope pointed to two new aspects of workers and others in contemporary society: the aspiration to equality and the aspiration to participation. These are expressions of human dignity and freedom (PP, 22-25). When these aspirations are made concrete in political and social structures, in the context of human community, they become part of the integral development of the whole person. It is interesting to note here that, with his persistent concern for the injustices of underdeveloped nations, Paul says justice in legislation for equality and participation is not enough for full human relationships. To care for those in want, charity is necessary as well.

The Gospel instructs us in the preferential respect due to the poor and the special situation they have in society: the more fortunate should renounce some of their rights so as to place their goods more generously at the service of others. (OA, 23)

Justice, equality, and participation are always needed in human community. This is part and parcel of the principle of human dignity. Yet there are times, Paul said, when more is needed. The love of neighbor, or charity, or preferential option for the poor, can motivate individuals and groups to give up voluntarily some of their rights, so that the needs of people worse off may be met. Again the pope returns to his leitmotif of the interdependence of people in community. And, what applies to people in a particular society applies, *mutatis mutandis*, to countries in the world family of nations.

In his two major documents on the social question, Pope Paul VI supported the teaching of the just wage. Though he did not directly develop it, indirectly he framed the issue in the wider context of the integral development of the human person. Material needs alone are not enough. The pope feared the exclusive pursuit of material possessions, which have the potential to harden hearts and nurture greed. The full development of human beings, who work and are co-creators of the world, is necessary. Those who work on behalf of justice are to be constantly aware of this. Furthermore, no people or nation is an island. Everyone, especially those in authority, who craft the new world order, needs to cultivate a global perspective. Human dignity is built up only within an interdependent world.

Pope John Paul II

In *Laborem Exercens*, his major writing on work, Pope John Paul says, "The present reflections on work are not intended to follow a different line, but rather to be in organic connection with the whole tradition of this teaching and activity." (LE, 2) Yet he goes on to say that he wishes to apply what is "old" (the issue of work and how it has been reflected upon by the magisterium in the 90 years since *Rerum Novarum*) to what is "new" (the contemporary world).

What is old is familiar. The dignity of the human person, and the specific rights which come from it, are to be protected by the church. Each worker, because he or she is a human being, has such dignity. The pope wishes to uphold each one's dignity, to condemn the structures and situations where that dignity and those rights are violated, and to offer some guidelines for human societies.

What is new is how the pope ties work to human dignity. Work is good, he says, because "it expresses [human] dignity and increases it." (LE, 9; CA, 6) From an exegesis of Genesis he offers that work is fundamental to human life, and universally familiar. He acknowledges the pain and hardship of work ("In the sweat of your face you shall eat bread") which he attributes to the breaking of covenant with God. However, he tends to emphasize the opportunities for "co-creation" with God ("Fill the earth and subdue it"), and for human beings to reflect the acts of the Creator through work. Work is a universal calling, and human life is built up through work.

> If one wishes to define more clearly the ethical meaning of work, it is this truth that one must particularly keep in mind. Work is a good thing for man--a good thing for humanity--because through work man not only transforms nature, adapting it to his own needs, but he also achieves fulfillment as a human being and indeed in a sense becomes "more a human being." (LE, 9)

In this sense, work can be ennobling. Its purpose is linked with the integral development of the whole person. Nicholas von Hoffman says the pope "insists that work must be ennobling, that it must be one of the ways people fulfill themselves, that its end and purpose is higher, better and other than profit."[88] The pope acknowledges that not all labor ennobles. However, when work builds up dignity it points to industriousness as a human virtue.

This aspect can be looked at negatively as well. John Paul says a fundamental error is committed, which he labels "economism," whenever human labor is considered solely for economic purposes. The result of such an error is a harmful juxtaposition and conflict between labor and capital. Such an error makes human work and activity, broadly considered, subordinate to the pursuit of material goods, the fruit of human labor. This is a failure to "recall a principle that has always been taught by the church: the principle of the priority of labor over capital." (LE, 12) Capital--that is, all elements of the means of production from most simple to complex--is only and always to be seen as the result of human work. Human beings and their work activity are the subject, not the object, of the means of production.

It is from the perspective of the priority of labor over capital that certain human rights have their source. In his address to the United Nations, during his first visit to the United States, Pope John Paul II repeatedly praised the 1948 Universal Declaration of Human Rights as a valuable expression of some of the inalienable rights of all people. Among the rights he specifically mentioned were: the right to life, liberty and security; to food, housing, health care, and leisure; to freedom of expression, culture, conscience, and religion, both privately and publicly expressed; to choose one's state in life, and to found a family; to private property, work, decent working conditions, and a just wage; to assembly and association; to freedom of movement; and to political participation. The pope said at that time:

> All these human rights taken together are in keeping with the substance of the dignity of the human being, understood in his entirety, not as reduced to one dimension only. These rights concern the satisfaction of man's essential needs, the exercise of his freedoms, and his relationship with others; but always and everywhere they concern man, they concern man's full human dimension.[89]

In this vision of human rights the pope says that a just wage is central to the question of human labor. In *Laborem Exercens* he writes:

> The key problem of social ethics in this case is that of just remuneration for work done. In the context of the present there is no more important way for securing a just relationship

between the worker and the employer than that constituted by remuneration for work. (LE, 19)

The pope's definition of the just wage clearly follows that of his predecessors. "Just remuneration for the work of an adult who is responsible for a family means remuneration which will suffice for establishing and properly maintaining a family and providing for its future." (LE, 19) In an earlier section of the encyclical John Paul had linked work and family. Specifically, he saw a unity in the personal dimension of human work and the family nature of human life. In a certain sense, human labor is a necessary condition for the founding of a family, and is an ingredient in the education of the members of the family. "In fact, the family is simultaneously a community made possible by work and the first school of work, within the home, for every person." (LE, 10)

Wages for work done are to be supplemented by other, necessary benefits. John Paul mentions medical assistance for work-related accidents, health care, a pension and social security for old age, and the right to rest, including at least Sunday each week and a vacation period each year. He also shows environmental sensitivity by stating a worker has a right to a healthy work environment.

In a largely negative assessment of *Laborem Exercens*, Stanley Hauerwas praised the pope for returning to the economic issues which generated previous papal social teaching. He particularly praised his treatment of the just wage, for it "has the virtue of being concrete and empirical" and "sober and realistic." He saw the just wage as a practical way of directing attention to the moral and social purposes economic systems are meant to serve. Hauerwas said, "This criterion reminds us that all economic questions are fundamentally moral questions."[90]

For the Holy Father, a just wage has more than an individual and family context. It is also crucial, and critical, to the economic system as a whole within society. Wages are a means to secure a just relationship between employer and employee. Wages are also an evaluation tool to judge the community's whole socioeconomic structure.

> It should also be noted that the justice of a socioeconomic system and, in each case, its just functioning, deserve in the final analysis to be evaluated by the way in which man's work is properly remunerated in the system. Here we return once more to the first principle of the whole ethical and social order, namely the principle of the common use of goods. In every system, regardless of the fundamental relationships within it between capital and labor, wages, that is to say remuneration for work, are still a practical means whereby the vast majority of

people can have access to those goods which are intended for common use: both the goods of nature and manufactured goods. Both kinds of goods become accessible to the worker through the wage which he receives as remuneration for his work. Hence in every case a just wage is the concrete means of verifying the justice of the whole economic system and, in any case, of checking that it is functioning justly. It is not the only means of checking, but it is a particularly important one and in a sense the key means. (LE, 19)

This assertion of the just wage as a "test" of the morality of a socioeconomic system is a link between the individual contract between employer and worker and the justice of a whole society. For in the background of John Paul's presentation of the just wage is the modern concern with the interconnectedness of economies and nations. In his encyclical on the twentieth anniversary of *Populorum Progressio, Sollicitudo Rei Socialis*, John Paul reaffirms Paul VI's insights on the need for development in an increasingly interdependent world. He is also more pessimistic about the progress, or rather, the lack of progress, in social, political, and economic development since Paul's letter. When John Paul speaks of rights, for instance, in *Sollicitudo Rei Socialis*, he addresses the respect due to human rights both within nations and on an international level. Among those rights is the right to justice in employment relations (SRS, 33).

In his commemoration of the one hundreth anniversary of *Rerum Novarum*, John Paul II affirms the centrality of the dignity of human work and of workers in socio-economic systems (CA, 6). He sees the right to a just wage, which is always a family wage, as one of several essential human rights.[91] According to what the pope calls "the principle of solidarity," nation-states must work to create "favorable conditions for the free exercise of economic activity" for the weakest and most vulnerable workers (CA, 15).

It should be noted that when John Paul spoke of labor in *Laborem Exercens*, he expanded the previous magisterial teaching's notion of who is a worker. Scholastic writers had in mind for the most part agricultural workers and indentured servants. Leo XIII was concerned with the workers in the factories and mines of the Industrial Revolution, those who came to be known as "blue collar workers." However, John Paul spoke not only of farmers, miners and factory hands, but also those who labor at "the intellectual workbench," for example, scientists, physicians, teachers, scholars, journalists, and office workers. This understanding of human labor is consistent with the pope's vision of work as co-creation. Human beings who labor, in whatever fashion, participate in the work of the Creator on earth.

Pope John Paul II in his major social teachings continued and expanded the understanding of the just wage. He explicitly supported the root of the just wage in the inalienable dignity due to each human being. Indeed, Donlon says, "The pope was not primarily concerned with the worker's pay, but with the person coming to realize his or her full personal dignity."[92] The just wage is linked to certain necessary physical, social and familial rights of the worker. John Paul understood the rights of the worker in the context of the society, nation, and world community of nations.

The full remuneration given to a worker is an important way of judging the justice of the socioeconomic system, as well as the particular employee-employer relationship. Such a just wage allows a worker the opportunity to develop his or her talents, to flourish as a human being, and to nurture his or her family.

Summary

This review of the Church's concern for the remuneration of the worker has shown much development through the centuries. The past one hundred years in particular have witnessed the grave concern of the Church for a just wage at the highest teaching level. It is worthwhile to note several summary points.

The teaching of the magisterium on the just wage is less about the economic value of work and more about the dignity of the human person. Each and every human being has worth and dignity. Because of this dignity, there are certain rights which are to be respected. Each person must have the means of fulfilling those rights and meeting his needs. Each person must be able to live in a manner befitting a human person. A key ingredient of the teaching on just wage is that each human being has a right to see that his family, as well as himself, is able to live in a similar fashion.

The concern for the dignity of the human person has led to the recognition that there are certain rights which are inviolable and inalienable and for all people. The remuneration for work is judged as just insofar as it permits a person to provide for those rights, for himself and for his family. There are other factors which must be taken into consideration as well. Yet if the wage does not allow the person and his family to live in a human fashion, it cannot be seen as just.

The enumeration of rights has grown longer and more detailed in the development of Catholic social teaching. The most extensive list of rights was given by Pope John XXIII. These rights need to be addressed and satisfied in an accounting of the just wage. Any listing of human rights would include: the right of workers to food, clothing, and shelter for themselves and for their families; the right to future security; the right to life, bodily integrity, and the use of property; the right to develop one's physical, moral, and spiritual life, including the right to education for oneself and one's children; the right to rest, medical care, and social services; the right to share in the goods of the earth and to participate in their development.

The right to a just wage has conditions as well. Even as it is concerned with the preservation of the dignity of the person, it must take account of the situation of the particular business, and its ability to pay adequately and still make a profit. The economic system of the community and the nation has to be taken into consideration as well. No individual wage contract can be viewed in isolation. Pope Paul VI expanded the vision of interdependence to include the entire world, and the ever more complex network of financial and social ties. The just wage must respect the dignity not only of the individual worker, but of all people. The conditions of the just wage will be examined in more detail in the next chapter.

This examination of the history of the church's teaching on the just wage has shown the growth of ecclesial concern for the concrete needs of human beings. The ordinary way most people are able to care for their needs, and the needs of their family, is through work. The just wage is an expression of the support for the dignity of each and every human person, and his or her practical ability to achieve a decent livelihood as well as realize his or her integral development.

NOTES

1. Tertullian, *Apologeticum*. XLII, 1-3, quoted in Igino Giordani, *The Social Message of the Early Church Fathers*, trans. by Alba Zizzamia (Patterson, NY: St. Anthony Guild Press, 1944), 279-280.

2. Tacitus, *Histories* V, 4. Quoted in Robert M. Grant, *Early Christianity and Society* (San Francisco: Harper & Row, 1977), 66.

3. Quoted in Grant, 77, 183. See also Clement of Alexandria, *Paedagogus* III, 11.

4. *Apostolic Constitution* II, 63, quoted in Grant, 77.

5. Epiphanius, *Adversus haereses* LXXX, 4, 1-5, quoted in Grant, 79. Cited in 2 Thessalonians 3:10 and Proverbs 6:6-11.

6. E.g., Ignatius, To Polycarp I, 3; Barnabas 10:41; Didache 12:3-5; Clement of Alexandria, *Paedagogus* II, 78, 2.

7. Origen, *Contra Celsum* IV, 76, quoted in Giordani, 282-3. Clement of Rome said that labor was a way of avoiding the indignity of begging. I Clement XXXIV, 1.

8. Ogmatois. To Polycarp V, 1, quoted in Giordani, 286.

9. Clement of Alexandria, *Paedagogus* III, 11, in *Clement of Alexandria: Christ the Educator*, trans. by Simon P. Wood (New York: Fathers of the Church, Inc., 1954), 258-9.

10. John Chrysostom, *De Anna* V, 3; *In inscriptionem altaris* II, as quoted in Grant, 95.

11. L. William Countryman, *The Rich Christian in the Church of the Early Empire: Contradictions and Accomodations* (New York: Edwin Mellen, 1980), 209-10.

12. Boniface Ramsey, *Beginning to Read the Fathers* (New York: Paulist, 1985), 191-2. Ambrose, 2 *Clement* 16, 4.

13. Clement of Alexandria, *Paedagogus* III, 6.

14. Thomas Aquinas, *Summa Theologiae* II-II, 58, 2c and 5c.

15. Leo G. Shields, *The History and Meaning of the Term Social Justice* (Notre Dame, IN: University of Notre Dame Press, 1941), 26-74; William

Ferree, *The Act of Social Justice* (Washington: Catholic University of America Press, 1942), 79-141; and Normand J. Paulhus, "Uses and Misuses of the Term 'Social Justice' in the Roman Catholic Tradition," *Journal of Religious Ethics* 15 (1987): 261-82.

16. Thomas Aquinas, *Summa Theologiae* II-II, 77, 4 ad 1.

17. John D. Callahan, *The Catholic Attitude Toward a Familial Minimum Wage* (Ph.D. diss., Catholic University of America, 1936), 8, referring to Albert the Great, *Opera Omnia*, Paris: 1891, vol. 7, Bk. 5, tract 9, cap. 10.

18. Frederick E. Flynn, *Wealth and Money in the Economic Philosophy of St. Thomas* (Notre Dame, IN: University of Notre Dame Press, 1942), 43-5.

19. Ibid., 44.

20. Thomas Aquinas, *Summa Theologiae* II-II, 77, 1, ad. 1. Translated by Marcus Lefebure, Blackfriars Edition, vol 38 (London: Eyre & Spottiswoode, 1975), 217.

21. Michael Fogarty, *The Just Wage* (London: Herder & Herder, 1961), 257-300.

22. Thomas Aquinas, *Summa Theologiae* I-II, 114, 1, and De Lugo, *De Iustitia et Iure* II, 29, 3.

23. See QA, 83, and RN, 16.

24. Fogarty, 261.

25. Fogarty, 264, notes that such an "honest" job need not be "honorable." He says, "The whore, too, is worthy of her hire," and refers to moralist A. Vermeersch, *Quaestiones de Iustitia*, who offers a general statement of the rule that a service in itself immoral can give rise to a legitimate claim for pay.

26. Fogarty, 263. See the parable of laborers in the vineyard, Matthew 20:1-15.

27. Bernardino of Siena, *Tome* II, Sermon 35, c .2, as quoted in Manuel Rocha, *Les Origines de "Quadragesimo Anno": Travail et Salaire a Travers la Scolastique* (Paris: Desclee, 1933), 81-2. Flynn, 45-9, quotes several commentators on Thomas (Cajetan, Billuart, Sandoz) who argue that a common, or social, estimate of the just price avoids the temptation to greed and is less prone to error.

28. Fogarty, 266.

29. Ibid., 267.

30. Henry of Langenstein, *Tractatus de Contractibus et Origine Censum* I, 12, quoted in Fogarty, 273.

31. E.g., Cajetan (1469-1534), Lessius (1554-1623), and Lehmkuhl (1834-1918).

32. Antoninus, *Summa* I, I, 3, 3, quoted in Callahan, 12.

33. Fogarty, 268. See also RN, 34, and QA, 69.

34. Langenstein, *Tractatus* I, 10-12, quoted in Fogarty, 267.

35. Fogarty, 270. He calls the effort of Rocha to do this "heroic."

36. Fogarty, 285.

37. James Healy, *The Just Wage 1750-1890: A Study of Moralists from St. Alphonsus to Leo XIII* (The Hague: Martinus Nijhoff, 1966).

38. Ibid., 226-227.

39. Ibid., 227.

40. Ibid., 434-6.

41. Ibid., 437-8.

42. One notes with dismay that this is decades after Bishop Wilhelm von Ketteler of Mainz, Germany, had addressed several economic and moral aspects of the social question.

43. Ibid., 455.

44. St. Antoninus, *Summa*, par. 3, tit. 8, cap. I., quoted in Healy, 455.

45. While still an Anglican archdeacon he had tried to have the Poor Laws of his parish revised and to have the hours of employment for girls regulated. But from his suggestions no improvement resulted. Joseph H. Fichter, *Roots of Change* (New York: D. Appleton-Century, 1939), 214.

46. Henry Cardinal Manning, *Miscellanies*, "The Dignity and Rights of Labour," 459.

47. Ibid., 468, 475-6, 482-4.

48. Quoted in John Cronin and Harry W. Flannery, *The Church and the Workingman* (New York: Hawthorn Books, 1965), 94.

49. Quoted in Fichter, 204.

50. Ibid., 211.

51. Ibid., 209. Pope John Paul II echoes this theme of human labor as capital in LE, 14.

52. See William E. Hogan, *The Development of William Emmanuel von Ketteler's Interpretation of the Social Problem* (Washington: Catholic University of America Press, 1946), 236, footnote 1, for a "history" of this statement. Leo also told Msgr. Liesen, von Ketteler's last secretary, in an audience on August 30, 1896: "Ketteler was a great bishop. He was the first to state openly the responsibility and the duty of capital and the state to the working men of our time."

53. Hogan remarks ruefully that it is almost impossible to find in the literature anything except praise for him, his writings, and his life. Ibid., xiii.

54. Quoted in Hogan, 38.

55. Quoted from Johnnes Mumbauer, *Wilhelm Emmanuel von Kettelers Schriften* (Munchen: Koesel und Pustet, 1924) in Hogan, 39.

56. Rupert J. Ederer, trans., *The Social Teachings of Wilhelm Emmanuel von Ketteler* (Washington: University Press of America, 1981), "The Labor Problem and Christianity," 313.

57. Ibid., 321-2.

58. Quoted in Fichter, 168.

59. Ederer, 359.

60. Ibid., 385.

61. Ibid., 387.

62. Hogan, 164.

63. Edward C. Bock, *Wilhelm von Ketteler, Bishop of Mainz: His Life, Times and Ideas* (Washington: University Press of America, 1977), 63-100, 185-212. See also the six demands of his *Christian Labor Catechism* in George Metlake, *Christian Social Reform: Program Outlines by its Pioneeer William Emmanuel Baron von Ketteler* (Philadelphia: Dolphin Press, 1923), 157-175. "The first demand of the working classes is: increase of wages corresponding to the true value of labor." Ibid., 160.

64. Hogan, 40.

65. Fichter, 231.

66. Richard C. Camp, *The Papal Ideology of Social Reform: A Study in Historical Development 1878-1967* (Leiden: E.J. Brill, 1969), 10. See also David Hollenbach, *Claims in Conflict: Retrieving and Renewing the Catholic Human Rights Tradition* (New York: Paulist, 1979), 43.

67. Interestingly in this same paragraph the pope also condemns those who "proclaim the absolute equality of all men in rights and duties."

68. RN, 40. Hollenbach, *Claims*, 45, points out that even as Leo supported equality for all people economically and before the law, he defended the legitimacy of unequal political rights. See also QAM, 1.

69. John F. Cronin, *Social Principles and Economic Life* (Milwaukee: Bruce, 1959), 206-10.

70. James I. Donlon, *The Human Rights of Priests to Equitable Sustenance and Mobility: An Evaluation of Canon Law from the 'CIC' to the Proposed Revision of the Code of Canon Law* (J.C.D. diss., Catholic University of America, 1984), 12-13.

71. RN, 13 and 46. See Joseph Husslein, *The Christian Social Manifesto* (Milwaukee: Bruce, 1931), 177, and Cronin, *Social Principle*, 210-16.

72. RN, 7, 9, 13, 34, and 42.

73. Camp, 87-93.

74. J.Y. Calvez and J. Perrin, *The Church and Social Justice: The Social Teaching of the Popes from Leo XIII to Pius XII, 1878-1958* (Chicago: Henry Regency, 1961), 232.

75. Oswald von Nell-Breuning, "The Drafting of *Quadragesimo Anno*," in Charles E. Curran and Richard A. McCormick, eds., *Readings in Moral Theology No. 5: Official Catholic Social Teaching* (New York: Paulist,

1986), 60-8.

76. For analysis and background to QA, 76-98, on the much controverted reconstruction of the social order, see Oswald von Nell-Breuning, *Reorganization of Social Economy: The Social Encyclicals Developed and Explained*, trans. by Bernard Dempsey (New York: Bruce, 1936), 194-263; Husslein, 221-31; Calvez and Perrin, 414-26; and Cronin, 120-39.

77. Von Nell-Breuning, *Reorganization*, 178.

78. Pius XII, Christmas address (December 24, 1955), trans. in Vincent A. Yerzmans, *The Major Addresses of Pope Pius XII*, vol. 2 (St. Paul, MN: North Central Publishing, 1961), 183.

79. Pius XII, Pentecost radio address (June 1, 1941), trans. in *Catholic Mind* 39 (1941): 11.

80. Pius XII, Christmas address (December 24, 1942), trans. in *Catholic Mind* 41 (1943): 45-60. It's importance is shown in being cited eleven times in Pope John XXIII's *Pacem in Terris*. See Hollenbach, *Claims*, 103, n. 46.

81. Christmas address of 1942, in *Catholic Mind* 41: 56.

82. Pius XII, address to Italian workers (June 13, 1943), trans. in *Catholic Mind* 41 (1943): 2.

83. Pius XII, address to United States delegates to the International Labor Organization (July 16, 1947), trans. in *Catholic Mind* 45 (1947): 578.

84. Hollenbach, *Claims*, 63.

85. Ibid., 64, emphasis in original.

86. Pietro Pavan, commentary on Declaration on Religious Freedom, in Herbert Vorgrimler, *Commentary on the Documents of Vatican II*, 5 vols. (New York: Herder and Herder, 1969), vol. 4, 63-8.

87. Hollenbach, *Claims*, 79-82, emphasis in original.

88. Nicholas von Hoffman, "Papal Economics," *The New Republic* (November 4, 1981): 18.

89. John Paul II, address to the General Assembly of the United Nations, New York City (October 3, 1979), no. 13, in *A.A.S.* 71 (1979): 1153. (The pope gave the address in English.)

90. Stanley Hauerwas, "Work as Co-Creation: A Critique of a Remarkably Bad Idea," in John W. Houck and Oliver F. Williams, eds., *Co-Creation and Capitalism: John Paul II's "Laborem Exercens"* (Washington: University Press of America, 1983), 52.

91. CA, 4, 8, 15, 34, 43, and 47.

92. Donlon, 47. See also CA, 15 .

CHAPTER TWO

THE THEOLOGICAL FOUNDATIONS OF THE JUST WAGE

This chapter attempts to present the theological foundations of the teaching of the just wage. It begins with an analysis of the dignity of the human person. Each person's dignity is preserved and promoted by support of human rights. The right to a just wage is situated within certain biblical and theological perspectives, and is expressed within the whole constellation of human rights. Within the order of rights, the right to a just wage is seen as a social mediation of the individual's right to work. Each right, including the just wage, has corresponding duties as well.

To properly locate just remuneration it is necessary to look at the context of the family and the common good. The traditional principles of justice provide specification in dealing with the conflicting claims of rights and the power struggles of people and institutions in society. Finally, the historic emphasis on love, in relationship to and supportive of justice, expressed the specific Christian moral claim to respond affirmatively to the concrete dignity of human persons.

The Dignity of the Human Person

The foundation of the Catholic Church's theological understanding of the just wage, indeed of all social issues, is the dignity of the human person. Each and every human being is created by God in God's own image and likeness. All human beings are capable of knowing and loving their Creator. The human person is the center of the created universe, under God, and was appointed by God as master of all earthly creatures, to subdue them and use them for God's glory.[1] The human being is made up of body and soul, in a unified whole, never able to be separated. The dignity of every person springs from this human nature. It is not conferred by society, nor is it a product of local custom or law. It may not be abridged or taken away by anyone or by any law.

Essential to an understanding of human dignity is the social nature of all people. Human beings are inherently social. The Book of Genesis expressed the interpersonal nature of humanity in God creating "male and female." Human beings are not created in solitary isolation, but as social beings. In his commentary on Vatican II, Pope John Paul II says it is apparent that the human person was made in God's image "not only because of the spiritual nature of his immortal soul but also by reason of his social nature if by this we understand the fact that he 'cannot fully realize himself except in an act of pure self-giving.'"[2] For human beings to live a fully human life, they must live in association with other human beings. Women and men need to relate with one another to develop their potential.

The family and society are two key places where the social human being meets and lives with others. The family and society are each a kind of "living unity" where a person can find the means to recognize another as a person, as an equal. Interpersonal relations in the family and in society demand respect for the dignity, and the equality, of each human person. As the Second Vatican Council expressed it:

> Since all men possess a rational soul and are created in God's likeness, since they have the same nature and origin, have been redeemed by Christ, and enjoy the same divine calling and destiny, the basic equality of all must receive increasingly greater recognition. (GS, 29)

Pope Paul VI saw that the aspiration to equality was a characteristic of the individual in modern society. Along with the aspiration to participation, the desire for equality flowed from the dignity of the human person (OA, 22). Two distinguished commentators noted this connection when they wrote, "The affirmation by the Church of the dignity of man is always completed by the affirmation of the equality in dignity of all human persons."[3]

The equality and dignity of all persons demand that more humane and just conditions of life be brought about in society. A person needs the resources of the community to fulfill his or her obligation to grow in truth, justice, faith, and charity. Yet it must also be acknowledged that within community, no human being can fulfill these obligations perfectly. Each human society is marked by the refusal to serve God and neighbor. Sin disorders human relationships and human communities.

Another way to acknowledge the dignity of the human person is to recognize that from God's love Jesus Christ redeemed humankind from sin. Through human nature human beings are over the whole of creation. They also have to arrange their families and societies in conformity to their destiny, in accord with human dignity.

One part of the arrangement of society must be freedom. Human beings by virtue of their dignity are endowed with reason and free will. Only when human beings are free can they take responsibility for their actions, and direct themselves toward what is good. From the Pastoral Constitution on the Church in the Modern World:

> Authentic freedom is an exceptional sign of the divine image
> within man. For God has willed that man be left "in the hand

of his own counsel" (Sirach 5:14) so that he can seek his Creator spontaneously, and come freely to utter and blissful perfection through loyalty to Him. Hence man's dignity demands that he act according to a knowing and free choice. Such a choice is personally motivated and prompted from within. It does not result from blind internal impulse nor from mere external pressure. (GS, 17)

In *Dignitatis Humanae* the Council Fathers spoke about the need for responsible freedom for all people. They identified freedom as a "value proper to the human spirit," (DH, 1) with its charter in the dignity of the human person.

In sum, human dignity is the source of all moral principles. It does not rely on any ethical human actions or groupings of peoples. It is not given by any law or person. Human persons have human dignity. They do not earn it or deserve it. Human dignity rather makes claims on others that it be recognized and respected.

Furthermore, human dignity is at one and the same time transcendental and concrete. Hollenbach says this well.

> Human dignity . . . has reality in all situations, independent of the kinds of actions and relations which give them structure. Dignity is thus a transcendental characteristic of persons. Human persons have a worth which claims respect in every situation and in every type of activity. Dignity is the norm by which the adequacy of all forms of human behavior and all the moral principles which are formulated to guide behavior are to be judged. Human dignity is therefore not primarily a guiding rule or principle which is formulated by and within reflexive human consciousness. It is a concrete reality which exists wherever persons exist.[4]

Because human dignity is found in concrete human persons, it needs specification to real and particular needs and relationships. Reflecting on Roman Catholic tradition, David Hollenbach states

> the bare notion of human dignity is nearly empty of meaning. . . . Unless the relations between the transcendental worth of the person and the particular material, interpersonal, social and political structures of human existence can be specified, human dignity will become an empty notion. The specification of the concrete conditions for the realization of dignity in action has been the continuing endeavor of the tradition since Leo XIII.[5]

The effort to identify concrete conditions of human dignity, lived out in family, state, and society, has been expressed in the Roman Catholic tradition of identifying human rights. This is an ongoing endeavor. Each generation and each particular expression of church must examine the human rights tradition and attempt to apply it in its own situation. For an understanding of the teaching on a just wage it is important now to look at the human rights which flow from human dignity.

The Rights of the Human Person

The fundamental expression of preservation, promotion, and protection of the dignity of the human person has been given in the Catholic human rights tradition. Each person because of his or her dignity has certain rights (and duties) which are universal, inviolable, and inalienable. They are part of the personal reality of every human being. They are seen and given expression in the context of the multitude of relationships human beings share in the world. The communities of family and society, and indeed the whole social order, must work to benefit and improve the situation of every person. The Council Fathers of Vatican II said, "This social order requires constant improvement. It must be founded on truth, built on justice, and animated by love; in freedom it should grow every day toward a more humane balance." (GS, 24)

David Hollenbach defines rights as "the conditions for the realization of human worth in action."[6] The Roman Catholic tradition of rights has identified many areas of concern. Some are human needs, such as life, bodily integrity, food, shelter, work, and medical care. Some refer to freedom and self-determination. Some regard human interrelationships in the family, in politics, economics, and religious expression.[7]

The teaching of the Catholic Church on the just wage is found within the human rights tradition. Chapter One reviewed the papal and conciliar statements on the worker's right to a just wage. To analyze this right to a just wage it is first necessary to examine briefly the biblical and theological reflection on work, the right to development, and the right to work. Then the right to a just wage can be seen in the context of several human needs and freedoms.

Work: Perspectives from Genesis

It is commonly assumed that the Bible contains only negative evaluations of work. Yet the first eleven chapters of Genesis contain several stories which illustrate positive, as well as negative, perspectives of work.

A prime example of the use of illustrations of the positive vision of work is contained in *Laborem Exercens*. John Paul II repeatedly refers to Genesis 1:26-28, from the priestly account of creation. He uses these verses to develop the theme of human work as a participation in the creative activity of God. Human beings are created "in the image of God," and are like God through their communion to subdue the earth and have dominion over the whole of creation. Hollenbach comments:

> The encyclical thus understands all the creativity of civilization and the economy as an expression of the image of the Creator in the human creature. Whether work be agricultural or industrial, physical or intellectual, more traditional in form or in the technologically advanced spheres of electronics and scientific research, the encyclical affirms that all forms of creative activity by which nature is brought to the service of human ends are an expression of the image and likeness of the Creator in the human creature.[8]

Claus Westermann in his examination of these Genesis texts comes to a similar conclusion. "All human work of whatever kind can participate in the cultivation and preservation of the space which the Creator has given man to live in." It is a fundamental and positive biblical view that "civilised activity and the growth of mankind both derive from God's blessing."[9]

Other texts from Genesis also point to a positive evaluation of work. The genealogy of Cain (4:17-22) represents the growth of cultivation of the fields and civilization in the city. These developments are regarded as signs of God's continuing blessing for human creativity. God promises to Noah (8:21-2) that this blessing shall continue "as long as the earth remains, in an everlasting covenant" (9:16).

It should also be noted that the positive biblical view of work is not applied only to "creative" activity. The biblical authors most often refer to ordinary, everyday, more or less monotonous toil. They saw work as a necessity. John O'Grady states the biblical writers saw that "work was and is a necessary and God-ordained function of human life. . . . Work is not a curse but a blessing. Human society benefits when people can work."[10]

Genesis, however, also brings out the limitations of human creative activity and the destructiveness of sin. Five major events are used to show the emergence of sin. These are the disobedience of Adam and Eve, and their expulsion from the Garden of Eden (3:1-24); Cain's murder of his brother, Abel (4:2-16); the marriage of the "sons of God" with the "daughters of men" and the limitation on the span of human life because of this (6:1-4); God's destruction of the earth by flood as a result of the wickedness of human hearts (6:5-7:24); and the confusion in languages and scattering of the peoples by attempting to build the Tower of Babel (11:1-9). It can be seen that the Yahwist author of these passages is considerably more attuned to the ambiguities of human creativity and work. The stories point to a failure to recognize the limitations of human nature. Adam and Eve want to be "like God." The builders of the Tower of Babel want to "make a name" for themselves through their building prowess. "The motif of the creation of human persons 'in the image of God' is thus held in tension with the powerful warning that human superiority over nature is the occasion of a perpetual temptation to try to become 'like God' through knowledge, sexuality, technology, or other human capacities."[11]

These Genesis narratives also illustrate the inability of human beings to live in perfect harmony within community. Mutuality and equality give way to domination and subordination. Alienation from God ("Adam, where are you?") is paralleled by alienation from one's fellow human beings ("Where is Abel, your brother?"). The Yahwist continually reminds us of our limits: "You are dust, and unto dust you shall return." (3:19)

Both the positive and negative biblical perspectives on human labor and creative activity need to be held in tension in reflecting on work.

Work: Perspectives from Christian Tradition

This same balance of tensions reveals itself in an examination of past theological reflections on the meaning of human work. Francis Schussler Fiorenza offers three influential perspectives.[12]

The medieval notion of work is seen within a theocentric universe. All creatures, including human beings, find their place in God's creation and cooperate in bringing the divine plan to consummation. Work is an individual's vocation. It is also a fulfillment of the individual's responsibility to community. Work has personal and social significance.

A second theological reflection occurs in the seventeenth and eighteenth century. Fiorenza attributes to the Jansenist mentality an appeal to fidelity in obligations, to hard work, and to self sufficiency. Riches are less important than gaining eternal life through a life of virtue. It was the preparation for a "middle class mentality." Work is a result of sin, according to this perspective. It unmasks the world's vanity. It is often difficult, weary, monotonous, and strenuous. Yet as work served as a penance for sin, it also aided human beings in the glorification of God. Work was not meaningful in itself, only in its religious end. Later, a "bourgeois attitude" grew out of this religious interpretation, namely, that work was to bring success and achievement in this life only.

A third interpretation of work, in the 1950s, took as a given industrialization and mass production, which had led to the loss of the human signification of work. Several theologians[13] therefore tried to stress the positive evaluation of work, from biblical sources and Christian anthropology. Through work, human beings participate in divine creativity. Work becomes part of the transformation of the material world into the order of grace.

After reporting these theological interpretations of work, and reflecting on their historical and social contexts, Fiorenza concludes that today's theologizing needs to confront past understandings.

> In the religious tradition, work has both a positive and negative evaluation. It is seen as creative, as a service to community, and as a divine vocation. Yet it is also negatively evaluated as a punishment for sin. In contemporary society, a similar ambivalence exists. On the one hand, work is seen as important for the individual's self-concept, sense of fulfillment, and integration into society. On the other hand, there is an increasingly instrumentalist attitude toward work: persons work not so much for the sake of work itself, but for the rewards of work.[14]

The Right to Development

The examination of the biblical and theological valuations of work has shown work as a positive expression of human creativity and work as a burdensome toil and punishment for sin. The right to a just wage must also be set in the context of the specific listings of rights, and their interpretation, in the papal and conciliar tradition of Catholic social teaching. Chapter One has shown that the right to a just wage has consistently been explicitly named as an important right in Catholic social teaching since *Rerum Novarum*. It has not been mentioned in isolation, nor can it be interpreted as such. Human rights are always seen as interconnected.

The best expression of the interconnectedness of human rights may be found in the 1971 Synod of Bishops document *De Iustitia in Mundo*. The Synod of Bishops was formed after the Second Vatican Council as an institutional expression of the Council's recognition of the contemporary church's international and multi-cultural reality. In the wake of the 1968 gathering of Latin American bishops at Medellin, Colombia, the Synod turned its attention to fundamental problems of so many developing countries: justice and human rights.

With its episcopal representatives from all over the world, the Synod saw human rights in a contemporary, worldwide perspective.

> The strong drive towards global unity, the unequal distribution which places decisions concerning three quarters of income, investment and trade in the hands of one third of the human race, namely, the more highly developed part, the insufficiency of a merely economic progress, and the new recognition of the material limits of the biosphere--all this makes us aware of the

fact that in today's world new modes of understanding are arising. (DI, 12)

The "new" mode of understanding justice and human rights was seen in the right to development. Development was defined by the synod as "a dynamic interpenetration of all those fundamental human rights upon which the aspirations of individuals and nations are based." (DI, 15) Hollenbach sees this as "a recognition that human dignity implies a constellation of rights which must be understood, not singly, but in dynamic interrelation with each other."[15] Rights must be seen and analyzed in their concrete form within the relationships--personal, social, national, international--which give form to human interaction. This right to development is not another added to the past listings of rights from the papal documents. It serves to emphasize that there is no mathematically precise yardstick which can be used to measure human dignity, or its protection by an institution or government. Hollenbach calls it "a comparative right. It's concrete content can only be discovered by regarding the individual person within his or her social context and in relation to other persons."[16] The right to development is made specific by the need for participation. Without participation in the economic, political, and theological institutions of society, people become marginalized. On the margins of society these people are "ill fed, inhumanly housed, illiterate and deprived of political power as well as of the the suitable means of acquiring responsibility and moral dignity." (DI, 10)[17] Respect for persons demands that people participate actively in the social movements, institutions, and processes of development.

The Right to Work

The right to a just wage needs to be set within the "social constellation" of the right to development in a particular historical setting. Now this becomes more precise. It also needs to be seen in the light of the personal right to work.

The word "personal" is used deliberately in the previous sentence. Older commentators saw work as both a duty and as a right. The duty to work shares the twin valuation of work in the biblical and theological traditions. John Cronin stated, "While the burden of work may be associated with God's punishment of man after the fall of Adam, it is at the same time an instrument of redemption. . . . Work participates in the miracle of creation, since man thereby brings into being new forms and materials not found in nature."[18] Individual human beings have an obligation, a duty, to "sweat" for their living, because of human nature.

But human nature also needs certain things. Leo XIII saw work as essential for human beings to live. *Rerum Novarum* put it this way.

> The labor of the workingman is not only his personal attribute, but it is necessary; and this makes all the difference. The preservation of life is the bounden duty of each and all, and to fail therein is a crime. . . . Each one has a right to procure what is required in order to live. (RN, 34)

Pius XII reiterated this statement in his radio address on the feast of Pentecost in 1941, and explicitly referred to a right to work. He used the same foundation: human beings have "a natural, grave, individual obligation to maintain life." This right was not granted by society but "imposed on and conceded to the individual . . . by nature." Commentators Calvez and Perrin neatly sum it up. "What we have just established is an inalienable and imprescriptible fundamental right of the human person."[19]

David Hollenbach places the right to work in perspective in a schematic interpretation of the rights listed in John XXIII's *Pacem in Terris*. He uses two perspectives at the same time: according to dimensions of the human personality and according to the kinds of relationships involved. Within the sphere of economic rights, he sees the right to work as primarily personal. The social expression of economic rights is the right to adequate working conditions and the right to a just wage. The instrumental expression is the right to organize unions and the right to property.

There is much wisdom in this analysis. The Catholic tradition of human rights is personalist. Yet it is not individualistic or libertarian. The understanding of human rights is always placed within social and institutional contexts. Rights must be mediated through duties which bind other persons, society, institutions, and the state.

Pope John Paul II gave a new expression to this tension of the personal and social in the organization of work with his distinction of an indirect and direct employer. In *Laborem Exercens* he wrote, "The indirect employer substantially determines one or another facet of the labor relationship, thus conditioning the conduct of the direct employer when the latter determines in concrete terms the actual work contract and labor relations." (LE, 17) Friedhelm Hengsbach gives these examples of the indirect employer: "governments, central banks, trade unions, employers' organizations, the International Monetary Fund, the General Agreement on Tariffs and Trade."[20] In the first place among indirect employers, *Laborem Exercens* says, is the state.

The role of indirect employers is to prevent unemployment, or positively, to provide "just and rational coordination" and overall planning for the differend kinds of employment. This planning, John Paul says, needs to affect not only the economic sphere but also the cultural life of society. And because of the interdependence of nation states and their economies, planning and organization cannot stop at the border. "Action in this important area must also be taken in the dimension of international collaboration by means of the necessary treaties and agreements." The very complexity of international relations demands a high level of effectiveness by indirect employers. The criterion of success for effectiveness by these agents responsible for the whole orientation of labor policy will be whether suitable employment is available for all who are capable of it and whether "the living standard of the workers in the different societies will less and less show those disturbing differences which are unjust and apt to provoke even violent reactions." (LE, 36)

Hollenbach concludes:

> These duties are not simply interpersonal bonds such as those which exist within families and other primary groups. They are also social and political. Consequently the recognition of the full richness of human dignity creates demands in the human community that the social and instrumental rights . . . be recognized through the appropriate structures.[21]

Therefore the right to a just wage is a social mediation of the individual's right to work. The right to a just wage is given to each person, but admits of many ways of being carried out in society, in varied economic and historical situations. Also, these particular economic rights cannot be seen in isolation from other human rights. "There can be no mechanical or mathematically perfect schematization of rights and their relationship. The realization of human dignity is possible only through a constant struggle to achieve a form of integrity which keeps many factors in a living unity with each other, a struggle for 'integral development.'"[22] This struggle for integrity and human dignity is a dynamic one. The papal and conciliar documents uphold the rights and their interrelationship. A later section will address the complex claims in light of the types of justice used in the Catholic tradition. The magisterial documents do not give hard and fast rules for implementing them in the many economic and political structures of the nations of the world. That will be the burden of the final chapter, to propose principles or criteria to judge whether wages and wage policies are just.

Rights Which Flow from a Just Wage

Before turning to the relationship of the family to a just wage, it is necessary to acknowledge the several rights which are supported by the right to a just wage.

When Leo XIII expressed his support for the individual's right to a just wage in *Rerum Novarum*, he stated that the worker was to receive a wage sufficient for himself and his family to live in a reasonable and frugal manner. He further spelled out what this meant for the family members:

food (13, 34), housing (34), clothing (34), physical well-being (34, 42), sufficient rest and leisure (42), provisions for children and their rearing and education (13), opportunity to own property (9), and guarantees for the future (7). As was pointed out in Chapter One, this was supported by Leo's successors. John XXIII expanded the list of rights, and gave the most complete listing in an encyclical letter, in *Pacem in Terris*. The first paragraph of that listing embraces the needs mentioned above, and several more.

> Man has the right to live. He has the right to bodily integrity and to the means necessary for the proper development of life, particularly food, clothing, shelter, medical care, rest, and finally, the necessary social services. In consequence, he has the right to be looked after in the event of ill health; disability stemming from his work; widowhood; old age; enforced unemployment; or whenever through no fault of his own he is deprived of the means of livelihood. (PT, 11)

Further on John affirms the right of parents to support and educate their children (PT, 16-17). He stresses the right to a just wage for workers in a set of paragraphs dealing with the economic sphere. "The amount a worker receives must be sufficient, in proportion to available funds, to allow him and his family a standard of living consistent with human dignity." (PT, 20)

This lengthy listing of rights which is proposed as a result of the worker's right to a just wage serves as one set of test questions to confirm or reject what is proposed as a just wage. The rights are related to each other, and are to be provided by the various parties who have the responsibility to uphold them. All economic and political actors are to work for the "integral development" of persons and of the structures of society.

Now it is time to turn to the duties of employees and employers in the right to a just wage.

Duties in the Right to a Just Wage

It is axiomatic that for every right there are corresponding duties. This section looks at the duties of the employee and the employer in the right to a just wage.

In *Rerum Novarum* Leo XIII explained the corresponding duties of workers and their employer. Workers are to

> fully and faithfully perform the work which has been freely and equitably agreed upon; never to injure the property, nor to outrage the person, of an employer; never to resort to violence

in defending their own cause, nor to engage in disorder; and to have nothing to do with men of evil principles, who work upon the people with artful promises of great results, and excite foolish hopes which usually end in useless regrets and grievous loss. (RN, 20)

It seems that Leo's understanding of the employee's duty is to act virtuously. This includes, but is not limited to, an honest and full day's labor, respect for the property of the owner and the person of the manager, obedience to civil law, avoidance of violence in addressing grievances, and prudence in the choice of one's friends and acquaintances. These seem to be plain and sensible requests, in keeping with the moral law.

Leo exhibited distrust of the motives of the employer. In the same paragraph, Leo warned the employer to treat each worker with the dignity becoming a human being. The pope made this very specific, and perhaps reflected prevailing understandings of the time, when he stated that employers must not "misuse men as though they were things in the pursuit of gain, or to value them solely for their physical powers--that is truly shameful and inhuman." There are other responsibilities the employer has: to give time to the worker for religious duties; not to tax workers beyond their strength, or employ them in work unsuited to their age or sex; not to defraud any worker of earned wages; in sum, the "great and principal duty is to give everyone what is just." (RN, 20) In another section Leo defended the right of the workers to form unions or associations to promote their just claims. Leo also upheld the responsibility of the employer (as well as the state) to allow such workers' associations (RN, 49-66).

These are important responsibilities which each worker and each employer must seriously consider, and strive to follow. They are the practical attitudes and actions which defend human dignity in the workplace.

Pope Pius XI supported the right to a just wage in *Quadragesimo Anno*. This right formed the first consideration of his reflection on the individual and social character of work. The second factor he discussed, the common good, will be addressed later in this chapter. The third factor directly relates to the duties of employers.

In article 72, Pius XI presumed that the owners of businesses have the responsibility to pay just wages for all workers. He accused as "guilty of a grievous wrong" those who "deprive workingmen of a just wage." In stating the duty of employers to pay a just wage he also set forth a distinction. The economic conditions of a particular business need to be considered. On the one hand, if the owners and/or managers of a business do not put forth sufficient effort to make a profit, or do not keep up with technical or economic progress, "that must not be regarded as a just reason for reducing the compensation of the workers." If there are outside factors which prevent profit, or even threaten a business with bankruptcy, then "it would be unjust to demand excessive wages which a business cannot stand without its ruin and consequent calamity to the workers." (QA, 72)

In these statements Pius XI recognized that the concrete historical situation of a business must be taken into consideration. Owners and managers have an obligation to put in a "full day's work" and to use all available technology, acumen, and expertise to make and keep the company competitive and profitable. "We've always done it this way" would seem to be a poor excuse for managers who fail to keep up with the times. Just as importantly, owners and managers cannot "bleed" an enterprise of its profits and assets, allowing top management to escape with large and extravagant "golden parachutes" while the rank and file workers are told there is no money available for wage increases. In some cases workers in this situation are even asked to accept pay cuts voluntarily.[23] The right to profits, i.e., a return on one's investment, is subordinate to the workers' right to receive a wage which is just. If the workers' just share of the return from the business has not been given to them, it is "a grave injustice" for the employer, owner, or majority stockholder to keep the workers' share as part of the profits.

The duty of each employer to pay a just wage does not deprive the owners and managers of a business of their own right to a fitting livelihood. Edward Reissner states, "The employer has no obligation in justice to deprive himself and his family of necessities in order to pay his workers."[24] If there are economic circumstances extrinsic to the business which would prevent the payment of a minimum just wage, the injustice forced upon the workers cannot be blamed on the employer. Pius XI condemned those who cause the loss of business "from the outside," as it were, and thereby cause the loss of jobs. The contemporary appreciation of sinful social structures, especially on an international scale, and John Paul II's notion of the indirect employer, referred to above, can help us to understand Pius' insight here.

But Pius does not offer any practical guidance to businesses or workers caught in this position. One solution is for the firm to go out of business, and for workers to seek employment elsewhere. Reissner states flatly, "An enterprise has no right to exist if it cannot pay just wages."[25] However, if there are no jobs available, the alternative might be for employees to work for a wage less than just. In this case some income could be better than none. The understanding of the right to a just wage would only seem to allow this for a short period of time. There would have to be well-founded hope that just or full wages would be returned soon.

For the just wage to be carried out in the real world, both employees and employers need to attend to their duties in their respective areas of labor.

The Just Wage in the Context of the Family

Human Dignity

One of the key insights the history of the doctrine of the just wage teaches is that a just wage must enable the worker to have and raise a family. This is foundational to a just wage. What is actually taking place in the world and in the church can and does conflict with this ideal. But the foundation of the just wage as a *family* wage still remains.

The theological link of the just wage and the family begins with human dignity. The preamble to the *Charter of the Rights of the Family* states, "The rights of the person, even though they are expressed as rights of the individual, have a fundamental social dimension which finds an innate and vital expression in the family."   All human beings are social in character. Our sociality is expressed in many forms, but in none so basic as the family. The Second Vatican Council called the family "the first and vital cell of society." (AA, 11) The family is seen as a natural society and exists prior to the state. The family possesses inherent rights which are inalienable. As a "community of love and solidarity" the family teaches and transmits cultural, ethical, social, spiritual, and religious values to its members, and is essential for the development of society. (CF, preamble)   Indeed, society in general, and the state in particular, need to defend and foster the family. Pope John Paul II wrote in *Familiaris Consortio*:

> In the conviction that the good of the family is an indispensable
> and essential value of the civil community, the public authorities
> must do everything possible to ensure that families have all
> those aids -- economic, social, educational, political, and
> cultural assistance -- that they need in order to face all their
> responsibilities in a human way. (FC, 45)

In light of the essential nature of the family, all human beings, by virtue of their dignity, have the right to marry and found a family, if they so freely choose and have the necessary capacity. Furthermore, "those who wish to marry and establish a family have the right to expect from society the moral, educational, social and economic conditions which will enable them to exercise their right to marry in all maturity and responsibility." (CF, 1b)[26] Human beings who have the right to marry also have the rightful expectation of cooperating with the conditions to make the right a reality. These conditions include the right to participation in social and political affairs, to stability, and to economic conditions "which assure [families] a standard of living appropriate to their dignity and full development." (CF, 9a) Article 10a reaffirms the church teaching on how this standard of living should be achieved.

Remuneration for work must be sufficient for establishing and maintaining a family with dignity, either through a suitable salary, called a "family wage," or through other social measures such as family allowances or the remuneration of the work in the home of one of the parents. (CF 10a)

In this assertion, the teaching on the just wage comes full circle. Papal and conciliar documents on work have shown that human beings have the right to a salary for their work which enables them to provide for a decent standard of living for themselves and their families. In the *Charter of the Rights of the Family*, the just wage is affirmed as the usual or key means to defend the rights of the family to health, stability, growth, and well-being.

Diverse Conditions Today

A grave lacuna in the church's understanding and expression of the just wage as a family wage is the recognition of the diverse situations of families today. The earlier Vatican documents which have been repeatedly cited generally presumed that the family consists of a husband who works outside the home and a wife and mother who does not have a paying job and who remains in the home nurturing one or more children. For example, Leo XIII spoke of the right of property belonging "to a man in his capacity of head of a family." He continued:

It is a most sacred law of nature that a father should provide food and all necessaries [sic] for those whom he has begotten; and, similarly, it is natural that he should wish that his children, who carry on, so to speak, and continue his personality, should be by him provided with all that is needful to enable them to keep themselves from want and misery. (RN, 13)

There is no mention here of a family picture other than working father, stay-at-home mother, and children. Later documents give more attention to the rights of women as individuals while still recognizing the importance of motherhood and child rearing.

Pius XI supported Leo's teaching on the just wage for the male head of the household (CC, 117). He could even see that other members of the family could contribute toward the support of the household. But his examples are limited to small farms and businesses. The wife/mother's place is in the home. A lengthy quotation from *Quadragesimo Anno* provides us with Pius XI's perspective on the family.

In the first place, a worker must be paid a wage sufficient to support him and his family. That the rest of the family should also contribute to the common support, according to the capacity of each, is certainly right, as can be observed especially in the families of farmers, but also in the families of many craftsmen and small shopkeepers. But to abuse the years of childhood and the limited strength of women is grossly wrong. Mothers concentrating on household duties should work primarily in the home or in its immediate vicinity. It is an intolerable abuse, and to be abolished at all cost, for mothers on account of the father's low wage to be forced to engage in gainful occupations outside the home to the neglect of their proper cares and duties, especially the training of children. Every effort therefore must be made that fathers of families receive a wage large enough to meet ordinary family needs adequately. (QA, 71)

There are several points to be noted in Pius XI's vision of family. He wants to protect children from hard labor in factories, which is abusive to their growth and prevents their proper education. He also wishes to protect the mother's physical strength (their "limited condition"). Her physical activity should be confined to child rearing, household duties, and--perhaps--unspecified work near the home. But the wife's work is not to include "gainful occupations." It is hard to decide whether Pius was referring only to hard manual labor here or included "white collar" or professional occupations. The presumption in the last sentence of the quotation is, of course, that mothers *were* working outside the home because of the lack of a just wage for the father/head of household. There is no acknowledgment of the possibility that wives and mothers would work because there was no adult male in the picture, or would choose *voluntarily* to work outside the home, in the pursuit of a career or profession.

With John XXIII there is the beginning of change in the notion of who the head of a household may be. John presumed the male as head of the household when he defended the just wage in *Mater et Magistra*. He wrote that among the essential personal rights "is a man's right and duty to be primarily responsible for his own upkeep and that of his family." A similar phrase is repeated in *Pacem in Terris*, supporting the just wage (MM, 55; PT, 20).

Yet John used language elsewhere which is ambiguous and can be interpreted to see the head of the household as either male or female. The plural form "workers" in the restatement of the just wage in *Mater et Magistra* allows for the interpretation that the head of the household could be male or female (MM, 71). In *Pacem in Terris* John did not condemn women's work outside the home. In a section entitled "Economic Rights" he warned against harmful and adverse working conditions. Children are not to have their development stunted by a harsh work environment. Women need to make prudent decisions which strike a balance between the demands of child rearing and motherhood and the work situation.

> The conditions in which a man works form a necessary corollary to these rights. They must not be such as to weaken his physical or moral fibre, or militate against the proper development of adolescents to manhood. Women must be accorded such conditions of work as are consistent with their needs and responsibilities as wives and mothers. (PT, 19)

John Paul II goes the farthest in acknowledging that women could be the head of a family. In his defense of the just wage he speaks of "just remuneration for the work of an adult [iusta remuneratio operis hominis adulti] who is responsible for a family." This inclusive language is confirmed in his definition of a family wage:

> . . . that is, a single salary given to the head of a family for work [capiti tributum familiae ob ipsius laborem], sufficient for the needs of the family without the other spouse having to take up gainful employment outside the home. (LE, 19)

In the language of this statement there is the acknowledgment that a wife can be employed outside the home and a husband can stay at home (perhaps to raise children). However, there is no mention here, or in any of the previous examples, of the popes recognizing the millions of women who are heads of households because of widowhood, separation, divorce, or single motherhood. There is no explicit statement that when these women (who are also heads of households) hold paying jobs, they deserve a wage which enables them to provide sufficiently for themselves and their children. This would apply as well to the statistically fewer cases of men who head the household and raise children without a wife.

One commentator even goes beyond this criticism. Elizabeth McKeown praises the magisterium of the church in its use of the family as an institution and as metaphor. She says, "The church fathers [of the last 100 years] have consistently taken family as the index of a well-ordered society and have extended it to address contemporary problems of international economics and political justice." But she criticizes the narrow vision of family, an expressed ideal which

> is static and in increasing tension with the realities of life in rapidly changing societies. Sooner or later, papal and episcopal

understanding of the family must deal with cultural pluralism and begin to take account of the fact that, while the monogamous and fecund family dedicated to the nurturing of children continues to be a prominent feature of social life, this form of intimate human social organization is but one among many. Even within the family properly so-called, a diversity of form is increasingly evident.[27]

One contemporary episcopal document which has attempted to be more sensitive to "the signs of the times," to the familial realities of a particular society, is the 1986 pastoral letter of the United States bishops, *Economic Justice for All*. The letter takes note of the large and growing numbers of women in the workforce, "not only in order to put their talents and education to greater use, but also out of economic necessity." (EJA, 144) The reality is that today many families in America need two incomes to survive.

The bishops acknowledge how the situation of female-headed households often leads to poverty. They are heavily dependent on the mother's income. The unemployment rate for female heads of households holds at 10%. Discrimination is a way of life for women seeking employment, in wages, salaries, job classifications, promotions, child care service, part-time benefits, and other areas. The fact that women bear the primary burden of child rearing often hinders hiring or job promotion. When marriages break up, women usually take custody of the children and bear the major financial responsibility for their support.

The American bishops make many concrete proposals to improve and foster dignity and justice for women. For example, the bishops call for an end to gender-based discrimination. They suggest pay equity, flex time, and affirmative action for women. They call for tax policies and programs to allow mothers of young children to remain at home. They challenge employers, governments, and private agencies (but not the church?!) to improve the quality and quantity of child care services, and to establish parental leave policies which would maintain job security.[28]

Ann O'Hara Graff acknowledges how the bishops recognize major affronts to the dignity of women in the economic sphere. Yet she pushes them to see the wider issue of institutionalized sexual discrimination. This affects the wife and mother at home, the mother who works, and children. Although she does not offer concrete solutions to these dilemmas, she articulates the conundrum working women and mothers face today.[29] Their dignity is directly upheld (or not) by the practices of economic justice in businesses, government, and the church.

If the church is to continue to express its support for just remuneration for workers and their families, church leaders must acknowledge and address the varied cultural and economic realities of families today. This is especially true as the number of two-income families, and female-headed households, continue to grow.

The Just Wage in the Context of the Common Good

It is important in assessing the teaching on the just wage to place it within the context of Catholic social teaching's understanding of the common good. Much of the discussion of the just wage in this chapter has been directly focused on the worker and the implication of his or her wages for the proper expression of human dignity. In the previous section it was necessary to point out the importance of the worker's family as integrally joined to the teaching on the just wage. In this section the context widens. Employees (and their families) and employers always work within a particular society, government, and economic system and need to consider the practical realities of the common good there.

In considering the just wage, then, there are four sets of emphases which must be balanced for economic actors to try to move in the direction of the common good. These are the communitarian and individualistic notions of society, the principle of subsidiarity and the role of the state, the ends of the state and society, and the growth and limitations of human rights language in contemporary Catholic social teaching.

It has already been pointed out how the dignity of each human being is essentially social. We live out our choices and decisions and identities in the midst of other people with whom we relate. The understanding of the common good is rooted in a communitarian vision of society. Society is essentially relational. The common good is made up of the civil and political liberties due each person, as well as their social and economic needs. The common good is not simply the aggregate of the welfare of individuals. *Gaudium et Spes* came very close to a definition of the common good:

> the sum of those conditions of social life which allow social groups and their individual members relatively thorough and ready access to their own fulfillment. (GS, 26)

The common good is a set of social conditions which are necessary for the realization of human dignity. Economist Charles Wilber comments:

> In short, individuals have rights to those things necessary to realize their dignity as human beings. These rights are derived from a person's membership in a community, not from his or her status as an isolated individual.[30]

In this vision, the common good must be deliberately sought. It should be "consciously willed and pursued in the design of social institutions and public policy [and] the whole institutional fabric of a society."[31] This includes, but is not limited to, a substantial role for government.

In contrast to the Catholic vision of interdependence and the common good, much of the modern economic thinking is rooted in an individualist concept of society. In this understanding

> society is seen as a collection of individuals who have chosen
> to associate because it is mutually beneficial. The common
> good is simply the aggregate of the welfare of each individual.
> Individual liberty is the highest good.[32]

In this vision, individuals make economic decisions based on their self-interest, and compete in the free market. The voluntary exchanges are supposed to lead to individual freedom and material welfare for all the members of society. Interventions by government and public authorities are viewed as hindrances to production. The sole judge of the worth and value of the common good is productive efficiency. John Paul II in *Laborem Exercens* (13) named this ideology "economism."

The just wage clearly is rooted in the communitarian vision of society. Each individual pursues his or her own path to fulfillment within society. The just wage enables each adult worker the means to achieve the minimum goods necessary for human livelihood. How this is achieved touches the second set of emphases in the common good.

The principle of subsidiarity "is intrinsically connected with the core of the common good tradition. This principle recognizes a rightful role for individual persons and for voluntary associations in society as well as for the state itself."[33] This principle tries to walk a path between collectivism and individualism. Individuals and small groups should do as much as possible to achieve practical justice in political, social, and economic affairs. The state should support individuals and smaller voluntary associations, not take over what individuals or groups can do. However, there are times when the state needs to intervene as a help ("subsidium") for the good of all concerned. In this understanding the state is not an evil, but has a positive, albeit restricted, role to play. "The state is not something negative which unduly restricts human freedom, but rather the state has the positive effect of promoting justice and true freedom for all."[34] The question within Catholic social teaching is not if the state can intervene, but when and to what extent.

The application to the just wage is clear. Individuals and owners of the smallest businesses are entrusted with the responsibility of enacting just wages. The state can and should intervene only when smaller groups or individuals do not move toward just remuneration. The debate over state intervention for just wages is not new in this country. It goes back to the turn of the century, before the enactment of national minimum wage legislation.[35]

A third concern in search of the common good is the difference between the state and society. Charles Curran notes this as one of the new developments in the understanding of the common good since Vatican II. The state can never be identified with society. The state is only one portion of society. The end of the state is the public order, an order of justice, public morality, and peace. This was also known as the temporal common good. The end of society is much wider--the common good, also called the spiritual common good. The church and religion in general are not private, but public realities, and influence the state and, indeed, all of society. However, in this approach to religious liberty, the common good in society does not call for the union of church and state. The state has no competency in matters of religion. In the protection of religious liberty Vatican II insisted on a more limited role for the state (DH, 6-7). In the concern for the dignity, freedom, and rights for the person John XXIII insisted on a greater role for the state (MM, 54-58). Curran remarks that contemporary Catholic social teaching has yet to recognize the conflict in both emphases and to show how they are compatible.[36]

Another important characteristic of the understanding of the content of the common good concerns the above-mentioned emphasis on personalism, in the dignity, freedom, and rights for the human person. John XXIII tried to avoid the pitfall of individualism by insisting on a balanced need for duties as well as rights. He also included economic rights, as well as political and civil rights. Paul VI recognized that the aspiration for equality is also part of today's personalism (OA, 22). The conflict comes in reconciling the desire for equality with the common and social nature of human existence. Paul VI was well aware of this problem: "Without a renewed education in solidarity, an overemphasis of equality can give rise to an individualism in which each one claims his own rights without wishing to be answerable for the common good." (OA, 23)

The just wage is very much caught up in these emphases. The promotion of the right to a just wage can pit one group of workers against other groups, in a clash of so-called special interest groups. To implement a just wage causes disagreement. Contemporary church documents are less sanguine about the possibility of conflict. Human sinfulness, the role of power, and the reality of conflict are all part of the pursuit of justice.[37] Yet the conflict can only be resolved in the context of the shared goal of the common good.

Each of these "balancing acts" involve very difficult decisions in the pursuit of the common good. The principle of subsidiarity and the recognition of the widely varying historical situations throughout the world only increase the complexity of concrete decision-making (OA, 4). Yet it is necessary to continue to keep before society the vision of the common good, for all people, even as human beings struggle imperfectly to achieve it.

The Just Wage and the Virtue of Justice

In the struggle to balance and judge competing claims to rights the Catholic tradition has an important resource. This is the understanding of the principles of justice. The documents of Catholic social teaching repeatedly refer to these principles to make specific how the exercise of rights by some persons is limited by the rights of others. The tradition's articulation of the principles of justice is presupposed by the acceptance of the dignity of each human person and the essential social nature of that dignity. The "truth" of the dignity and needs of each person are judged in comparison to the "justice" of the relative weight of the claims which come from this dignity and need, in relation to the competing claims of others. David Hollenbach sets out the conceptual framework:

> The entire theory of rights is developed within the framework of a complementary theory of justice. Rights represent claims to those things which are due individuals. The notion of justice is an indispensable means in the process of judging which of these claims takes priority over others in situations of conflict. The language of rights, therefore, focuses on the dignity, liberty and needs of all persons in society regarded disjunctively or one at a time. The language of justice, on the other hand, focuses on the dignity, liberty and needs of all persons regarded conjunctively or as bound by obligations and duties to one another.[38]

The right to a just wage for a worker and his or her family is an individual right. In judging how to implement this individual right it is necessary to see this right within the social situation of the worker. The tradition has worked out three types or modes of justice to deal with the competing claims of individuals and social groups. These are commutative justice, distributive justice, and social justice. Each of these types of justice is distinguished by the nature of the human relationship and interdependence to which they refer. The practical implementation of a right to a just wage needs to take into consideration all three of these modes of relating.[39]

For a long time commutative justice was the primary, sometimes only, principle used to judge the morality of a wage contract. Commutative justice is concerned with the relationships which bind individual to individual in the sphere of private transactions. At the center of this principle is the equal dignity and freedom of each person involved. Each person's dignity and freedom must be upheld for a contract to be judged morally just. For example, when a person enters into a wage contract, the agreement is equally binding on the employee and employer. The standard used is one of strict equality. No one in the contract has a privileged claim on the wage-for-work transaction. Pius XI said, "Mutual relations between capital and labor must be determined according to the laws of strictest justice, called commutative justice." (QA, 110) Hollenbach notes that "strict" in this understanding refers to what Aristotle called an "arithmetical" proportion. "The wage/labor exchange creates an obligation which is equally binding on worker and employer and the exchange itself must be one of strict equality."[40]

The notion of commutative justice is based on the direct relation of one person to another. It is not concerned with social, political, or wider economic questions of equality. Depending on one's understanding of the structures of society, the appeal to commutative justice can have progressive or reactionary effects. Leo XIII and his successors have used the notion of equality, which is at the core of commutative justice, as a defense of the equal right of all persons to work. Also, it has been used to conclude that slave wages, which do not support the basic needs of a worker, are fundamentally a denial of the rights of a worker. The payment of inadequate wages denies the equal dignity of employee and employer.

Yet it must be acknowledged that the private transaction is only one aspect of each person's life-in-community. The uniqueness of each human person, and his or her dignity, cannot be seen in isolation from the person's relationship with the wider community and society. There are many goods which cannot be realized by an individual alone. They transcend the sphere of the private contract. Such goods as the productivity of an industrialized economy, the fertility of the earth, and the national systems of social insurance and health care are public goods, the products of the social system as a whole.

Distributive justice and social justice concern the relationship and claims of persons in society as a whole. Distributive justice specifies the claims of individuals on these public goods. It limits the claims of commutative justice by placing these claims within a relational and societal context. Not only do individuals in contracts have a claim to equality, all citizens have an equal claim to a share in public goods (RN, 44). Distributive justice specifies that claim in two ways: first, it promotes the equality of opportunity for participation or entry into the social, economic, cultural, and political relationships which make up the common good (DI, 18). No societal benefits should be monopolized by a particular privileged class.[41] Second, the needs of all persons for the preservation of human dignity take precedence over the rights of the wealthy and majorities in a society. The resources of the common good are given by God to all human beings for the benefit of all the members of the human race.

> Distributive justice will be realized when social patterns are so organized that they meet the minimum needs of all persons and permit all an equal opportunity to participate in the public activities which meet these needs. These claims take priority over claims arising from merit, private ownership, social status, or de facto political power.[42]

With regard to the just wage, commutative justice recognizes the rights of owners and employers vis-a-vis the rights of workers. Distributive justice can limit the rights of employers by the just insistence of workers to participation in the economic life of society and to an adequate, human dignity-upholding wage. Obviously, this understanding of distributive justice does not produce an "arithmetic" equation for justice. The three understandings of justice in the Catholic tradition reflect the fact that all genuine rights exist in ordered relationship with each other. Distributive justice orders fundamental human rights. In a complementary manner, too, does social justice.

Social justice works in the opposite direction as distributive justice. It does not presume the common good. It rather looks at what is necessary for individuals to do to build and protect the common good. Hollenbach defines social justice as the measure or ordering principle which seeks to bring into existence those social relationships which will guarantee the possibility of realizing the demands of distributive justice. This calls for the creation and support of those institutions or structures which will support human dignity and human rights, participation in the social, economic, cultural, and political spheres of society, and assistance to genuine human needs. Prime among these institutions is government. Social justice appeals to the power, juridical and political, inherent in government to bring about changes which order the society more justly. Social justice makes claims on individuals as well. It asks that people cooperate in the formation of those structures, laws, and institutions which are needed for the protection of the rights of all.

The conclusion of John A. Ryan's groundbreaking work, *A Living Wage*, was an exercise in the practical application of social justice. He wrote, "As an abstract proposition, the State has both the right and the duty to compel all employers to pay a Living Wage."[43] One of the goals he worked toward for over twenty years after the publication of *A Living Wage* was that the federal government pass legislation mandating a minimum wage. Since that time, even more has been legislated in the name of social justice: restriction on child labor, disability payments, minimums of occupational safety, protection of retirement pensions, protection of the opportunity to found or join a trade union. This body of legislation is part of the practical expression of political power to promote the right to a just wage for workers and their families. Current legislation and the mechanics of governmental support of the right to a just wage also need to be judged today by the number of unemployed persons, the concerns and needs of workers, the changing economic conditions, and the goal of a more just society.

Each of these modes of justice--commutative, distributive, and social--is necessary to examine adequately whether and how the right to just remuneration is carried out. All three forms taken together provide a general framework for seeing the interrelationship of employee and employer, state and society. They also assist in the assignment of priorities for social, political, and economic action.

The Just Wage and the Virtue of Love

In 1971 Pope Paul VI wrote:

> If, beyond legal rules, there is really no deeper feeling of respect for and service to others, then even equality before the law can serve as an alibi for flagrant discrimination, continued exploitation and actual contempt. . . . In this field, everyone sees the highly important contribution of the Christian spirit, which moreover answers man's yearning to be loved. (OA, 23)

The exposition of the Church's teaching on the just wage in this chapter has been an attempt to explicate and apply the tradition's theological categories upon one particular issue. It has used the documents of modern Catholic social teaching and the commentary of theologians to bring to light "reason informed by faith."

This theological analysis, however, would be incomplete without touching upon the place of love. Without a "deeper feeling of respect" or sense of the "Christian spirit," the presentation of philosophical presuppositions and principles of justice would be without the heart of the Christian religious quest.

> Critical knowledge--the source of moral principles--reveals different aspects, dimensions and interrelationships of persons. But without the response of love to that concrete call of personal dignity the moral life would not exist at all. We would have only ethics--a set of principles of somewhat indeterminate content, suspended somewhere above the circumstances and particularities of actual human life.[44]

It is love which summons the motivation for human beings to use their critical knowledge in concrete moral decisions. Love reveals the *ought* which can drive us to enact and embody the dignity and worth of real human beings.

This is not a new idea in Catholic social teaching. Leo XIII tried to place love in relationship to justice when he said, "The law of mutual charity . . . completes the law of justice," and bids us "not only to give all their due . . . but also to do kindness to one another." Pius XI did not see justice and love as supplementary to each other but as different ways of expressing a single obligation. Pius XII expressed the relationship of justice to love as organic and mutual, analagous to matter and form, body and soul. For example, Pius XII said:

> On this organic conception which alone is living, in which the noblest humanity and the most genuine Christian spirit flourish in harmony, there is marked the Scripture thought, expounded by the great Aquinas: *Opus Justitiae Pax*--The work of justice shall be peace--a thought which is applicable to the internal as to the external aspect of social life. It admits of neither contrast nor alternative such as expressed in the disjunction, love or right, but the fruitful synthesis of love and right. In the one as in the other, since both radiate from the same spirit of God, we read the program and the seal of the human spirit; they complement one another, give each other life and support, walk hand in hand along the road of concord and pacification, which right clears the way for love and love makes right less stern and gives it higher meaning.[45]

One may quarrel here with Pius XII's romantic view of society, hierarchical and stratified, without conflict or power struggles in the community. But the complementary nature of justice and love "in the spirit of God" means one should not bring to action one without the other.

Since the Second Vatican Council, one important development of the theme of love in relation to justice has been the need to see love in relation to the concrete needs of people. This has been accompanied by a corresponding shift in the understanding of society. From the organic order of society of Leo XIII and Pius XI there has been a shift to a social model which envisions conflict and community as dynamically interrelated. The summons to love is prior to the reasoned reflection on how to formulate principles and strategies. "The Conciliar breakthrough also called for a recognition of the fact that the call to love in action extends further than the limits of organic harmony. Indeed, the obligation to love can be a call to engage in conflict."[46]

When Christians respond to the needs of their brothers and sisters, it is the duty of these Christians to flesh out the moral principles in concrete actions. The papal teaching of the past thirty years has been critical of all societal models. Therefore the popes have hesitated to offer any one detailed plan (or ideology) as *the* form of social action to follow. Christians, individually and joined in local churches, have the responsibility of assessing the signs of the times, the needs of people, and the resources at hand, in the light of reason (e.g., the Catholic social teaching) informed by faith and love. In an important admission Paul VI said it plainly.

> In the face of such widely varying situations it is difficult for us to utter a unified message and to put forward a solution which has universal validity. Such is not our ambition, nor is it our mission. It is up to the Christian communities to analyze with objectivity the situation which is proper to their own country, to shed on it the light of the Gospel's unalterable words and to draw principles of reflection, norms of judgment and directives for action from the social teaching of the Church. (OA, 4).

Concrete love has to take into consideration the historical situation of needy and hurting people, a critical analysis of the economic and political system, and a sense of the mutual interdependence of all peoples. Pope John Paul says it this way: "For the church does not propose economic and political systems or programs, nor does she show preference for one or the other, provided that human dignity is properly respected and promoted, and provided she herself is allowed the room she needs to exercise her ministry in the world." (SRS, 41) Love is not without content therefore. The appeal to love unites people to support human rights and dignity "and to establish progressively a justice which will be less and less imperfect." (OA, 15)[47]

The call to love in solidarity and in particularity is an important aspect of the right to a just wage. There is no one dogmatic application or formula of this right (or of any other right). Christians who have responsibility for setting and administering wages and benefits must take into account the laws governing labor and wages. They also have to see the needs of their employees in light of their common human dignity. The right to a just wage becomes an "in-principled" expression of love and solidarity.

Summary

This chapter has attempted to show that the right to a just wage is grounded in the basic themes of Catholic social doctrine. A fundamental presupposition is the dignity of the human person. Each person's dignity is both transcendental and concrete. Each person's dignity is lived out and upheld within a social context. The human person is social in nature. The concrete expression of human dignity is best found in the human rights tradition. Human rights have been continually espoused and expanded over the last one hundred years. They form a constellation of "the conditions for the realization of human worth in action," in a kind of order or arrangement. This order is characterized by interconnectedness and integral development. No one right can be singled out without acknowledging its relationship--personal, social, instrumental--to other human rights. The order of human rights is directed toward the full and integral development of persons, as individuals and within human communities.

The right to a just wage needs the perspectives from the bible and from theology as a background for its explication as a human right. The myths of Genesis reveal the positive and negative sides of human work. Theological reflection notes the changes in the understandings of work in the context of various historical situations. Within the order of rights, the right to a just wage is a social mediation of the individual's right to work. When workers receive fair remuneration they are empowered to carry out other rights, to bodily integrity, to the support of their families, to the contribution of the common good.

Like other rights, the right to a just wage is not without its own duties. Each worker has responsibilities to his or her employer, family, and the society as a whole. Employers as well have the responsibility to give workers just remuneration and appropriate benefits.

To take seriously Paul VI's call for people to look at the situations in which they live and apply Catholic social teaching to them requires examination of the contexts of the family and the common good. The family has an indispensible and essential role in the building of society. The just wage has repeatedly been expressed as that set of monetary payments and benefits which allows workers to support themselves *and their families*. The variety of families in each culture must be taken into consideration in the application of the just wage. The social teaching's support of the common good allows employers, employees, and the state to live their vision of the economic and political system beyond individualism. The human person is a person in community. The principle of subsidiarity assists each level of society in determining who should do what to support the dignity and rights of each person.

Another richness of the Catholic social tradition which needs to be applied to the right to a just wage is the three-fold division of the principles of justice. The just wage is first of all a contract, subject to commutative justice. Fundamental equality governs the parties to the contract (employee and employer). But the reflection on justice does not stop with individuals. The common good in its many elements must also be taken into consideration. The principles of distributive and social justice also affect the wage agreement. They help to give order to the structures and institutions of civil government and society as a whole, so that the right to a just wage for an individual worker can be enacted.

Finally, the virtue of love provides a point of religious reference in order to avoid a sterile and abstract application of ethical principles. The faith community of Christians, called into being by our loving God, passes on this love in mutual interdependence, with participation in all the structures of society, and in practical concern for the concrete needs of people. What John Paul II calls "the virtue of solidarity" is the movement of individuals, groups, and the church going beyond themselves in love for others. Love gives content by its comfort of hurting human beings, its challenge to structures of injustice, and its movement toward unity and peace in human communities. Those who apply the just wage need to carry it out in a spirit of love.

NOTES

1. See John F. O'Grady, "The Biblical Doctrine of Work," *Chicago Studies* 28 (1989): 69-76.

2. Karol Wojtyla, *Sources of Renewal: The Implementation of the Second Vatican Council*, trans. P.S. Falla (San Francisco: Harper & Row, 1980), 61. Inner quotation from GS, 24.

3. Calvez and Perrin, 106.

4. Hollenbach, *Claims*, 90.

5. Ibid., 90-1.

6. Ibid., 91.

7. For an historical analysis of human rights in the Catholic tradition, see Hollenbach, *Claims*, 41-107.

8. David Hollenbach, *Justice, Peace and Human Rights: American Social Ethics in a Pluralistic Context* (New York: Crossroad, 1988), 41. Also see LE, 4.

9. Claus Westermann, "Work, Civilisation and Culture in the Bible," in Gregory Baum, ed., *Work and Religion* (New York: Seabury, 1980), 83. See also O'Grady, "Biblical Doctrine," 65-78.

10. O'Grady, "Biblical Doctine," 68-70.

11. Hollenbach, *Justice, Peace*, 44.

12. Francis Schussler Fiorenza, "Religious Beliefs and Praxis: Reflections on Catholic Theological Views of Work," in Baum, *Work and Religion*, 92-102, and idem, "Work and Critical Theology," in W.J. Heisler and John W. Houck, eds., *A Matter of Dignity: Inquiries into the Humanization of Work* (Notre Dame, IN: University of Notre Dame Press, 1977), 23-44.

13. Fiorenza mentions H. Rondet, J. Lacroix, M.D. Chenu, J.H. Oldham, A. Auer, J.J. Illanes, and E. Kaiser. Fiorenza, "Religious Beliefs," 101-2.

14. Ibid., 98.

15. Hollenbach, *Claims*, 85.

16. Ibid., 87.

17. The Second Synod of Bishops also say, "Participation constitutes a right which is to be applied both in the economic and in the social and political field." (DI, 18)

18. Cronin, *Catholic Social Principles*, 315. See also Calvez and Perrin, 235-7.

19. Calvez and Perrin, 236.

20. Friedhelm Hengsbach, "The Church and the Right to Work," in Jacques Pohier and Dieth, *Unemployment and the Right to Work* (New York: Seabury, 1982), 42.

21. Hollenbach, *Claims*, 97.

22. Ibid., 99.

23. The decline of the American steel industry in the 1980s could be used as an excellent and frustrating case study on the dilemmas of this situation. See among many books David Bensman and Roberta Lynch, *Rusted Dreams: Hard Times in a Steel Community* (Berkeley, CA: University of California Press, 1987), John P. Hoerr, *And the Wolf Finally Came: The Decline of the American Steel Industry* (Pittsburgh: University of Pittsburgh Press, 1988), and William Serrin, *Homestead: The Glory and Tragedy of an American Steel Town* (New York: Times Books, 1992).

24. Edward Reissner, *Canonical Employee-Employer Relationships: Canon 1524* (Washington: Catholic University of America Press, 1964), 34. See also von Nell-Breuning, *Reorganization*, 184.

25. Reissner, 34.

26. Sources cited in this document are RN, 9; PT, 15; GS, 26; CIC canons 1058 and 1977; and the Universal Declaration of Human Rights, 16. John XXIII adds as a gloss to this right, "in the founding of [a family] both the man and the woman enjoy equal rights and duties." (PT, 15)

27. Elizabeth McKeown, "The Seamless Garment; The Bishops' Letter in the Light of the American Catholic Pastoral Tradition," in R. Bruce Douglass, ed., *The Deeper Meaning of Economic Life: Critical Essays on the U.S. Catholic Bishops' Pastoral Letter on the Economy* (Washington: Georgetown University Press, 1986), 133-4.

28. EJA, 147, 167, 199, 207, and 208.

29. Ann O'Hara Graff, "Women and Dignity: Vision and Practice," in Charles R. Strain, ed., *Prophetic Visions and Economic Realities: Protestants, Jews, and Catholics Confront the Bishops' Letter on the Economy* (Grand Rapids, MI: William B. Eerdsmans, 1989), 220-5.

30. Charles K. Wilbur, "Individualism, Interdependence, and the Common Good: Rapprochement Between Economic Theory and Catholic Social Thought," in Strain, *Prophetic Visions*, 230.

31. R. Bruce Douglass, "First Things First: The Letter and the Common Good Tradition," in Douglass, *Deeper Meaning*, 25.

32. Wilbur, "Individualism," 231.

33. Charles E. Curran, "The Common Good and Official Catholic Social Teaching," in Oliver F. Williams and John W. Houck, eds., *The Common Good and U.S. Capitalism* (Lanham, MD: University Press of America, 1987), 118.

34. Ibid. See also Cronin, *Social Principles*, 75, and Calvez and Perrin, 121-4, 328-37.

35. John A. Ryan, *A Living Wage: Its Ethical and Economic Aspects* (New York: Macmillan, 1906), 297-323.

36. Curran, "Common Good," 120-2.

37. Congregation for the Doctrine of the Faith, *Instruction on Christian Freedom and Liberation* (Washington: United States Catholic Conference, 1986), 46-8.

38. Hollenbach, *Claims*, 144. In this section I will substantially make use of his discussion of the principles of justice.

39. For further discussion of the three types of justice, see thse examples, among the extensive literature of Catholic social teaching: John A. Ryan, *Distributive Justice: The Right and Wrong of Our Present Distribution of Wealth*, 3rd ed. (New York: Macmillan, 1920), chapter 16; Calvez and Perrin, *Social Justice*, chapter 6; von Nell-Breuning, *Reorganization*, 170-91; Johannes Messner, *Social Ethics*, rev. ed (St. Louis: B. Herder, 1965), 314-24.

40. Hollenbach, *Claims*, 146. In a footnote he refers to *Nicomachean Ethics*, 1132a, and Thomas Aquinas, *Summa Theologiae*, II-II, 61, 2.

41. For discussion of how the preferential option for the poor relates to distributive justice and the common good, see Curran, "Common Good," 126-7, and Anthony Tambasco, "Option for the Poor," in Douglass, *Deeper Meaning*, 37-96.

42. Hollenbach, *Claims*, 151.

43. Ryan, *A Living Wage*, 301.

44. Hollenbach, *Claims*, 168.

45. Christmas address of 1942 in Yzermans 2:56-7.

46. Hollenbach, *Claims*, 172.

47. Richard McCormick notes that two of the important shifts in moral theology since Vatican II are the tentativeness of moral formulations and the dual nature as teachers and learners of the moral magisterium. Richard McCormick, *The Critical Calling: Reflections on Moral Dilemmas since Vatican II* (Washington: Georgetown University Press, 1989), 16-21 and passim.

CHAPTER THREE

CHURCH TEACHING ON THE JUST WAGE
IN ITS OWN INSTITUTIONS

The previous chapters have tried to examine the right to a just wage in the major moralists of the Middle Ages and in the papal and conciliar documents of the past one hundred years. Analysis of the Catholic Church's human rights tradition has helped to flesh out what is meant by the right to a just wage, its demands and limitations. It is now time to move to the heart of the argument. What does the Catholic Church say about its responsibility to be consistent in its own teachings, what is necessary "in house"? This chapter will review the brief texts that are available, from Pope Leo XIII, the 1917 Code of Canon Law, the Second Vatican Council, the 1971 Synod of Bishops, the 1983 Code of Canon Law, and the hierarchy of the United States of America.

Pope Leo XIII

In his landmark encyclical, *Rerum Novarum*, Pope Leo XIII did not explicitly refer to a just wage for church employees. However, in two sections he referred to the Catholic Church as a teacher and guide of the commandments (26-29 and 63). The church is a teacher of its own people, through the instruments of its bishops and clergy. Leo saw that only the voluntary acceptance of the instruction he was proposing would be effective. The church "strives to influence the mind and the heart so that all may willingly yield themselves to be formed and guided by the commandments of God." (RN, 26) His concern was to apply the teachings of the Gospel to the industrial working classes. Charity was one element of this application. He said, "The Church, moreover, intervenes directly in behalf of the poor, by . . . maintaining many associations, which she knows to be efficient for the relief of poverty." (RN, 29)

Another concern Leo had was the practical application of virtue, for individuals and for the agencies of the state. The pope stated:

Neither must it be supposed that the solicitude of the Church is so preoccupied with the spiritual concerns of her children as to neglect their temporal and earthly interests. Her desire is that the poor, for example, should rise above poverty and wretchedness, and better their condition in life. (RN, 28)

This work of the Church in the temporal world was urgent. It was to be carried out forcefully by the bishops and clergy ("Every minister of holy religion must bring to the struggle the full energy of his mind and all his power of endurance."), and by those who have power to effect change for the good of the people (RN, 63).

With this intensity of feeling, and an optimistic vision of the efficacy of virtue applied, one line of the encyclical stands out with particular force. "But the Church, not content with pointing out the remedy, also applies it." (RN, 26) Leo was not talking specifically about the just wage here. Yet he was speaking to the church's responsibility to be consistent. The bishops and clergy and faithful in Christ need to apply the teachings he was proclaiming in the world and in the church. It would take many years for the bishops to be more explicit on the application of the church's social teachings to its own institutions and agencies, especially the right to a just wage.

1917 Code of Canon Law

Pope Benedict XV promulgated the Roman Catholic Church's first official codification of all its universal legislation for the Latin Church, on May 27, 1917. The *Codex Iuris Canonici* was the fruit of thirteen years work, having been initiated by Pope Pius X in 1904. It repealed all other extant universal canonical legislation. Commentator John Alesandro says, "As such, its 2414 canons represented the most radical revision of law the Church had ever effected."[1]

Only one canon addresses the issue of just compensation of workers. Canon 1524 reads in translation:

> All administrators of ecclesiastical goods, and especially priests and religious, must pay the workmen whom they employ good and fair wages, and must see to it that at a convenient time they are free for prayer; must not in any way dissuade them from their domestic duties and thrift; and not impose on them more work than their strength can bear, nor work which does not agree with their sex or age.

This canon is part of a group which contains instructions on the administration of ecclesiastical goods. The fundamental understanding of good administration is seen in Canon 1523, where administrators are obliged to fulfill their office with the care and diligence of a "paterfamilias." Canon 1524 is not limited to bishops, priests, or religious, but applies to all

Catholics who administer church goods and agencies. Only one commentary noted the influence of *Rerum Novarum* on the canon (even though the Latin edition of the Code refers to this encyclical in a footnote). Yet this commentator also seemed to water down the "ought" ("debent") of the canon by remarking, "In the present sociological conditions, the question of just and fair wages (or of a so-called living wage) is a very big and difficult problem, especially in a country as large as the United States."[2]

It is interesting to compare the treatment of just compensation for church workers and for priests in the 1917 Code. The just wage for lay employees was not identified as a right. But the clergy were entitled to receive sufficient remuneration by virtue of the canonical "title" of their ordination. The ordinary forms of title in the Code were title to an ecclesiastical benefice, pension, or patrimony. Two qualities which were necessary were that the title provide sufficient income for the priestly candidate's livelihood and that it be secure for the entire life of the cleric. If the bishop did not provide a candidate for orders with such a title, he was to ordain him to the title of "service of the diocese" or "service to the missions." (CIC/17 Canon 981) Here the bishop assumed, both for himself and his successors, the responsibility of providing for the priest's livelihood. Of course, the Code also allowed for the priest to receive stipends for the celebration of Mass and "stole fees," voluntary offerings on the occasion of the administration of the sacraments (CIC/17 Canons 840 and 463). James Donlon summarizes the attitude of the 1917 Code of Canon Law on the equitable sustenance of the priest:

> The Code did not so much speak of the right of the priest, as a person, to support and a decent livelihood, as it spoke of the need to maintain the clerical state and respect for it. The well-being of the priest as an individual, while not disregarded, takes a secondary position. . . . The end result of the Code's concern in many ways would coincide with the end result of adherence to the teaching of Pope Leo in *Rerum Novarum*. . . . Unfortunately, however, the motivation of the Code in this matter is at variance with that of Pope Leo. One seeks to protect a class, a state, and respect for it, while the other was concerned with protecting respect for the dignity of the individual.[3]

Vatican Council II

In two documents the Fathers of the Second Vatican Council affirmed the right to a just wage for those employed by the church. The right to a just wage for workers, in general, is affirmed in *Gaudium et Spes*, article 67.

In the Decree on the Missionary Activity of the Church, there is a discussion of a growing phenomenon: full time lay catechists in the missions. The Council Fathers praise these men and women. The catechists are affirmed as important to the spread of the Gospel, and are deserving of thorough training, with due respect for understanding and appropriating local culture. Pastors are to provide catechists with both academic and spiritual formation. This training aids catechists in study of the Catholic faith and growth in holiness of life, which are both essential to their mission. Also essential to their work is proper remuneration for adequate living conditions.

> In addition, for those who dedicate themselves entirely to this work, a decent standard of living and social security should be provided through a just salary. (AG, 17)

In calling for a just salary for the catechist and his or her family, the document is only asking for church leaders to put into practice the very principles of social justice which the catechists proclaim and teach. Some Council Fathers recognized the difficulty financially-strapped missionary bishops would have raising sufficient funds for just remuneration of their catechists. They proposed a foundation for the support of catechists, similar to the "Opus Sancti Petri," which supports native priests. This wish was written into the document in article 17 as a demand on the Congregation for the Propagation of the Faith.

Of wider application is the paragraph in the Decree on the Apostolate of the Laity, which calls for justice for layfolk who work for the church. The full article is worth quoting in its entirety.

> Deserving of special honor and commendation in the Church are those lay people, single or married, who devote themselves and their professional skill either permanently or temporarily, to the service of associations and their activities. The Church derives great joy from the fact that every day an increasing number of lay persons offer their personal services to apostolic associations and activities, either within the limits of their own nation or in the international field, or especially in Catholic mission communities and in regions where the Church has only recently been planted.
>
> The pastors of the Church should gladly and gratefully welcome these lay persons and make sure that their situation meets the demands of justice, equity, and charity to the fullest extent possible, particularly as regards proper support for them and their families. Pastors should also see to it that these lay people enjoy the necessary formation, spiritual consolation, and

incentive. (AA, 22)

There is nothing grudging about the spirit of this text. The Council Fathers see laity who work in service to the church as a blessing. Pastors (diocesan bishops as well as pastors of parishes) are to show their happiness as well as their gratitude by how fairly they treat these co-workers in ministry, "quam maxime." Remuneration is only just if it considers the lay worker's family as well as the worker. There is concern for full or integral development of the person, too, in the call for pastors to provide academic training, spiritual formation, and pastoral support and care. There is to be a future dimension to their work. Incentive offers the opportunity of possible promotion to a position of greater responsibility as well as a greater salary. What is called for is not charity, but justice. In his commentary on this passage, Ferdinand Klostermann notes that there were several proposals by Council Fathers "to tone down the accentuation given to just requirements and adequate payments for families." All were rejected, in favor of the approved text.[4]

If there is a cloud hanging over this text, it is that praise is directed only to those laity who have professional skills to give in service to the church. They are obviously worthy of praise and deserving of a just salary and proper benefits. Yet the "ordinary worker," whose skill is manual, not professional, is not mentioned or praised. It is always risky to read into what is lacking in a particular statement. It would be easy, nevertheless, for some to see a difference between the laywoman who may be a theologian or physician or sociologist, working for an international church agency, and the layman, who is a janitor for a small parish. The chance of misinterpretation of this text, and possible failure to apply justice to all workers in and for the church, dampens the effect of this valuable passage.

1971 Synod of Bishops

The most explicit declaration of the church's responsibility to practice what it preaches is found in one of the two documents issued by the 1971 Second General Assembly of the Synod of Bishops, *De Iustitia in Mundo*. This document is often known by its Englist language title, *Justice in the World*. Although the two documents issued by the Synod are not technically papal or conciliar teaching, it is significant that they were published in the *Acta Apostolicae Sedis*. This was done at the direction of Pope Paul VI, who confirmed all conclusions in the documents that conformed to current usage. His order that they be published indicated that he was in general agreement with the contents of the documents. The Synod declared in the Introduction of *De Iustitia* its affirmation of the link of the work of justice and the proclamation of the Word, in these well-known words:

Action on behalf of justice and participation in the transformation of the world fully appear to us as a constitutive dimension of the preaching of the Gospel, or, in other words, of the Church's mission for the redemption of the human race and its liberation from every oppressive situation. (DI, 6)

The Synod demonstrated this concern for justice with concrete and realistic analysis of the structures of injustice in the world. It spoke of all the members of the church becoming leaven in the world to promote the common good in an increasingly interdependent world.

But the above quoted sentence needs to be linked to another, less well known, passage from the third chapter, on the practice of justice.

While the Church is bound to give witness to justice, she recognizes that anyone who ventures to speak to people about justice must first be just in their eyes. Hence we must undertake an examination of the modes of acting and of the possessions and life style found within the Church itself. (DI, 40)

Here is the clearly expressed commitment of the church to be consistent: what it says for others it also must do. The human rights of all people in the church are affirmed. No one is less deserving of the protection of human rights because she or he is a member of the church. Several rights are explicitly named: to participation (especially by women), to freedom of expression, to due process, to consultation in decision-making, and to a just wage for employees of the church in its institutions.

Those who serve the church by their labor, including priests and religious, should receive a sufficient livelihood and enjoy that social security which is customary in their region. Lay people should be given fair wages and a system for promotion. (DI, 41)

This statement is clear that a just wage is a right for all who work in and for the church. It clarifies the ambiguity of *Apostolicam Actuositatem*, which mentioned only those who have and give professional skills to the service of the church as deserving a just wage. The sufficient livelihood recalls earlier, more explicit, papal statements on the needs of human beings, which a just wage ought to provide, for self and for family. These include food, clothing, shelter, medical care, rest and relaxation, and the opportunity for education for oneself and one's children. The wage earned by a church worker should allow the individual to live in a manner befitting the dignity of the human person.

In this text there are also two recognitions of future developments which flow from the just wage due an employee of the church. These are social security and a system for promotion. Each person needs assurance of aid when he or she is disabled, unemployed, or in old age. Paying employees "under the table" to avoid taxes and social security would seem to deny the rightful expectation of this statement, and the need of the laborer. Participation in an already established governmental program, such as Social Security in the United States, would be a prudent course for employers in church institutions. The second future consideration, a system of promotion, would appear to be quite a challenge. It makes the reasonable presumption that some workers, by education or ability or acquired skill, have the potential for advancement. It also presumes that their talent and abilities are valuable for the church, and should be encouraged and cultivated. One area of expertise is suggested in the text by the Synod of Bishops: administration of church property. Others, such as education, pastoral ministry, and social service, come easily to mind. Since there are many parishes, and indeed even in this country not a few dioceses, with very small staffs and rosters of employees, the opportunity for, and even more, a "system" of promotion, would have to encourage movement of some employees from parish to parish, from diocese to diocese.[5]

This has to have an impact on the managerial style of pastors, at many levels in the church. A genuine concern for the development of lay workers in the church would encourage pastors to support continuing education and, where it furthers the mission of the church, job changes for promotion. It would also call for increased cooperation among church parishes, institutions, and dioceses.[6]

The recognition in the text that religious and priests are workers in the church and as such deserve a just wage is supported by the second document issued by the 1971 Synod of Bishops, on the ministerial priesthood. The Synod said,

> The remuneration of priests, to be determined certainly in a spirit of evangelical poverty, but as far as possible equitable and sufficient, is a duty of justice and ought to include social security. (DSM, 14)

They ask that determination of what is just and sufficient for priests be done in a spirit of solidarity, within dioceses and regions. Excessive differences in priests' remuneration should be removed, within dioceses and ecclesiastical jurisdictions.

The witness of the church to the practice of justice is linked in *De Iustitia in Mundo* to the process of educating to justice. Education to justice is conducted on many levels, with several means. The family, the parish religious education program, schools, even trade unions and political parties impart education for justice. Participation in the work of societies devoted to justice and contact with the reality of injustice make this education practical. Education for justice only "works," however, when there is a renewal of heart. This renewal

> will likewise awaken a critical sense, which will lead us to reflect on the society in which we live and on its values; it will make men ready to renounce these values when they cease to promote justice for all men. (DI, 51)

The core content of this critical sense is respect for human beings and their dignity. The Synod reaffirmed the magisterial teaching on social concerns expressed in the social encyclicals from *Rerum Novarum* to *Octogesima Adveniens*, in the Word of God, and in the liturgy, as three sources of the principles of justice in the world.

The articulation of this critical sense as essential to education to justice is a challenge to look anew at church employment practices, especially wages, salaries, and benefits. It is part of the scrutiny of the signs of the times (GS, 4). It is also a call to action.

> The examination of conscience which we have made together, regarding the Church's involvement in action for justice, will remain ineffective if it is not given flesh in the life of our local Churches at all their levels. (DI, 72)

Action includes theological research, ecumenical collaboration, and study by curial bodies and episcopal conferences around the world. Church leaders and members must constantly reassert[7] and flesh out the gospel's call to justice in the world and in the church.

1983 Code of Canon Law

On January 25, 1983, Pope John Paul II promulgated the new Code of Canon Law for the the members of the Latin rite of the Catholic Church. He did this on the twenty-fourth anniversary of Pope John XXIII's surprise announcement, in which he revealed his pastoral plan for *aggiornamento*. John's vision was for a synod for the diocese of Rome, a new Code of Canon Law, and an ecumenical council for the Roman Catholic Church.

Because of John's brief pontificate, it was left to Pope Paul VI to carry out the vision. On several occasions Paul set the course for the task of revision of canon law. Specifically, he said that the revision was not to be a mere reworking, but a reformation, of the 1917 Code. The new Code must be accommodated to a new way of thinking proper to the Second Vatican Council. Both Paul VI and John Paul II often stressed the interrelationship of church law and the conciliar teaching. This is important to realize when reading the Code. "The canons, many of which repeat or summarize the Council's texts, must be interpreted in light of its teaching; they cannot properly be isolated from their historical sources."[8]

This process of applying the conciliar teaching to the new Code of Canon Law is carried out in the expression of the right to a just wage for a worker employed by the church. There are two canons which specify this right. The more general one addresses social justice in labor relations. Canon 1286 reads in translation:

> Administrators of goods
> #1. are to observe meticulously the civil laws pertaining to labor
> and social policy according to Church principles in the
> employment of workers;
> #2. are to pay employees a just and decent wage so that they
> may provide appropriately for their needs and those of their
> family.

This canon does not see any necessary opposition between ecclesial law and civil law. Civil law is to be carried out in labor relations. There is the presumption here that civil law benefits workers. However, there may be times when the limitation of church principles comes into play. Generally the canon takes the position of supporting the civil law which governs social order.

Of specific interest is the second point of the canon. The right to a just wage is affirmed for employees hired or contracted by administrators of church goods. This is to be a family wage, for the decent support of those for whom the worker is responsible. In canon 1282 it is noted that administrators can be either clerics or lay persons. They are bound to a position of trust in the church, and need to recognize that their duties are to be carried out in a manner which will bring credit and credibility to the church. Canon 1286 specifies that the social teachings of the church, including the rights of workers, must be followed in the administration of church goods.

Canon 231 lays down the fundamental norms for lay people employed by the church. The full canon reads in translation:

> #1. Lay persons who devote themselves permanently or
> temporarily to some special service of the church are obliged to
> acquire the appropriate formation which is required to fulfill
> their function properly and to carry it out conscientiously,

zealously, and diligently.

#2. With due regard to can. 230, #1, they have a right to a decent remuneration suited to their condition; by such remuneration they should be able to provide decently for their own needs and for those of their family with due regard for the prescriptions of civil law; they likewise have a right that their pension, social security, and health benefits be duly provided.

This canon comes in the context of several canons on the obligations and rights of lay Christian faithful. Canon 1286 refers to *anyone* employed by the church. Canon 231 is more specific as it refers to those laity who devote themselves to service in and for the church. This canon follows the spirit and letter of *Apostolicam Actuositatem*, article 22. The full development of lay persons employed in church service is seen as their own responsibility. However, if they are bound to proper formation (academic, professional, spiritual), they have a corresponding right to the opportunity to receive this. (This right is supported by canon 217, on Christian education, and canon 229, on theological formation.) These laws encourage the lay workers to carry out their function zealously, and are consistent with the generous tone of the passage from the Decree on the Apostolate of the Laity.

Canon 231 distinguishes lay persons employed by the church from the general apostolate and liturgical ministries mentioned earlier in canons 225 and 230. The workers may or may not hold an ecclesiastical office; the just wage applies in either case. The canon does not distinguish between full-time and part-time employment, so both can be understood as included.

Even as the church worker has certain responsibilities to keep abreast of new developments in his or her field, there is the corresponding responsibility on the church administrator to pay a just wage. This applies to both men and women in church service. The benefits of a pension, social security, and health care form an integral whole with decent remuneration. Both are characterized as a right ("ius"). Provost notes that this is stronger than the claim clergy have to just remuneration (canon 281) in the Code of Canon Law.[9]

A brief review of the *fontes*, or sources, published with each canon provides the link between the canons and previous church teaching on the just wage. Paragraph 2 of canon 231 has references to *Apostolicam Actuositatem*, 22, and *Ad Gentes*, 17. These have been reviewed earlier, in the section on the Second Vatican Council. Canon 1286 has several references: canon 1524 of the 1917 Code; *Quadragesimo Anno* and *Divini Redemptoris* of Pius XI; the Christmas message of 1942 and the address to Italian workers on June 13, 1943, of Pius XII; John XXIII's *Mater et Magistra*; and *Apostolicam Actuositatem* and *Gaudium et Spes* from Vatican II. The only two notable absences from this list, on the teaching on a just wage, are *Pacem in Terris* and *De Iustitia in Mundo*.[10]

The 1983 Code of Canon Law faithfully echoes the papal and conciliar teaching of the church, with regard to the right to a just wage, for all workers hired by church administrators and for those employed in church service. Canons 1286 and 231 adequately treat this right. In keeping with the principle of interpretation that the canonical texts must be understood in light of the Vatican II teaching, "the right to a just remuneration" are the words which open up the full articulation of this right as expressed in previous documents. On this subject, the Code does seem to embody church teaching in law, with the diligence of a wise householder (canon 1284).

Economic Justice for All

Background

In 1986 the Catholic bishops of the United States approved in final form and published its second long pastoral letter in three years. *Economic Justice for All: Pastoral Letter on Catholic Social Teaching and the U.S. Economy* was the result of six years of work by an ad hoc committee of American bishops. The committee was chaired by Milwaukee Archbishop Rembert Weakland. It was initially charged with writing a study of the relationship of Christianity to capitalism. This was suggested by some bishops after the NCCB's letter on Marxism in 1980.

In a report to the U.S. bishops at their annual meeting in 1983, Archbishop Weakland said that the committee members and staff had decided not to approach capitalism on a theoretical level. Also, because of the many forms of capitalism found throughout the world, the committee chose to focus primarily on the American economy, and only to a lesser degree on how American capitalism affects the world's economy.[11]

The committee members and staff followed the same "open" process of text development as was used to complete the 1983 pastoral letter on war and peace, *The Challenge of Peace: God's Promise and Our Response*. Beginning in 1981, the committee held "hearings" to listen to over 120 business people, farmers, congressional staff members, sociologists, economists, politicians, theologians, and representatives from social justice organizations. Then they invited wide consultation from their fellow bishops, all Catholics, and interested Americans, on three drafts. The document was amended and approved at the annual meeting of the U.S. bishops in November of 1986.

As with the 1983 pastoral letter on war and peace, the bishops stirred up fierce argument and public debate. A group of Catholics, under the leadership of Michael Novak and William E. Simon, even wrote and published their own, business-oriented letter on the American economy and the social teachings, entitled *Toward the Future: Catholic Social Thought and the U.S. Economy.*   However, in the wealth of symposia, sermons, reports, and articles published, this writer found that the topic of a just wage for church employees seems to have stirred up no debate whatever. Nowhere is there to be found mention of, much less disagreement with, the assertion of the right to a just wage for those men and women employed by the church.

Seventy Years of Support
        Perhaps the reason for this lack of critical comment is that the U.S. Catholic bishops have a solid history of supporting the right to a just wage. James Cardinal Gibbons, the archbishop of Baltimore from 1877 to 1921, was a stalwart supporter of the working class, especially their right to form unions. In the 1919 statement, *Program of Social Reconstruction,* issued by the Administrative Committee of the National Catholic War Council (forerunner of the NCCB), the bishops urged no lowering of wage rates after the war. Instead, they echoed *Rerum Novarum* and called for wages for all adult male workers sufficient for the maintenance of a family. This would include future as well as present needs. A legal minimum wage enacted by states should provide at least for a just wage. They went even further, and said, "After all, a living wage is not necessarily the full meaning of justice."[12] Specific references in pastoral letters in 1933, 1940, and, most recently, 1975, reaffirmed the right of a worker to a wage adequate for the needs of self and family. Through these letters, and the outstanding work of priest staff members John A. Ryan, Raymond McGowan, John A. Cronin, and George G. Higgins, who served as staff and advisors to the bishops' conference on labor and on economic issues, the Catholic bishops supported the papal teachings on social concern and attempted to apply them to the United States.[13]

        John Pawlikowski also notes a sub-theme to the twentieth century history of the statements on economic policy by the American bishops. After World War II, they turned their attention outward, beyond the immigrant boundaries of American Catholicism. The statements urged newly affluent Catholics to join in the efforts to aid the remaining poor in the United States. A 1966 statement on racism, and the 1970 resolution to begin the Campaign for Human Development, marked a new posture for the bishops. Pawlikowski says,"Defense of the poor may now mean speaking words of judgment to important elements of the Catholic community."[14]

        Economic Justice for All is very much in the tradition of these statements by the American hierarchy. It also continues the critical concern, as the bishops call themselves, and all members of the church, to be just among their own workers and in their own agencies and institutions. The 1986 letter is the most explicit challenge to the church for justice in all of the American bishops' statements on economic policy.

The Drafts

A review of the three published drafts of this pastoral letter[15] shows that the section on the church being challenged by its own teaching on justice is substantially the same from the first draft to the final, approved document. There are, nevertheless, a few changes through the process of revision which are worth noting.

In the first draft, the general tone of self-criticism is set. The church is identified as an economic actor in its own right. The bishops are responsible for stewardship of the many resources of the church. Therefore, "All the moral principles that govern the just operation of any economic endeavor apply to the church and its many agencies and institutions. Indeed the church should be exemplary in its fidelity to the principles of economic justice." The bishops quote articles 40 and 41 from *De Iustitia in Mundo*, to support the need for the church to be just even as it calls others to justice. Article 41 specifies just remuneration for all in the church. The bishops state that this demand will cause considerable strain on the church's resources. Nevertheless, they acknowledge their responsibility to carry this out, and quote canon 231, 2, from the 1983 Code of Canon Law. Church employees have a right to decent remuneration for themselves *and their family members*.

This is the only draft in which the bishops quote this canon from the new Code. It is the most specific of the references to a just wage and sufficient benefits, for the worker and his family. The bishops affirm the right to a just wage, for the worker and his family, in the body of the letter. This support carries through to the final approved document (EJA, 80, 103, 196). But the explicit recognition that a just wage is also a family wage, for the employee of the church, is not spelled out in the subsequent drafts nor the final text.

The second draft moves the section on challenges to the church to the end of the text, where it remains through subsequent revision. It is curiously noteworthy that this draft omits both quotations from the 1971 Synod of Bishops, as well as canon 231, 2. The text does emphasize with italics, the sentence "All the moral principles that govern the just operation of any economic endeavor apply to the church and its many agencies and institutions. Indeed the church should be exemplary in its fidelity to the principles of economic justice." This important sentence, with its highlighted emphasis, remains in the third draft and the final document. A footnote to this sentence refers to canons 231, 2, and 1286 of the 1983 Code of Canon Law. This is the last time these canons are quoted. There is no reference to them (in this section) in the third draft or the final work. A paragraph is added on the need for conversion of heart in the process of transformation of structures. Also, a Vatican II "mini-ecclesiology" is added in another paragraph. It sees the church as a communion of people called to transcendence, yet carrying out its mission in the world through visible structures.

The key phrase in this draft states, "We bishops commit ourselves to the principle that those who serve the church--laity, clergy, and religious--should receive a sufficient livelihood and enjoy the social benefits common in our nation." This is a close paraphrase of article 41 of *De Iustitia in Mundo*. It is repeated in the third draft (and the final version) with only the phrase "common in our nation" changed to "provided by responsible employers in our nation." As noted above, it omits reference to the wage supporting the needs of the family of the worker.

For the third draft, the bishops bring back and reprint the quotation from *De Iustitia*, article 40: "'While the Church is bound to give witness to justice, she recognizes that anyone who ventures to speak to people about justice must first be just in their eyes. Hence we must undertake an examination of the modes of acting and of the possessions and life style found within the church herself.'" The third draft text in this section hardly changes from the previous draft. There are, however, two other additions.

A new section of three paragraphs, "Supporting the Family," is added, immediately in front of "The Church as Economic Actor." This section is a litany of the difficulties contemporary economic life has on marriage and the family in our society. It calls for the church to support the family by fighting against certain unjust economic structures. This brief section ends by stating, "Economic arrangements must support the family and promote its solidity. We would do well in our society and in our own lives to ask whether such arrangements are the norm." It is unclear whether this is a reference to a just wage which would support the needs of family members.

The second noteworthy addition reaffirms articles 42 and 43 from *De Iustitia in Mundo*. In these paragraphs the Synod called for women to exercise responsibility and their share of participation in society and in the church. After noting the right to collective bargaining, and calling for "new creative models of collaboration" and "fruitful modes of cooperation" between labor and management, the bishops say, "In seeking greater justice in wages, we recognize the need to be particularly alert to the continuing discrimination against women throughout church and society, especially reflected in both the inequalities of salaries between women and men and in the concentration of women in jobs at the lower end of the wage scale." This is a theme absent from the previous drafts, and perhaps long overdue. Sexism as well as racism is often found in the actions of church members and in church structures. It is most appropriate for the bishops to include a condemnation of sexism in the church.

The Approved Document

A review of the section entitled "Challenges to the Church," in the fifth and final chapter of *Economic Justice for All*, shows that little is changed from the third draft. All the members of the church, gathered in smaller faith communities and always a communion of people in Christ, are to participate in the mission of the church: in education, in support of family life, and for justice in the church as an economic actor. Economic arrangements by the church need to support the family (339). At all times the church must apply its own principles that govern the just operation of any economic structure to its own workings. "Indeed, the Church should be exemplary." (347) The 1971 Synod of Bishops document on justice is quoted to support a critical self-examination of the justice of the church in its own practices, possessions, and style of life. Renewal in the church is most definitely needed in the economic life of the church (349). The bishops commit themselves to paying a just wage for all church employees. For this they will need the support of all the baptized, not just the users of services or staff members. Many of the faithful will have to increase their contributions (with the encouragement for some of sacrificial tithing) to move toward more adequate wages and benefits (351). Discrimination against women is totally opposed, in the form of unequal wages for similar work and for inadequate opportunities for responsible positions and promotion. The church needs to use its resources wisely, to be a servant to the poor (356). The bishops rejoice in the work of church volunteers (352), the efforts of many individuals to promote economic justice in their workplaces and communities (357), and the excellent network of human services delivery systems (356). The church needs to become a model of collaboration, participation, and economic justice to American society (358).

Summary

Leo XIII's teaching on the worker's right to a just wage, to support himself and his family, has been the primary influence on subsequent documents to promote this right for men and women employed by church agencies and institutions. The 1917 Code of Canon Law specified this in canon 1524. This was one of several requirements for administrators of church goods to follow, if they were to be faithful to their office and responsibilities. The just wage was an expression of support for the workers' dignity and worth. The Second Vatican Council supported just wages for church employees in two documents. *Ad Gentes* encouraged the ministry of lay catechists in missionary areas. For them to accomplish their work effectively it was necessary to pay a salary which provided for the catechists' basic needs, and those of their household. *Apostolicam Actuositatam* offered a broader mandate. It spoke to all laity who serve the church, in full time or part time employment. Pastors are to welcome these workers gladly and give them their fullest cooperation. Fundamental to supporting these employees is paying them an adequate salary and appropriate benefits.

The document on justice from the 1971 Synod of Bishops holds a special place among these writings. It not only supports the right to a just wage for employees of the church. It calls the church itself to be self-critical, to carry on a continual process of examination of conscience. If the church wishes to call others to justice (and it must, for this is constitutive to its mission), then it must *be* just. Witness to justice is linked to effective education to justice. Those who teach must first do.

The 1983 Code of Canon Law is faithful to the papal and conciliar teaching. It affirms the church worker's right to a just wage, with necessary benefits, for oneself and one's family. Like the earlier Code it makes someone responsible for putting this right into practical action: administrators of church goods.

Finally, the 1986 pastoral of the bishops of the United States, *Economic Justice for All*, stands in the American episcopal tradition of supporting workers and their rights. The bishops reaffirm the right of all workers, in the world and in the church, to a just wage, for themselves and their family members. If there is a small dark cloud here, it is that the bishops do not explicitly state that the wage for a church employee also is to cover the needs of the employee's family. This is clear from other, general references in the text. But it is disappointing not to see footnotes to the most recent texts, namely *De Iustitia in Mundo*, 41, and canon 231, 2, of the 1983 Code.

There would seem to be little doubt that workers employed by any institution, agency, or structural expression of the church are to receive wages and benefits, for themselves and for their families, which support a decent human living. "Indeed, the Church should be exemplary." There should be nothing grudging on the part of pastors and church administrators. People engaged in the ministry and works of the church, whether lay faithful, religious or clergy, whether janitors, musicians, support staff, pastoral assistants, catechists, parish priests, or skilled administrators, deserve to have their dignity upheld in concrete actions, by visible structures. Receiving a just wage is foundational to upholding dignity.

NOTES

1. John A. Alesandro, "General Introduction," in James A. Coriden, Thomas J. Green, and Donald E. Heintschel, eds. *The Code of Canon Law: A Text and Commentary* (New York: Paulist, 1985), 4.

2. Stanislaus Woywood and Callistus Smith, *A Practical Commentary on the Code of Canon Law* (New York: Joseph F. Wagner, 1952) vol. 2, 205-6. Also reviewed were Stanislaus Woywood, *The New Canon Law: A Commentary and Summary of the New Code of Canon Law* (New York: Joseph F. Wagner, 1918); John A. Abbo and Jerome D. Hannan, *The Sacred Canons: A Concise Presentation of the Current Disciplinary Norms of the Church*, Rev. ed. (St. Louis: B. Herder, 1957); and T. Lincoln Bouscaren, Adam C. Ellis, and Francis K. North, *Canon Law: A Text and Commentary*, 4th Rev. ed. (Milwaukee: Bruce, 1963).

3. Donlon, 106-8. See also James H. Provost, "Ecclesial Rights," *Proceedings of the 44th Annual Convention of the Canon Law Society of America* (1983): 56-60.

4. Ferdinand Klostermann, commentary on Decree on the Apostolate of the Laity, in Vorgrimler, 3:368.

5. There are many church related agencies in various professional fields which carry out this function, e.g., the National Catholic Educational Association, the National Conference of Catechetical Leadership, Catholic Charities USA, and the National Association of Church Personnel Administrators.

6. One topic frequently mentioned for lay employees in this regard is the "portable pension." See Barbara Gartland, *Compensation: A Manual for Administration of Church Systems* (Cincinnati: National Association of Church Personnel Administrators, 1986), 110-2, 119-20.

7. The 1974 Synod of Bishops, which discussed the topic of evangelization, issued a statement at its conclusion jointly with Pope Paul VI, in which they said, "From her own experience the church knows that her ministry of fostering human rights in the world requires continued scrutiny and purification in her own life, her laws, institutions, and policies. . . . In the church, as in other institutions and groups, purification is needed in internal practices and procedures, and in relationships with social structures and systems whose violations of human rights deserve censure." Synod of Bishops, Third General Assembly, *Human Rights and Reconciliation, Origins* 4 (1974): 318-9.

8. Alesandro, "General Introduction," in Coriden et al., *The Code of Canon Law*, 5.

9. James H. Provost, "Canons 204-231," in Coriden et al., *The Code of Canon Law*, 170. See also Donlon, 122-51, and Valasio De Paolis, "The Maintenance of the Clergy: From the Council to the Code," in Rene Latourelle, ed., *Vatican II: Assessment and Perspective Twenty Five Years Later* (New York: Paulist, 1988), 660-97.

10. CIC/83 Canon 281, on just remuneration for priests, includes among its references two other documents: *De Sacerdotio Ministeriali*, from the 1971 Synod of Bishops, and the *Directory on the Pastoral Ministry of Bishops*, from the Sacred Congregation of Bishops (1973).

11. Rembert Weakland, "Church Social Teaching and the American Economy," *Origins* 13 (1983): 447-8.

12. Administrative Committee, National Catholic War Council, *Program of Social Reconstruction* (February 12, 1919), 19 and 24, in David M. Byers, ed., *Justice in the Marketplace: Collected Statements of the Vatican and U.S. Catholic Bishops on Economic Policy, 1891-1984* (Washington: United States Catholic Conference, 1984), 375 and 377.

13. For a detailed examination of the bishops' public statements, see David J. O'Brien, "The Economic Thought of the American Hierarchy," in Thomas M. Gannon, ed., *The Catholic Challenge to the American Economy: Reflections on the U.S. Bishops' Pastoral Letter on Catholic Social Teaching and the U.S. Economy* (New York: Macmillan, 1987), 27-41.

14. John T. Pawlikowski, "Introduction to Five Postwar Statements," in Byers, 444-5.

15. First Draft, "Catholic Social Teaching and the U.S. Economy," (November 15, 1984), *Origins* 14 (1984): 336-83; Second Draft, "Catholic Social Teaching and the U.S. Economy," (October 7, 1985) *Origins* 15 (1985): 257-96; Third Draft, "Economic Justice for All: Catholic Social Teaching and the U.S. Economy," (June 3, 1986), *Origins* 16 (1986): 33-76.

CHAPTER FOUR

SURVEY OF PARISH WORKERS' WAGES AND BENEFITS
AND COMPARISON WITH OTHER LOCAL WORKERS

The previous chapters have reported and examined in detail the magisterial teaching on the just wage both for all workers in general and for church employees in particular. Before drawing practical conclusions for the church as an employer from these admittedly general statements, it seemed important to look at the actual wages and benefits received by some church workers. Many questions come to mind. What is the actual compensation picture of church workers? What are they paid? What benefits do they receive? Are the terms of employment clear to the employees? Do pastors have employment policies? If so, do they follow them? How are the policies established? Do the workers contribute to the formation of employment guidelines? How do the wages of various job classifications compare to one another? How do the wages of church workers compare against a fair standard of living in the United States?

This chapter attempts to answer some of these questions and provide some insight into the reality of workers employed by the church.

A Survey of Local Parish Workers

To try to answer some of the above questions, I conducted a survey by mail of Pittsburgh area church workers in 1989. There were several limitations which determined the shape of this survey, in order to make the data manageable. The survey of church workers was limited to the 199 Roman Catholic parishes located in Allegheny County, Pennsylvania. Allegheny County includes the city of Pittsburgh and 133 smaller municipalities. By restricting the pool of workers to one county it is easier to compare the data against other workers employed in the same metropolitan area. It is not necessary to cross-reference the cost of living differences of various cities or metropolitan areas. Allegheny County is one of the four counties, and the largest, in the Pittsburgh Primary Metropolitan Statistical Area (PMSA).

Whom to survey came next. There are several jobs in the church which have local and/or national organizations which propose salary and benefit guidelines. For example, organists are supported by the American Guild of Organists, parish musicians have the National Association of Pastoral Musicians, directors of religious education have the National

Conference of Catechetical Leadership (formerly known as the National Conference of Diocesan Directors of Religious Education). In the Diocese of Pittsburgh, Catholic school teachers in all secondary schools and some elementary schools are represented by the Federation of Pittsburgh Diocesan Teachers. Each of these organizations sets guidelines (or in the case of the union, signs contractual agreements) for salary scales and benefits.[1] Pastors and church administrators can chooe to ignore these guidelines, but only at the peril of employing a less than competent or unskilled worker in that field. They may also incur the ire of neighboring parishes by "lowering the going rate" for a particular job. The guidelines do not prevent a church employer from paying less than the proposed scale, but they do give evidence of clearly unacceptable wages. The union contracts similarly influence the salaries and benefits of nonunion workers in the same field.

Fundamental to the understanding of the just wage articulated in the magisterial documents is that the just wage provides a *minimum* on which to live. By a minimum here is meant the practical expression of those basic economic rights which are due to human beings by virtue of the dignity of the human person. They have been articulated in fullest fashion in the magisterial social doctrine by Pope John XXIII (PT, 11-27). Despite the glaring injustices of salaries and benefit packages for church professionals,[2] these professionals are better paid than their support staff. Therefore, the survey of workers was aimed at those workers employed by the 199 Catholic parishes in Allegheny County who are not covered by a union, a diocesan liaison office, or a professional-directed national organization. The jobs focused on were: bookkeeper, cook in rectory, food service worker, housekeeper, janitor, receptionist, and secretary. It is in these and other nonprofessional job classifications that one finds the lowest paid church employees.

The Procedures for the Survey

The survey was conducted in the fall of 1989 in two stages. A letter was addressed to the pastor or priest-administrator of each parish in Allegheny County (Appendix One). He was asked to provide the author with the names and addresses of each parish worker in the above mentioned job classifications. Pastors from 113 parishes (56.8%) responded. They provided 627 names of workers in the above mentioned jobs.

Each of these workers was sent a letter (Appendix One) asking for their cooperation by completing a one page set of questions (Appendix Two). Each worker was also invited to write personal comments or expansions of their replies. Four hundred fifty-eight (73.0%) answered the questionnaire. Let's take a look at how the respondents identified themselves.

The Respondents

More than three quarters of the respondents were female (Appendix Three, Figure 1). Over 80% of the respondents were over 40 years of age, with the categories 41-55 and 56-70 almost equally represented (Figure 2). The largest number (34.1%) identified with the job of secretary (Figure 3). Janitor and housekeeper (24.2% and 14.8%) were also well represented. Almost half of the respondents (44.7%) had been in their current job five years or less (Figure 4). At the other end, however, there were 29 workers (6.3%) who had been in their current job 20 or more years. The worker with the longest tenure reported 43 years in the same job.

Approximately one quarter of the respondents (Figure 5) were part time employees (20 or less hours per week). There were also 74 respondents who reported that they worked more than 41 hours per week, although only 57 reported that they were salaried. There were 376 who replied in the negative when asked if they received overtime pay (Figure 6). Only five of the 75 respondents who gave a rate for their overtime pay said it met the legal minimum in the Commonwealth of Pennsylvania (Figure 7).[3]

The survey shows that the workers in the job classifications targeted are overwhelmingly female.[4] This confirms the often heard conventional wisdom that the church employs many more women than men (when clergy are excluded). The median number of years the respondents had been on their particular job is six, while the median number of years the respondents were employed by the church in any capacity is eight. Most of these workers are fairly new to their jobs, despite the handful of workers who have been employed for more than two decades. More than three in ten had been on the job three years or less. Yet it is not a young work force. Less than one in five of the respondents was under 40 years of age. With the wages which will be reported, it would seem to be a gross violation of fairness--to say nothing of being illegal--that only 76 of the respondents report they would be paid for overtime work. If you subtract the salaried workers from the number working 31 or more hours per week, you have 178 who would have the potential for regularly receiving overtime. Yet only 75 gave an overtime rate. And of this number who said they were paid for overtime, more than three quarters receive only the same hourly rate.

Wages

Each respondent was asked to give his or her hourly rate of pay. The range of wage rates was $1.15 to $11.79 per hour. They were put into four groupings: $1.15 to $3.79; $3.80 to $6.99; $7.00 to $8.99; and $9.00 to $11.79. Twenty-five of the respondents failed to answer this important question.

Figure 8 shows that 10.5% of the respondents received an hourly wage under the federal minimum wage ($3.80 per hour) at the time of this survey.[5] Only 6.3% were in the top grouping of wages reported. The median rate of the respondents was $5.45, which is in the middle of the second grouping, where there were 63.3% of the respondents.

If these hourly rates are translated into annual wages, the majority of workers (Figure 8) made between $7,904 and $14,539. The average wage rate of all who responded is $11,909 annually. The highest paid worker among all the respondents made a total of $24,523 for the year. The lowest was paid at an annual rate of only $2,392. (The annual wage is determined at the rate of 40 hours per week for 52 weeks.)

These annual wages can be compared to 1987 data for average annual wages in Pennsylvania (Figure 9). The average worker in Pennsylvania earned $20,408. The average worker in the Pittsburgh area earned $21,018 in 1987. The average worker in Allegheny County earned slightly higher, at $21,795. Allegheny County's average was fifth among the 67 counties of Pennsylvania. The highest average annual wage was $23,271 in Montgomery County (a suburb of the city of Philadelphia); the lowest was $14,112 in rural Pike County. Therefore, the annual average wage of the survey respondents from Allegheny County was $2,203 less than the lowest county in Pennsylvania, and $9,886 less than what the average worker in Allegheny County received.

The accompanying text in the 1988 *Pittsburgh PMSA* report notes that the high average wage in the Pittsburgh area is due to the concentration of jobs in durable goods manufacturing and such nonmanufacturing industries as health services and mining. Hourly wages are higher in goods producing industries. They are lowest in these nonmanufacturing service industries: retail and food stores, hotels and lodging places, personal services, apparel and accessory stores, domestics, and eating and drinking places. Annual wages in Pennsylvania work forces ranged from mining ($39,373) and primary metals ($36,054) to domestics ($8,483) and eating and drinking places ($6,451).

Who received what rate among the respondents? Figure 10 shows the rates compared with the job title. Only five job classifications had any workers at the highest level: janitor (12), secretary (11), housekeeper (2), bookkeeper (2), and business manager (2). Dealing with money certainly helped when being employed by the church: three of the six business and office managers and six of the eleven bookkeepers were in the two highest levels. Dealing with food did not help. There were no rectory cooks or food service workers at the highest level, and only one of the 25 rectory cooks and three of the 39 food service workers at the second to highest level. The two job titles with the largest respondents, secretary and janitor, offered the widest range. Two thirds of each job title were in the median grouping, yet these also had a small portion in the highest category: secretary, 11 of

150 (7.3%), and janitor, 12 of 105 (11.4%).

Benefits

Several of the questions on the parish workers survey focused on benefits. Despite the fact that 330 respondents worked more than 20 hours a week, which usually distinguishes part time from full time, there were only 162 who said they received paid health care (Figure 11). Six did not answer the question and 290 said they did not receive paid health insurance. The primary health carrier was Blue Cross/Blue Shield, with 140 cases. There were also 13 who said they were covered by their spouses' health insurance.

Figure 13 shows that 237 replied affirmatively that they received a pension benefit. However, there might seem to be some confusion here, because only 58 of the 237 of the respondents who said they received a pension identified how much the parish contributed toward their pension. There were 185 workers who said their parish did not pay toward their retirement. It is possible many, if not all of them, did not know how much was contributed toward their pension by the parish. Also, 36 people failed to give any response to the question.

There was a wide range of amounts contributed to the pension plan for workers, from $14 a year to $4,700. The median amount for the 58 replies was $435, the average contribution $573. This low median came about because there were only five contributions to pension plans over $1,000 per year (two at $1,300, $1,840, $2,193, and $4,700).

There was similar confusion over the number of years to become vested. There were 176 replies (Figure 12), with the majority of those (120) citing ten years to become vested for their pension. Yet this left 61 who either did not know how long it took, or simply decided not to answer the question.

The question which asked how many days the worker received for being sick and unable to work, for personal reasons, and for parental leave, largely went unanswered. Figure 14 shows that only a few knew how many days they received in these areas: sick days (44), personal days (26), parental leave (1). About two dozen in each case said that because they were employed part time, they were not entitled to these days. In a case of brutal honesty, one soul stated that the policy for sick days was "will of pastor." There were more who knew exactly how many vacation days they received (263, 57.4%). The large number of blanks to each of these questions strongly suggests the absence of any written personnel policy or manual, or even any verbal agreement between the employer (here, the pastor or parochial administrator) and the employee. That 53 replied "as needed" for sick days and 29 for personal days suggests a somewhat trusting relationship between employee and employer. This lack of explicit policy can also open the door to paternalism or tyranny on the part of the employer, and either fearfulness to request or abuse of privilege on the part of the employee.

Among those who knew their vacation allotment, 36 received either one or three weeks, and 109, almost a quarter (23.8%) of all the respondents, received two weeks. There were even 18 who were receiving four weeks of paid vacation. But given the longevity of some of the respondents (38 with 20 or more years in the current job), this should not be surprising.

A mixed signal is given on the issue of whether part time employees receive paid vacation days. There were 235 who reported working more than 30 hours a week, yet 263 reported on how many days of vacation they received. One would suppose that almost all full time workers would know their precise vacation allowance. So at least 28, and possibly more, of those who worked part time knew that they were receiving vacation days, and how many. On the other hand, 22 replied that precisely because they were part time, they did not receive any paid vacation days.

One lone worker knew that he or she could receive a full month for parental leave (although usual proposals for parental leave urge from three to six months).

There were isolated instances of generosity. One worker was entitled to 15 days a year for sickness. Two workers said they had an unlimited number of sick days available to them. Three workers received ten personal days and one worker an unlimited number of personal days.

Comparison with Other Workers

The wages and benefits given to the workers employed by Catholic parishes in Allegheny County cannot be understood in a vacuum. The contexts of other workers in similar occupations in their area and around the country must be considered. It can be instructive to see how the survey respondents' wages measure up (or down) to certain groups of workers in the Pittsburgh PMSA and around the country, and to workers in another Catholic institution, the Mercy Hospital of Pittsburgh.

Figure 15 lists the job titles of the respondents to the survey and their average hourly rate. The top three paying jobs had few respondents. The three business managers averaged $7.97 per hour, the one pastoral associate made $7.80, and the social worker made $7.00 per hour. As was noted above, the other handlers of money, bookkeepers, came next, at an average rate of $6.92 per hour. Then came the two largest groups in the survey, janitors and secretaries. Both were above the average for all the respondents by about fifty cents more per hour.

Ten of the job titles were under the survey average of $5.73 per hour. Even though these respondents were only 36.3% of all the cases, their wage rates were so low that they balanced the larger number of workers who were above the survey average.

How do the respondents to the survey compare to workers in the four counties of the Pittsburgh PMSA? There are three categories (Figure 15) available for comparison. In all three the Pittsburgh PMSA workers fared better. Accounting clerks/bookkeepers in the area were slightly ahead (15.6%) of their counterparts in the parishes. But secretaries and receptionists were paid substantially better. The receptionists had a average wage 52.5% greater than the parish receptionists. Secretaries were paid a whopping 63.7% more on average than parish secretaries. This final job comparison is even worse when it is noted that the Pittsburgh PMSA identifies five levels of secretary. These classifications are determined by the level of the secretary's supervisor and the level of the secretary's responsibility.[6] The level of secretary with the lowest median wage received $8.74 per hour. Then each level ascended at rates of $9.72, $10.07, $11.20, to a top rate of $13.40. These were from 42.9% to 118.9% higher than the secretaries in the survey of parish workers.[7]

Comparison with figures for all U.S. workers in seven job classifications shows a similar story. In six of the seven the median wage of the U.S. workers is higher than the Catholic parish workers. Figure 15 reveals that the food service workers in the parishes were paid at a rate five cents per hour higher than U.S. workers in a similar job classification. For the other occupations the percentage of difference ranged from 5.8% to 43.0%. The housekeepers, janitors, and bookkeepers employed by the parishes were exceeded by their counterparts nationally by modest increases (5.8%, 7.4% and 13.7% respectively). But the receptionists and secretaries were paid on average one third more than those who work for Allegheny County parishes.

A comparison can also be made with the wage ranges of several jobs in the largest Catholic hospital in the Pittsburgh PMSA, the Mercy Hospital of Pittsburgh.[8]

The wage scale in Appendix Five applies to both part time and full time employees. Each employee is evaluated once a year. Raises are on a pay for performance basis. Each employee also receives the following benefits: health insurance, dental coverage, life insurance, short- and long-term disability, educational assistance (up to $1,400 per year), and hospital contribution to a pension, with five years needed for vesting. The hospital policy for wages for these employees is to try to keep up with the market of other large hospitals in the Pittsburgh area. They do not want to lead, but also they do not want to be at the bottom of any comparisons. The wage scale is reviewed annually.

None of the average hourly rates of secretaries, receptionists, housekeepers, and food service workers among the parish workers comes close to the minimums of Mercy Hospital's wage scale. There would have to be increases of from $1.31 to $2.84 per hour to bring the average of these workers to the *minimum* of Mercy Hospital. Figure 10 notes that there are two housekeepers and eleven secretaries among parish workers who would be at the high end of the Mercy Hospital scale. But these are a small percentage (3.1% and 7.3%, respectively) of the total number of workers in each category. To bring the averages in each of these four job classifications to the mid point of the Mercy wage scale would mean substantial increases: from $2.42 per hour for housekeepers to $4.14 for receptionists. This means an increase of from 48.2% to 90.8% over the present average wage.

The Mercy Hospital figures show a definite improvement compared to the income of the respondents to the parish worker survey. Also, the minimums in the Mercy wage scale exceed the figures for U.S. workers. In Allegheny County, the beginning salary for Mercy receptionists is 43 cents higher than the average of their local counterparts. But the beginning salary for Mercy secretaries is almost $2.00 less than the average of all Allegheny County secretaries. These comparisons would seem to bear out the desire of Mercy Hospital to be in the middle of
market comparisons.

One benefit offered by Mercy to its employees stands out. The $1,400 educational benefit available to each employee is quite generous and in keeping with Catholic social teaching that a just wage should support the full development of a worker. It is a strong statement about Mercy's commitment to encouraging adult education and personal development. Nothing remotely close to it was reported by the respondents to the parish workers survey.

These three sets of comparisons point to the obvious disparity in the wages paid to parish workers, against local and national wage surveys in similar occupations, and against a local Catholic hospital. If these local PMSA and national wage surveys offer examples of "the market," it is clear that the pastors and parochial administrators are not trying to use them as benchmarks in their employment decisions. The parish workers do not come close in most cases. Receptionists and secretaries in this market comparison are particularly slighted and underpaid by the parishes which employ them.

Wages and Ordinary Economic Rights

Figure 15 also converts the hourly average rates of the survey respondents in the different job classifications into annual wage rates. These annual wage figures are useful to compare against attempts to put dollar amounts on what is necessary for a decent living in this country, as determined by the Liberato and Schervich report, *Just Wages*.

Just Wages did not try to define precisely what it terms "ordinary economic rights." These rights are well known as they have been listed in the social encyclicals, especially in *Pacem in Terris*. They include adequate food, shelter, clothing, health care, education for children, rest and leisure, security for unemployment, disability, and retirement, opportunity for worker associations and unions, and healthful working conditions. It is obvious that not all of these rights can be measured in cash. Nevertheless, the authors of the report settled on two slightly different benchmarks in order to have a dollar figure with which to make comparisons. The first is the median standard of living for persons in the United States. The second is the "thrifty" budget for a family of four. In the view of the authors of the NCDD report, these offer a reasonable approximation in dollar figures for the cost of the ordinary rights envisioned in the magisterial teaching. It is recognized that different countries, and even many cities and parts of our country, will have varying amounts for the same basic needs. These two benchmarks for family expenditures, namely, the median standard of living and the thrifty budget for a family of four, will be used in this chapter.

The median point of ordinary economic rights was determined by Liberato and Schervich by using data from the Bureau of Labor Statistics and the U.S. Department of Commerce on income and expenditures of families. These data are put into five "levels of living," corresponding to the quintile breakout of the distribution of income in the United States (Figure 17). The authors took the 1987 available figures and adjusted them by means of the Consumer Price Index to the last quarter of 1988.

The pre-tax income of households in the five quintile breakouts are $3,738, $11,460, $21,725, $33,754, and $66,208. It is the median level of expenses for ordinary rights which is used as an approximation of what is necessary for a decent standard of living. According to the Consumer Expenditure Reports of the Bureau of Labor Statistics, the median household in the general population is made up of 2.6 people, 1.4 of whom are income earners. The median age for the head of the household is 46.8 years. The annual income for this household is $27,388, and the expenses for ordinary economic rights is $25,226.

In noting this median, it has to be pointed out that these expenses are covered by 1.4 wage earners. One can safely presume that in actual practice the income in many, many households will come from two or more wage earners. In a certain sense, this violates the ideal in the papal expression and articulation of the just wage as that which *one worker* brings home in order to support self and the whole family. Nevertheless, this provides one way of looking at what might be met in a just wage for one worker.

By comparing the median figure for ordinary economic rights with Figure 15, one can see grave disparity. The highest wage among all 433 respondents who name a wage figure is $24,523. This one church worker would be $703 under the median figure for a household of three. (Again, I am presuming in all of these cases only the one income of the respondents in the survey for the support of the worker himself and the family.) This is the best comparison that can be made here. The highest wage grouping of workers (Figure 8) had 29 church employees making between $18,720 and $24,523. These 29 (6.3% of respondents) are several thousand dollars below the median for ordinary economic rights.

The comparison gets more embarrassing if one uses the overall average or the averages of the various job titles. The average of all 433 church workers was an annual wage rate of $11,909 (Figure 9). This is $13,317 less than the median ordinary expenses. In other words, *immediately doubling* the average wage of the church worker would still not reach the expenses for a household of three persons in the United States! One would fall short by $1,408. The comparisons of the top five averages are almost as bad. Business managers ($8,635 short, 52.0% raise needed), pastoral associate ($9,002, 55.5%), social worker ($10,666, 73.2%), bookkeeper ($10,823, 75.1%), and janitor ($12,218, 93.9%) all fare poorly. One cringes to go to the bottom of the list. The sacristans and laundresses would almost have to have their wage rate *tripled* (185% and 197%) to meet the median figure for ordinary economic rights.[9]

This benchmark for household expenses indicates not only the church employers' poor pay rates. It also touches the ridiculousness of the term used by the state and federal government, the minimum wage. This wage may be a legal minimum, but that cannot be construed to mean meeting minimum needs of a household. The federal minimum wage prior to March 30, 1991, was $3.80 per hour. It is now $4.25 per hour. Pennsylvania's minimum wage is $3.70. The federal minimum wage preempts the state's lower figure. The federal minimums are translated for a 40 hour work week for 52 weeks into annual wages of $7,904 (1990) and $8,840 (1991). These figures fall short of even the expenditures needed by the lowest quintile of households in Figure 16. These figures are below even the worst average wage of the local church workers. (However, the survey revealed that there were 48 church workers who said they were paid at an hourly rate of less than the 1990 U.S. federal government minimum wage.)

The comparisons are differentiated with more precision, but do not get any better, when the second standard of the *Just Wages* report is used. This benchmark is reached using a four-tier approach to family budgeting by the U.S. Department of Agriculture. This is based on the cost of items relative to the cost of food. The four tiers are labeled "low-cost," "thrifty," "moderate," and "high-cost." The budget presumes all items are purchased at the same level of consumption. This allows for individual choice in the cost and quality of items, while maintaining a uniform line of minimums necessary for the ordinary household. It also allows for separate costs for an individual, a couple, and a family of four. Again, in these comparisons it is presumed that there is only one wage earner in the family. This is not the reality of the working world in which we live, but it offers insight into how far certain wages (and employers) are from meeting a just wage for the head of a household.

Figure 17 shows the costs for ordinary economic rights for a family of four, using the four-tier approach of the U.S. Department of Agriculture. If one believes these 1988 figures, it becomes immediately obvious how terribly misguided and low are the federal and state minimum wage rates. The minimum wages do not even come near to one third of the low-cost figure.

Using the thrifty budget, these costs are broken down further in Figure 18 for a single person, a married couple without children, and a family of four. The single person needs $17,396 to take care of the ordinary economic rights, on a thrifty budget. The couple needs $32,266, and the family of four needs $37,124.

There is even greater disparity than the first standard if one uses the costs for a family of four on a thrifty budget, according to these 1988 USDA calculations, and compares $37,124 against the figures in Figure 15 for annual wages of the church workers. Now the highest paid worker in the survey needs $12,601 to reach the thrifty budget for a four person family, or a 51.3% raise. The average wage for all the respondents would need $25,215, or a 212% raise, more than triple the wage. The two largest groups of respondents, janitors and secretaries, would need nearly the same amounts ($24,116, 185% raise; $24,397, 192%) to bring them up to this mark.

The difference with this second attempt to put a dollar sign on ordinary economic rights is that not every worker in the local survey supports a family of four. There were no questions on the survey for marital status or whether the respondent was the head of the household and, if so, how many people he or she was supporting. In this thrifty budget figure one gets closer to the understanding of the just wage as the Catholic social teaching articulates it in principle. Three aspects of the complex application of a just wage directly apply here. One consideration is that there is no single just wage. The remuneration has to be adjusted not only to a thrifty budget, but also to the size of the household supported.

Another consideration is that the just wage means benefits based on need. This recognizes that there are other than cash benefits which assist in the provision of ordinary economic rights. Two of these benefits which a Catholic employer might provide could be family health coverage and payment of Catholic school tuition for the children's education. This "floating" benchmark reflects a third consideration, that the just wage means equal work for equal pay. There were serious proposals for an adjustable "family wage" in companies three decades ago.[10] Pay equity, as a philosophical concept and as nondiscriminatory law, would probably today rule out such a plan in this country. The salary is only part of the just wage, albeit the major part. This is linked to the level of responsibility of the job as well as years of seniority.

The second attempt at an economic measuring rod for ordinary economic rights reflects higher costs, even with a thrifty budget, than the median expenditures for the general population. Both are far above the average salaries for the local church workers in the Allegheny County survey. Both point to the gross inadequacy of the wages paid by pastors in the food service, clerical, and janitorial occupations. Both comparisons also challenge the faithful to substantially increase donations if they expect their leaders to pay just remuneration to their employees. The USDA budget does reflect as well the "messiness" and complexity of attempting to implement a just wage, which covers the basic human needs of the worker and his or her family.

Comments from the Survey of Local Church Workers

Among the 458 respondents to the survey of local church workers, 116 took advantage of the offer at the end of the survey to write any additional comments they wished to make on the back of the page. Many were simply explanations or clarifications of their answers. But there were several which are worth quoting in their own honest and unpolished words, because they provide the attitudes and feelings of some of the respondents.

One surprise among all the comments was that several workers thanked me for sending them a survey. The act of sending them a survey seemed to show them someone cared about them and their work. "Thank you for your interest," "Thanks, Father, for undertaking this worthwhile topic!" and "Thank you for the opportunity to contribute to your survey" were three responses in this vein. Another lengthy tirade concluded, "Thank you for this opportunity to spill my guts."

There were a dozen people who wrote to say they were happy and satisfied with their jobs and their employers. A sacristan described his flexible work hours and concluded, "All things considered, I am very pleased with my situation." A maintenance man said simply, "I like my work here." Three workers acknowledged their own dedication through extra hours and hard work. A (school?) secretary wrote, "I feel I am qualified to make more money, but I love my job and believe in Catholic education and I know the parish doesn't have the funds to pay more." A school business manager/secretary recognized the complexities of the situation. "I know that the pastor has always lamented the fact that the staff is grossly underpaid but what do you do when the money isn't there? Most of the parish staff are dedicated to the cause--but who couldn't use more money? Say what you will about Catholic education--but the guts of the system come from the underpaid, dedicated employees who are maintenance, receptionists, housekeepers, and yes, even secretaries!!"

Two cooks both recognized their inadequate wages but appreciated the "extra benefits from heaven" which they receive for working for the church and for priests. A new pastor was cause for rejoicing for one janitor: "Our present priest of 2 months is tremendous & has given all the employees a 6% raise & isn't cheap . . ." A letter which would warm the heart of any cold church administrator came from a director of food services. She said, "My 12 years with this program have been very gratifying ones in the sense that it is more of a ministry to me than a job. We 'feed the hungry' twice a day in an area that is poverty stricken. We receive government donated food and funds, and this is how the program stays alive. . . . Please remember our school and our 'feeding' program in your prayers."

The flexibility and kindness of several pastors were recorded. A maintenance worker/bus driver contributed, "I do admire the fact that when I was injured and laid up for weeks that I was still able to receive a monthly pay check from work. Without this benefit I couldn't possibly manage with monthly living and necessities." A parish secretary praised what she saw as often overlooked benefits of working for the church, including the opportunity to attend Mass on a daily basis. She added, "I feel that in any emergency the pastor is quite compassionate and understanding and again a flexible schedule would come into play--should the need arise."

There were more critical comments than complimentary ones among those who took the time to write. In a long note on the difficulty of his work load, a janitor summed up the criticisms by stating, "There have been many inequities over the years concerning raises and duties which do not reflect the 'so-called social justice for labor' in the Church."

Six comments were directed toward tuition assistance for workers with children in a Catholic school. One said it would be an enormous incentive to keep workers in the church's employ. Another saw tuition assistance as a substitute, non-cash benefit. "I feel I'm worth more than I get paid for even if it's only made up in tuition assistance." A female secretary saw a relationship between being a church worker and a member of the church. She was working on a college degree in religious education, but did not receive assistance from her pastor. "I would feel it beneficial to the Parish and to the entire Catholic Christian Community to help assist in this area those people, like myself, who will eventually put back into the Church far more than what they will receive." Another parish secretary said she will soon be looking for a new job. With her present salary, she and her husband will not be able to afford to send their 7th grade son to Central Catholic High School.

Two comments offered an example of the freedom pastors have in making decisions on benefits, and the lack of any professional or diocesan guidelines. A school secretary of 14 years experience did not like teachers receiving cash re-imbursement for hospitalization not used. That she felt strongly on this issue is in her emphasis: "If a benefit is offered to someone (like hospitalization)--<u>THEY SHOULD NOT</u> get reimbursed for not using it. It could save the school a lot of money . . . That's money in their pocket & the Catholic School is going down the drain!" Another secretary, however, noted that she did not receive paid health insurance, but would if she were not covered by her husband's policy. She noted casually, "As it is, I am given the money as a benefit rather than coverage." It is impossible to determine from this survey, or from other sources, what the general parochial practice is on this issue.

There were two dozen respondents to the survey who used the invitation to make comments to express their anger. Four were in the category of "sins of the pastor." One man, a newly hired janitor, 11 months on the job, wrote, "I was told at the start of my employment that I would receive one dollar an hour increase after one month. I have yet to receive it, even though I was told what a great job I was doing." This employee stated for the survey that his hourly rate of pay was $4.00. Another janitor, on the job for nine years, told this story: "In the first five years that I was working, I got a vacation pay, then the last four years, we got a new administrator and he took everything away from us. That meant no more vacation pay."

In a third case, a housekeeper employed 12 years (who identified her age group as 26-40) explained her situation. She put down that she was employed 1-10 hours a week and explained on the back page of the survey, "You see, Father, I was hired 12 yrs. ago in a full time capacity even tho I have always cleaned in the same manner [one day a week for 2-4 hours, or however long to complete her work]. It takes 10 yrs. to become vested for pension--at yr. 9 I was dropped to part time title. . . . My coverage for Health Ins. also dropped. I was receiving Major Medical as a full time employee. Now I pay my own BC/BS." Amazingly, this woman continued, "I am not angry at this, as I consider this job charity as well." She went on to say she also has other clients for whom she cleans house.

A secretary summed up her feelings with the comment, "So many pastors are out of touch with everyday living expenses involved in a lay person's life, especially when children are involved."

One self-identified "disgruntled employee" felt a major injustice was that the church rarely promoted from within. He continued, "Haven't had pay raise for 3 or 4 yrs. now. try to raise family of 4 making between $13K to $14K." This man, between 26 and 40 years old, was on the maintenance job for almost 6 years. He said he had no personal days available to him, and that four years previously the pastor cut the number of sick days from ten to three. Any more than three was up to the pastor's discretion.

Several workers felt the work load was unfair in comparison to their wages. An extreme example of anger was the comment, "I only get paid for 2 hrs. a day but in demand for 48 hrs. a day." A younger female janitor, on the job only four months and hired at a rate of $3.70 per hour said she will be leaving soon because of the low wages. She said her co-workers were "the greatest" but "this job is good for two kinds of people 1) soup kitchen persons 2) just released jail persons." A cafeteria worker, who said she was paid for 30 hours a week, stated, "I would like to get paid for all the hours I work. . . . I put in at least another 10 hrs. a week UNPAID. After 11 yrs. it is wearing thin."

A couple of workers compared their situation to other workers and found it wanting. A parish secretary complained how difficult it was for her to find a replacement to enable her to take vacation. She said, "Sometime, I wish we could have a work schedule similar to the Diocesan employees--they even get holidays off like Veterans Day, Presidents Day, etc. Also, we should be allowed so many 'sick days' and not have to come in when you don't feel too great." (Diocese of Pittsburgh central administration employees currently receive 14 paid holidays/holydays each year.) Two noted the disparities between their wages as church employed janitors and those of janitors in local public school districts. One concluded ruefully, "Another pastor has commented that my position and duties I perform are worth $30,000 annually." He identified his wage, after five years on the job, as $6.00 per hour ($12,480 a year).

There were five perceptive respondents who noted the absence of diocesan guidelines for the lowest paid of church workers. One long time secretary, who is well paid by the standards of this survey ($11.00 per hour, $22,880 annually), saw this omission. "My personal opinion is that the employees of the Church who are its backbone, i.e., Secretaries, Maintenance, Housekeepers, Bookkeepers, have been, and are continuing to be, set aside by the Diocese. I mean by that, that there is no Diocesan regulations regarding benefits, salaries, sick days, etc. as there are for CCD employees, teachers, elementary and high school, and organists." The writers felt a salary scale, set increments for service, and periodic reviews by one's supervisor should be included in these diocesan guidelines.

The words of a parish sacristan, employed four years, summarized the angry and critical comments. "Many excellent employees are lost by the diocese and parishes because of the lack of a just wage and the other injustices in the church. I have seen several [leave] and I will be one soon. The Diocese of Pittsburgh and its churches would be a lot better if the lay people that work for it, and for the most part hold it together, got the pay they deserve."

Summary

The survey of church workers in the parishes of Allegheny County, Pennsylvania, revealed low wages and confusion over benefits. The average wage for all workers in the survey, $11,909, was only 56.7% of the average wage for all of Pennsylvania, and 54.6% of the average wage for all workers in Allegheny County. The wages of the local church workers who responded fared worse against two cost-of-living standards used by the National Conference of Diocesan Directors of Religious Education's *National Project on Just Wages*. The two standards of income needed for ordinary human economic rights for a small family were $25,226 (median of all households in U.S.A., according to the Bureau of Labor Statistics) and $37,124 (thrifty budget for families of four persons, according to the U.S. Department of Agriculture). The average wage for respondents to the survey drops to 47.2% and 32.1% of these two standards of living, respectively.

Nor were the disparities of these averages matched in any one job classification. The highest average among all jobs, $16,578, for three business managers in the survey, was thousands less than any of the above Pennsylvania or national standard figures. The two job classifications with the largest number of respondents, janitor and secretary, were only about one thousand dollars above the survey median.

Confusion over benefits was evident in the many who were not receiving paid overtime above their hourly rate; the lack of knowledge for days for paid vacation, sickness, and personal needs; and minuscule amounts of pension contributed. The anecdotal comments which some respondents took the time to write strongly suggest the widespread lack of clear policies regarding benefits.

In sum, these figures point to severely underpaid employees, by several standards. There are indications of great ambiguity with regard to health care coverage, vacation and sick days, and policies for promotion or wage increases. The survey did not include the tools to judge the ability to pay of each of the 113 parishes whose pastors offered the names of workers for this survey. Nevertheless, it is clear that the parish churches and schools which employed the workers in this survey are paying unjust cash compensation and inadequate and somewhat arbitrary benefits. These churches who employ are inadequate to the mandates of economic justice, and their workers are paid unjust wages.

NOTES

1. For examples of salary guidelines for musicians and directors of religious education set by liaison offices for the Diocese of Pittsburgh, see Appendix Four.

2. See C. Michael Liberato and Philip H. Schervich, *National Project on Just Wages and Benefits for Lay and Religious Employees* (Washington: National Conference of Diocesan Directors of Religious Education, 1990).

3. Pennsylvania labor law states that work done by non-salaried employees in excess of 40 hours per week is to be paid at a rate not less than time and a half.

4. In Allegheny County 44% of the work force is female, in the Pittsburgh PMSA 42.5%, in the United States, 44.8%. Department of Labor and Industry, Bureau of Research and Statistics, *Annual Planning Information Report for Pittsburgh PMSA* (Harrisburg, PA: Commonwealth of Pennsylvania, Fall 1988), 43 and 45.

5. The federal minimum wage was increased to $4.25 on April 1, 1991. The Pennsylvania minimum wage was set at $3.70 on February 1, 1989. Federal law preempts state law in this case, unless and until Pennsylvania law sets a higher than federal minimum wage.

6. Bureau of Labor Statistics, *Pittsburgh, Pennsylvania Metropolitan Area Wage Survey* (Washington: U.S. Department of Labor, 1990), 27-9.

7. Ibid., 3.

8. Interview with Diane Kyle, compensation analyst, Personnel Department, The Mercy Hospital of Pittsburgh, October 16, 1990. Maintenance workers at Mercy are represented by the Operating Engineers. The wage scale in their contract with the hospital is confidential.

9. It must be acknowledged that many of the local parish workers are not full time employees. Yet their rate of payment, and list of benefits received, can still be judged woefully inadequate.

10. Michael Fogarty, "The Catholic Theory of the Family Living Wage," *Review of Social Economy* 15 (1957): 91-103, and Cronin, *Catholic Social Principles*, 309-15.

CHAPTER FIVE

CRITERIA FOR A JUST WAGE
FOR CHURCH EMPLOYEES

The preceding chapters have attempted to explicate and analyze the historical and magisterial teaching of the Roman Catholic Church on the the just wage and a theological grounding for the teaching. Chapter Three demonstrated that it is the explicit intention of the magisterium to apply this teaching on the just wage to all workers employed by church institutions, dioceses, and parishes. Examination of the actual wages and benefits which are currently paid to church workers in Allegheny County in the Diocese of Pittsburgh suggests that the church falls short in many, many instances of providing a reasonable and decent compensation package to workers who have been traditionally "at the bottom" of the wage scale.

The burden of this chapter is to use the preceding information and magisterial guidance in order to provide practical criteria for the administration of a just wage by church leaders and pastors.

It is not easy to jump from general magisterial pronouncements to specific personnel policies and wage scales. One begins by recognizing the value of stating an ideal situation in the form of a general moral principle. David Hollenbach says, "For the church, moral principles retain an important role in shaping the decisions, reached by practical reason, for they represent a theoretical crystallization of theological reflection on the past experiences of the Christian community."[1]

These moral principles are arrived at by a correlation of theological, philosophical, and social science insight. But that is not enough. Citing Karl Rahner and Edward Schillebeeckx, Hollenbach says the prophetic dimension of being church in the world demands creative imagination, charismatic insight, and the lived experience of social struggle. Making policy decisions is the art of translating an ideal into the real. It is not enough to express negative judgments on what policies are unjust or out of bounds for Christians. Using imagination, charism, and experience, it is necessary to present specific positive directions for ecclesial policy. These concrete proposals do not take the place of normative, general principles of Christian morality. But they do express the content and shape of Christian faith. Hollenbach adds: "Efforts toward the fulfillment of minimum human needs and the realization of structures of genuine mutuality are consequences of faith in Jesus Christ. They are religious obligations of all Christians and of the church as an organized actor in society."[2] The United States bishops expressed a similar idea in 1986: "Explicit reflection on the ethical content of economic choices and policies must become an integral part of the way Christians relate religious belief to the realities of everyday life." (EJA, 21)

Therefore, rather than give merely a monetary figure for the just wage, or some simple formula to calculate a just wage, this chapter will offer what I judge to be the foundational axioms of the just wage, axioms which are rooted in church teaching and practically applicable for this country and time. There will be twelve statements which explicate what is involved in the application of the just wage. The teaching on the just wage has many dimensions. These twelve statements need to be part of a process, which respects the right to participation of all parties. Both the twelve statements and a participatory process must be taken into consideration when arriving at concrete decisions. Concrete decisions are part of the responsibility of real people in the real world. This distinction between axioms of the just wage and a concrete just wage for today is in keeping with "the general norms of theological interpretation," which distinguish between the statements of recent popes and Vatican II (magisterial social doctrine) and the application of moral principles to specific cases.[3]

In the second section of this chapter I will explain the special issues involved in just compensation for vowed religious who have the church as an employer. Finally, the chapter will conclude with reflections on the virtue of industriousness.

Axioms[4]

The Just Wage is a Compensation Package

As was pointed out in the Introduction, the term "just wage" has been used in the magisterial documents, and throughout this book, to refer to the entire compensation package of wages and benefits owed to the employee by the employer. Synonyms for the term "just wage" are living wage, family wage, just compensation, just remuneration, and equitable sustenance. A just wage, therefore, includes all benefits as well as salary. These benefits might include financial bonuses, paid vacation and personal days, insurance policies, meals provided without cost by a parish or institution, and assistance for children in Catholic education. A just wage can be composed of an almost limitless constellation of wages and benefits.

The justice in a compensation package has to be met by an equitable balance of both wages and benefits. An employer cannot make up for inadequate wages with implicit permission to do shoddy or lackadaisical work, or with an unusually large number of paid personal days. Wages and benefits are not continually interchangeable. Both the wages and the benefits need to meet basic human needs, as presented in the listing of human rights in the magisterial documents.

There is no Single Just Wage

The papal and conciliar documents of the Roman Catholic Church in which the term just wage is explained are addressed to the faithful dispersed throughout the world. Both the general nature of the teachings set forth in these documents and the many nations, cultures, and economic systems in which the faithful live rule out that in principle there can be a single precise just wage for all nations and peoples. Each economic system is different. Each culture is different. Standards of living change over time.

The just wage, as explained in these pages, is an attainable ideal, one which must be examined, explicated, and brought up to date at periodic intervals by all employers concerned for justice. It will mean different wages and different benefits for workers in various countries, even for workers in different parts of the same country. At all times, however, the just wage means a concern to meet the basic human needs, as the next axiom attests. But there is no one, universal, fixed, just wage.

The Just Wage is a Minimum

Critics have sometimes accused popes and bishops of interfering in the decision-making power of owners and managers by telling them what to pay their employees. This is a false view of the teaching on the just wage. The magisterial social doctrine does not dictate the practical decision making of owners and managers. Indeed, this would be a violation of the principle of subsidiarity. The right to a just wage makes a claim about the human person, namely, that each human being has dignity and rights by virtue of his or her humanity. This dignity must be expressed concretely, by responding to certain personal, social, and instrumental rights. The just wage is simply the way of responding to the economic rights of every person which lay claim to adequate food, clothing, shelter, education, working conditions, health care, retirement protection--all that is needed for the full and integral development of the human person. The just wage is not interference in the internal administration of a business or institution. It is instead a statement of who the human person is, what is needed to express that identity, and how human labor, and compensation for it, make it possible to provide for actual human needs.

In the major documents of Catholic social teaching, the doctrine of the just wage has been expressed as requiring the minimum needed for integral human development. Some of the expressions of this minimum have been "to enable [workers] honorably to keep themselves from want and misery," (RN, 10); "reasonable and frugal comfort," (RN, 14); "adequate to meet ordinary human needs," (OA, 71); "sufficient to lead a life worthy of man and to fulfill family responsibilities properly," (MM, 71); "give . . . a standard of living in keeping with human dignity," (PT, 20); and sufficient for "establishing and properly maintaining a family and for providing security for its future." (LE, 19).

What is asked for in these quotes is more than subsistence, more than what is necessary to avoid starvation and eke out a living. It is to offer the worker the opportunity to cultivate life in all its human dimensions. The just wage has also been called a "saving wage." This refers to the opportunity of the frugal worker to set money aside from his wage for the future. This could mean the opportunity for growing in prosperity, e.g., home ownership, college education for children, or enhanced retirement income.

In the survey of church workers in Allegheny County almost three out of four respondents received less than $14,539 in annual wages (Appendix Three, Figure 8). It is hard to see how an individual person, much less a family of several persons, would be able to save enough on this salary to purchase a home or to pay the costs of a college education for several children. Such low salaries do not allow for full human development, for the worker or for the worker's family.

The just wage attempts to draw a line, or better, a border or no-man's land. In justice one cannot go below the border's standards. The U.S. bishops call this "a floor of material well-being on which all can stand." (EJA, 74) This floor or no-man's land is not a clear zone. It is not able to be determined with a specific arithmetical formula. It is a grey area open to differing opinions.

Therefore, a just wage is *at least* a minimum. To go below it is to be clearly unjust. Basic justice includes the motivation to rise above this floor and grant more than the bare minimum needed for human survival and future needs.

The NCDD project on a just wage attempts to spell out these minimum needs which lead to integral human development. The authors of the report call these "ordinary economic human rights" and spell them out in detail:

1. Health care for self and dependents, including medical, dental, mental and visual.
2. Life insurance of a face value equal to the dollar value of an employee's annual salary.
3. Personal leave, e.g., sickness and parental leave.
4. Unemployment compensation and disability insurance.
5. Retirement contribution equal to at least five percent of annual salary, with full vesting in five years, portability among the dioceses in the United States, and with non-mandatory employee contribution.
6. Vacation time.
7. Time and finances for educational development.
8. Catholic educational benefits for dependent children.

9. Liability insurance (where applicable).
10. Ability to add other family or dependents benefits at cost to employee.[5]

This listing is an effort to put into practice the lengthy list of "universal and inviolable" rights which flow from human dignity first presented by Pope John XXIII in *Pacem in Terris*, 11-27. A similar list was enumerated by Pope John Paul II in *Familiaris Consortio*, 46. The ten benefits proposed above leave room for legitimate employer discretion. Yet they try to cover the basics of human need. The only rights the popes present which are not covered in the benefits are the rights to respect and a good reputation, to assembly and association, and to representation. These are not able to be addressed in a listing of economic benefits. More properly they are preserved in the political order.

It was pointed out in the previous chapter how the Allegheny County survey respondents seemed to be confused and did not understand what benefits they were supposed to receive (Figures 11-14). In some cases it is clear that the employers of many of the respondents failed to provide some necessary benefits, e.g., paid vacation, paid legal overtime, health insurance. In a sense the bigger failure is the absence for most of these church workers to have an opportunity to sit down with their pastor, and to learn about and discuss what benefits they do receive. The large number of blanks in the survey, which appear as "no response" in the graphs in Appendix Three, attests to the shallowness of knowledge of the workers' conditions of employment.

There are also hard choices in trying to judge what is more than necessary, extra to basic living, not-quite-but-almost a luxury. Here are a few examples. Transportation in our society is needed. Does this mean a family must own a car? New or used? One or two? Time for rest and relaxation is a right. Is a yearly trip to the Jersey Shore frugal or extravagant? To Florida? To Hawaii? Future security is a right also. Worker and employer both contribute to the Social Security program. Should the worker also expect a partially paid company-contributed pension? A fully paid pension?

This study has been critical of parish and church structures, in their application of wages and benefits for employees. It is also appropriate to address briefly the economic choices individuals and families make every day. The call to bring the light of the Gospel to economic affairs has positive elements, e.g., a process of consultation and participation which leads to setting a just wage for all employees. The call to holiness and justice also has negative ramifications. The U.S. bishops state, "At times we will be called upon to say no to the cultural manifestations that emphasize values and aims that are selfish, wasteful and opposed to the Scriptures.

Together we must reflect on our personal and family decisions and curb unnecessary wants in order to meet the needs of others." (EJA, 334) This call is part of a movement to a simpler style of life. This is also a Christian prophetic witness to the world, in the face of the ever more wasteful and greedy accumulation of material goods that characterizes an affluent society.

Christians who make family and personal decisions which move toward a simpler lifestyle require prayer, reflection, and dialogue on the ethical norms involved. Such decisions may involve sacifices as well. Parishes and church institutions are not exempt from these decisions. Individuals, families, and communities of faith alike must reflect on what material goods are necessary and what are unnecessary, in order to instill a moral and ethical dimension to economic questions in the marketplace and in the church.

The just wage must provide the minimum needed for decent living. The demands of biblical justice would also urge church employers to go beyond the minimum. Here are opportunities for employees to strive for excellence and to work for promotions, and employers to provide for greater education, human development and participation.

The Just Wage is a Family Wage

One of the key themes throughout the modern Catholic social teaching is that the just wage must be adequate for the worker *and the worker's family*. This is consistent and clear. It is also very often overlooked in the real world of labor relations. If a worker is single, the just wage is to allow him or her the financial room for savings, so that planning for marriage and a family is a realistic possibility. One aspect of the ideal in the family wage is stability, in the sense that the worker can reasonably plan ahead for the creation and formation of a family. One can express this idea of stability by saying that in the ideal, a just wage enables a worker to make a career out of his or her job. There is the possibility that even without promotions to higher job classifications, the wages and benefits allow the worker to take care of himself and his family over the years.

This is an extremely touchy point for pastors. Many pastors make employment and wage decisions on the presumption that the church workers take home the "second income" in the family. The pastors presume their workers, most often women (see Figure 1), are not heads of households. The reasoning follows that it is not necessary to pay a "real" salary, comparable to the market. This job, and its income, is only extra income. It is not meant to cover the basic human needs of the family.

Decisions based on this understanding ignore the magisterial teaching on the just wage as a family wage. Even in those cases where it is clear that the church worker is receiving a second income for the family, the church administrator cannot presume to thereby offer lower wages. Both national statistics and anecdotal experience tell employers that one of the reasons why the second spouse works is because of the poor compensation (a wage that is not a living wage) of the first spouse's job.[6] If there is income exceeding the basics of human living, because of two salaries, life style decisions are to be made by the working spouses and their family members, and not by the employers.

It has previously been pointed out how the earlier documents of Leo XIII and Pius XI were insensitive to any model of the family except husband-worker and wife-mother at home with children. There is at least some ambiguity in later documents which allows the authoritative teaching to apply the family wage to the woman working outside the home or the woman being the head of the household. The diverse conditions of the family today necessitate an ever stronger assertion that the just wage is a family wage, whether a man or a woman is the head of the household. Two income families (with the children in day care) often are a response to the lack of a just wage. (It can also be true that the two incomes could be part of the pursuit of a more luxurious life style, or the career paths of two professionals.) Female-headed households are particularly prone to poverty when the woman does not receive a just wage for her employment. For all these situations, and many others, the church administrator in charge of employees must heed the long and strong tradition of Catholic social teaching that the just wage is a family wage.

The Just Wage is set within a System of Administration
The Just Wage includes a Signed Agreement

One of the practical conclusions contemporary personnel managers have arrived at, who are trying to implement a just wage, is that a publicly organized system of salary and benefits is necessary. This is in response to two enemies of good labor relations, arbitrariness and secretiveness. Wages are not to be decided arbitrarily by the employer. It is unfair for the manager to favor one or a few employees with a higher salary without any principled criteria for such differentiation. This practice is also destructive of the morale of a work force.

Secretiveness is also harmful to good labor relations. Financial decisions cannot be done in the dead of night. Both the reasons for the decisions, and the decisions themselves, must be available for scrutiny by the members of the church. Vatican II teaching urges and the 1983 Code of Canon Law mandates consultation in financial matters for diocesan bishops, pastors, and administrators of church goods (LG, 33 and 37; CIC/83 canons 492, 537, and 1280). Members of finance councils and committees have to take seriously their role to judge the moral adequacy, as well as the fiscal sanity and stability, of wage and benefit decisions.   Equitable sustenance does not just happen. The justice in a just wage does not lie only in dollars.

It is also to be found in the total process of knowing the magisterial teaching, consulting all involved parties, becoming informed about the local and national markets, and then making decisions in the light of the these sources of wisdom. A system of administration is necessary to insure clarity, fairness, participation, and integrity for employee and employer alike.

What would be the chief elements of an administrative system of salary and benefits?[7]   Such a system begins with solid, objective information about each position and job in the system. This information is used to organize and write job descriptions. A job description sorts out principal duties from secondary ones. It helps in comparison with other positions in the organization and in the market. The job description makes it easier for a superior to set performance goals and to perform an adequate evaluation.

Job description leads to job evaluation. This step determines the criteria for evaluating the performance of an individual worker and the distinctions among jobs in the system. It is usually necessary to use both qualitative and quantitative methods in job evaluation.   For example, confidentiality cannot be measured by quantitative data. Yet it needs to be considered and judged because of its importance in many church positions. Other factors, such as required experience, complexity of job, responsibility for relationships with others, supervisory skills, and effectiveness, can be judged using a combination of both methods.

With this information the employer is ready to design a salary structure and place all the jobs within the salary structure. The ranges of the salary structure are determined using both internal and external data, i.e., the ability of the employer to pay and the usual salary range for a particular job in the market. It is also necessary to determine how often and with what mechanisms the worker evaluation is performed. A prudent application of a just wage would seem to call for each worker to be evaluated at least annually. Supervisor and worker need to have criteria for that particular job as a basis for determining the quality of performance on the job. If a conflict arises over a sharp disagreement of the evaluation, the employee should have recourse to a higher level supervisor or an impartial court of due process.

The salary structure and benefits package should be reviewed annually or bi-annually to ensure that changes in cost of living, medical costs, and the organization's financial picture are taken into consideration. In addition, supervisors should be trained and evaluated themselves to support a fruitful and fair evaluation process. It goes without saying that such a system should adhere to all applicable state and federal laws.

The process of setting a salary and benefits system of administration is certainly not easy. It may also seem unnecessary to some pastors or church administrators who only employ a handful of people. It is here that individual dioceses, or regional groupings of dioceses or church institutions, can apply the principle of subsidiarity and perform a service for smaller church entities by providing the professional services to put a system into effect. Participation of all who are touched by this system is critical for its success. An open process of consultation, which includes comments from the workers and from those who "pay" for church services, the laity, builds knowledge of the principles according to which the system works and confidence and support of its conclusions. A system of administration prevents paternalism and purely arbitrary appropriation of jobs and funds. It prevents a newly appointed pastor or administrator from firing current employees without cause and hiring new ones. The just system can support job security for church workers. It also protects workers from having managers set wages only on the basis of the institution's fiscal situation at a given moment.

Very much linked to a system of wage and benefits is a signed agreement or contract. It is astonishing to see how many church employees do not have some form of written contract. Sometimes pastors argue that a written agreement erodes trust. "We're all Christians. Isn't my word and a handshake good enough?"

A contract need not undercut the integrity of the relationship between employer and employee. In fact, it can build a foundation for trust by stating principles, clarifying unspoken assumptions, and dealing with "what if" situations.[8]

The agreement binds both parties. The employee knows what are the hours of work, wage scale, job grade and description, benefits package, evaluation procedure, opportunities for promotion, and due process option. The employer knows what work he or she can expect from the employee, how and when payment is made, the minimal work environment conditions, and steps for lay off or termination. When principles and specifics are agreed to in writing by worker and employer, conflict is lessened; clarity can improve worker productivity; and sound relationships can build worker morale.[9]

The Just Wage means Equal Pay for Equal Work
The Just Wage means Benefits Based on Need

A first glance at these two axioms placed together can make one conclude they are opposites. The application of each of these concepts separately can lead to contrary conclusions. Yet in assessing the labor laws and economic history of the United States and Catholic social teaching on the just wage it is necessary to treat these two axioms as a unit. Liberato and Schervich conclude,"Principles of just compensation need to weave these two concepts simultaneously into a consistent interpretation of justice when applied to compensation."[10] By considering the polarities of these axioms together in a compensation system the church employer can move toward a just wage.

The United States in this century has gradually accepted the principle of equal pay for equal work in its labor laws and bureaucratic policies. This principle is also known as comparable worth.[11] The National War Labor Board defined this in 1942 when it authorized employers to "equalize the wage or salary rates paid to females with rates paid to males for comparable quality and quantity of work."[12] The 1963 Equal Pay Act narrowed "comparable" to "equal", and set the stage for many court battles over a generous or narrow interpretation of equal work.[13] For the purposes of this study, equal work means work valued equally by a job evaluation system. It does not have to be virtually identical work.

For moral and legal reasons, it seems clear that there can be no discrimination in the salary of church employees based on race, sex, national origin, handicapped condition, age, or marital status.[14] Equal pay is to be given for equal work. At all times the compensation is to be in compliance with local law.

With this in mind, Barbara Garland concludes that "the wage is the pivotal determination of the justice of a system of employment."[15] The wage is the largest piece of the compensation package. It is the prime factor in defining differences in the salary or wage scale of a system (in addition to the more abstract job responsibilities). It determines the right of access to economic activities in the society for the worker and his or her dependents. A particular wage needs to be set by adjusting other axioms noted in this section: that the wage (and compensation package) must meet at a minimum level those needs which support human dignity, for the worker and the worker's dependents; the condition of the region's economy and the employer's financial situation; the market value of a particular job.

To adjust for the needs of individuals, the church as an employer can best implement a just wage by fitting the benefits to the needs of the worker and his or her family. In this axiom the church begins to model a "counter-cultural" system of compensation. The church employer recognizes that to support the livelihood and dignity of a worker it may be necessary for one worker to receive a greater compensation package, at the same time that wages are equal for comparable jobs.

This is the paradox of treating these two axioms together. The value of one's work is measured monetarily within a stable and fair system of job grades and wage scale. The job description and classification determine the wage rate. The size of one's income from the total compensation package is measured by the needs of the individual and family, and any special circumstances. The costs of personal and family circumstances are explicitly part of the employer's system of salary administration and managerial decision making. This dual system tries to promote fairness in hiring and to allay fears that employers will be biased against workers with large families. In the joint treatment of these issues there is fidelity to the understanding of Catholic social teaching on the just wage, and compliance with current U.S. law and nondiscriminatory practice.

The Just Wage is conditioned by the Employer's Ability to Pay

The second axiom presented in this chapter, that there is no single just wage, acknowledges that context is important for this moral issue. The employer's ability to pay is one specific context which is often mentioned in the magisterial teaching. Two others, market forces and the common good, also need to be addressed.

For a business to employ, it must minimally over the short run balance losses with revenue, and over the long haul make a profit. Workers in their demands need to take into consideration the fiscal situation of a firm.

Not-for-profit organizations and institutions, which include the many manifestations of the church, do not make a profit as such. In many ways their fiscal situation is more precarious than businesses. They operate on minimal capital, usually with fewer reserves than businesses. Labor costs are often their greatest expense. They rely on unstable revenue sources: federal and state grants, bequests from wills, and donations from individuals. The fiscal picture of the ecclesial employer is vital to assessing a just wage.

Data from the survey of local church workers show that some parishes do not pay a just wage. This confirms other studies.[16] Pius XI implied that those businesses which pay an unjust wage would do better to go out of business and let their now unemployed workers have a chance to seek a job at a fair wage, or receive governmental assistance (QA, 72-73). Should the church employer stop employing if the church institution cannot pay a just wage? Again, by implication from Pius XI the answer would be in the short run, no, but in the long run, yes. Cooperation among owners, manager, and workers can sometimes adjust the productivity of the workers as well as their wages and businesses expenses.[17] But it is an unjust situation to employ workers at a wage which does not enable them to meet the needs of human dignity.

This has implications for the members of the church. They (we) are the people of God, whose generosity supplies the funds which allow the church in its many structures to operate. Andrew Greeley has documented how Catholicism in the United States--the religious group with the highest average income--gave 50% less in 1984 (by percentage of income) than in 1963.[18] Greeley and McManus suggest reasons for this drop, but Greeley does not foresee any changes in giving patterns for Catholics. At the same time that giving (by percentage of income) is down significantly, many members of the church are coming to see the need for more ministries, and more paid ministers. If the faithful are serious about employing these ministers, then it is the obligation of the whole church (leaders, administrators, and people together) to increase their financial contributions to ensure these new ministers are paid a fair and living wage. It is inconsistent when church members and leaders call for their structures to be just to workers in the wage they are paid, at the same time that their donations are inadequate to put just wages into practice. Even as church leaders, administrators, and workers must be held accountable for their service or ministry, they have the responsibility of calling for the Catholic people as a whole to contribute adequately for the workers' just support.

A just wage is an expression of faith. It is the imperative of the church (leaders, managers, and people together) to practice in its own house what its moral principles urge others to do. It is an expression of the justice all Christians are called to put into action.

The Just Wage interacts with Market Forces

A second element which makes the just wage complex to determine is the relationship of market forces to what the ecclesial employer pays. Can a numerical figure specify this relationship? After briefly examining the market in the United States, Bishop McManus proposes in his 1987 reflection that Catholic school teachers, and any college educated professional, be paid a minimum of $400 per week ($20,800 per year), and others employed by the church, $300 per week ($15,600).[19] This simplistic solution does not answer whether such a wage is just. He admits he proposes it as a way of stirring up arguments about what the church should pay and how the church might pay for a just wage.[20]

How to compare church institutions and the market is a complex question. There are many factors to take into consideration. For example, what market do you look at? One must decide: do you include all businesses or only service organizations?; profit making businesses and not-for-profit institutions together, or not-for-profits alone?; are federal and municipal employees included? Then one has to examine the salary scale, the benefits package, the process of compensation administration, and the principle of equal pay for equal work.

Whether to compare with the market at all is another question. In the lower levels of wages it seems clear that the church should not be governed merely by the legal minimum or by the market, but by what the local church judges reasonably just to support with dignity the worker and his or her family. It is in the middle and highest levels that comparisons with the market can be fruitful, without betraying the understanding of the just wage.[21] In certain occupations, skilled personnel are at a premium, and their scarcity can dictate to church employers what the market will bear. Examples are attorneys and high-level educational and fiscal administrators. Church employers have to balance the need or desire to attract and retain excellent personnel with the demands of the budget and the wage scale as a whole.

The Just Wage interacts with the Common Good

It is in recognition of the wage scale as a whole that one aspect of the common good enters the picture. All church institutions live within tight budgets. There is only so much money to apply to the labor force as a whole. The question of justice is applied not only to how much each individual worker is paid, but also how the scale is set and weighted. Is a top level administrator worth in salary the same as five janitors? This is perhaps an unfair way of asking if is it reasonable or just for a top level administrator to be paid five times as much as the lowest paid janitor. It seems excessive to this author if the highest paid employee receives ten times the wage of the lowest paid employee. It is necessary to have a system of promotion with commensurate salary increases. But if the church employer starts the salary scale at a higher wage than the market because of the demands of offering just compensation, it seems consistent (and practical) in the interests of the common good of all the employees to offer top level salaries, which are less than the best the market offers, while still remaining competitive.

The Just Wage applies to All Employees,
Including Church Employees

From the social doctrine of the church which has been reviewed in Chapters One and Four, the conclusion of this axiom is clear. A just wage and purposeful labor enables the worker to live in dignity with his or her family. If there are any exceptions, they would come in those cases where a business is struggling because of unforeseen expenses or a poor market. There have been many cases in recent years where unionized workers have been asked to voluntarily forego wage increases, or even to accept wage reductions. Many workers have experienced great difficulty giving up what their hard work and seniority had earned. The results of these voluntary reductions have been mixed. The Chicago-based Business Executives for Economic Justice suggest that businesses might carry people over the short term to avoid layoffs and terminations. They do acknowledge that this is easier for privately owned companies than publicly owned ones.[22] It is only a stopgap until an upturn in sales and revenue occurs.

If a church employer cannot afford a just wage, and if the people who donate to that institution or parish do not respond to appeals for greater support for this purpose, the only recourse is not to employ. The church administrator can ameliorate the effects of layoff or termination by offering retraining and outplacement services, insuring that benefits are stretched as far as possible between employment, and handle the process of termination or layoff in a manner which ensures the ongoing dignity of the worker. This very hard decision--employment only with just compensation--respects the integrity of the church's position as a teacher as well as a fair employer. Such a decision should be discussed thoroughly with the members of the church or board of directors of the institution. It may move them to restructure the work load, to use more volunteers, or explore other options for its ministerial needs to safeguard just wages for all workers.

What is the nature of the moral obligation of the church as employer to fulfill this teaching? The process of answering this question is inferred in the full panoply of Catholic social teaching by the magisterium. Charles Curran suggests in a comparison of the methodologies of Catholic social and sexual teaching that, unlike the sexual teaching, Catholic social teaching recognizes significant grey areas in the determination of right or wrong choices.[23] He cites the apostolic exhortation of Paul VI, *Octogesima Adveniens*, which respects a pluralism of options and the need for discernment. Curran identifies this as a relationality-responsibility ethical model. The historical character and dynamism of the church's social teaching are stressed. The pope appealed to conscience in the light of the gospel, not law. Service, concerns for the poor, and "creative innovations" are the touchstones of a faithful Christian. Paul VI said:

> It is with all its dynamism that the social teaching of the church accompanies men in their search. If it does not intervene to authenticate a given structure or propose a ready-made model, it does not thereby limit itself to recalling general principles. It develops through reflection applied to the changing situations of this world, under the driving force of the gospel as the source of renewal when its message is accepted in its totality and with all its demands. It also develops with a sensitivity proper to the church which is characterized by a disinterested will to serve and by attention to the poorest. Finally, it draws upon its rich experience of many centuries which enables it, while continuing its permanent preoccupations, to undertake the daring and creative innovations which the present state of the world requires. (OA, 42)

The historical character and the dynamism of Catholic social teaching are stressed in this passage. The pope does not see conscience in the light of obedience to law. There is a gospel call for "discernment" in light of the historical conditions and teachings of Christ and the church. Paul VI exhibited in this work a bias toward shared and participatory decision making, a bias for action in the midst of complexity, and the methodological importance of utopias (OA, 37 and 47-48).

These axioms are not proposed "to authenticate a given structure or to propose a ready-made model." They are offered in lieu of a definition of a just wage and as general principles grounded in magisterial and papal teaching. It would seem imperative for every bishop, pastor, and administrator to take as seriously as any other expression of the church's moral teaching Catholic social teaching in general, and the right to a just wage for every worker in particular. This means a full familiarity with the principles involved here. These teachings need to be passed on to the faithful, to priests, and especially to church workers.[24] Bishops, pastors, and church administrators have a serious moral obligation to make good faith efforts to work for the full implementation of a just wage for every employee and a system of compensation to assure that right into the near future.

In the course of research and writing this book, numerous friends, parishioners, and priests commented, "It certainly will be easy to prove the church doesn't pay workers a just wage." Furthermore, not only did they take it for a fact that church employers did not pay justly, they presumed as well that the ones in power had *no intention* of doing so now or in the future. This cynical attitude among many members of the Catholic Church is real and widespread--and unfortunate. This cynicism, I believe, relates to the lack of seriousness which the leadership of the Catholic Church treats its own social doctrine, and its reluctance to teach it and implement it.

Curran says, "There is a general impression, both within and outside the Catholic Church, that Catholic moral teaching in social and sexual areas appears to be somewhat different."[25] If his thesis that there are significant methodological differences in these areas is correct, then there may be reasons for the failure to put social teachings into practice. Curran again:

> There can be no doubt that the documents in official Catholic teaching on sexuality employ the law model as primary. . . . In a legal model, the primary question is the existence of law. If something is against the law, it is wrong; if there is no law against it, it is acceptable and good. Within such a perspective, there is very little grey area. Something is either forbidden or permitted. Within a relationality - responsibility model, there are more grey areas. Here one can recognize that in the midst of complexity and specificity one cannot always claim a certitude for one's moral position.[26]

The practical conclusion many Catholics and many church administrators seem to reach today is that if one cannot claim a "certitude" for one's moral position in the area of social ethics, it is acceptable to ignore any honest critique. One concludes that in the absence of certitude one is not bound to a standard of morality. This is not the position of Paul VI, who called for "daring and creative innovations" in applying the principles of Catholic social teaching (OA, 42). This is a struggle in which Christians must engage in order to build up the Kingdom of God. "At the heart of the world, there dwells the mystery of the human person discovering oneself to be God's child in the course of historical and psychological process in which constraint and freedom as well as the weight of sin and the breath of the spirit alternate and struggle for the upper hand." (OA, 37)

At the conclusion of *Sollicitudo Rei Socialis*, John Paul II notes the many negative forces in the world which threaten the dignity of the human person. After calling upon all men and women without exception to work for and support human dignity, he says, "In this commitment, the sons and daughters of the church must serve as examples and guides . . . It is their task to animate temporal realities with Christian commitment, by which they show that they are witnesses and agents of peace and justice." (SRS, 47)

Summary

The popes and bishops of the last one hundred years have urged in the strongest terms the practical and imaginative application of the principles of Catholic social teaching in the temporal order. The church itself is to be an example, a shining light, of what it asks all others to do. Pastors and administrators, with the cooperation and assistance of their employees and the church as a whole, need to take the teaching on the just wage, expressed in these twelve axioms, and begin the strenuous yet fruitful task of implementing it today.

A Just Wage for Religious

If the right to a just wage applies to all workers, including those employed by church agencies and jurisdictions, does it also apply to religious vowed to a life of voluntary poverty? This question has been raised often recently. One spur to its timeliness is the financial difficulties many religious congregations in the United States are facing because of the sharply increasing number of retired members and sharply decreasing number of younger, working members.

In 1986 the National Conference of Catholic Bishops joined with the Leadership Conference of Women Religious and the Conference of Major Superiors of Men to work cooperatively on ways to address the serious unfunded retirement liability that some religious congregations were facing. An outgrowth of that collaboration, called the Tri-Conference Retirement Project, was the formation of a subcommittee to put together data about compensation by religious, to evaluate the philosophies of various models of compensation, and to propose changes which improve compensation for active religious and assist needy religious communities, especially in their funds for retirement support. The report of the subcommittee concludes that there is impetus to move away from current forms of compensation, but there is no consensus around any one model for practically implementing what they call just compensation for religious.[27]

This section will outline the major issues of a just wage for religious women and men. It will begin with brief glances at magisterial teaching and canon law. Then the history of compensation for religious will be reviewed, which places in context the present widespread use of the stipend system of compensation for religious. Four areas which apply to vowed religious vis-a-vis a stipend system of compensation are noted. Finally, I conclude that the criteria for a just wage for church employees must be applied as well to the special situation of members of religious congregations.

Magisterial Teaching

Just as there were few explicit citations of the right to a just wage for the church worker, there are fewer still for religious men and women. The 1971 Synod of Bishops document *De Iustitia in Mundo* stated, "Those who serve the church by their labor, including priests and religious, should receive a sufficient livelihood and enjoy that social security which is customary in their region." (DI, 41) The only other explicit reference is in the 1986 economic pastoral of the United States bishops. The bishops write, "We bishops commit ourselves to the principle that those who serve the Church--laity, clergy, and religious--should receive a sufficient livelihood and the social benefits provided by responsible employers in our nation." (EJA, 351)

It is easy, and correct, to assume that when the documents of Catholic social teaching speak about the right to a just wage for all workers, and especially for workers in the church, that this teaching applies to religious men and women as well. But the absence of explicit mention of religious, except in the above two instances, points to a lack of reflection on and application of this principle to the situation of religious. The Decree on the Appropriate Renewal of the Religious Life has fine words to speak to the need for religious to embrace and cultivate voluntary poverty. But except for an affirmation that each religious should regard himself or herself "as subject to the common law of labor," it does not explain how the religious are to make "necessary provision for their livelihood and undertakings." (PC, 13)

Canon Law

The revised 1983 Code of Canon Law does not contain any explicit references to religious receiving a just and decent wage. Canon 231, 2, which refers to lay persons, certainly would apply to vowed religious who work for the church who are not clerics. Religious who are ordained priests would be affected as well by canon 281.

A different approach is to look at the care of temporal goods by religious. Canon 635 reads in translation:

> #1. The temporal goods of religious institutes, since they are ecclesiastical goods, are regulated by the prescriptions of Book V, The Temporal Goods of the Church, unless it is expressly stated otherwise.
> #2. Nevertheless, each institute is to determine appropriate norms for the use and administration of goods so that the poverty appropriate to the institute is fostered, protected and expressed.

This canon points directly to the section on the temporal goods of the church. This section contains the admonition in canon 1286 to all administrators of church goods to pay employees of the church a just wage.

While there are no references to religious with regard to a living wage, their situation is covered by the canons which refer to all employees of the church.

History of Compensation in the U.S.

The history of how religious were compensated for their ministry in this country is rooted in their missionary spirit. "Congregations came to the U.S. or were founded here expressly to minister to the needs of the poor immigrant Catholic population."[28] The primary work of religious, especially women religious, in the 19th century was staffing parochial schools. Pastors, parents of school children, parishioners, and religious all made sacrifices to support Catholic parochial schools. It is in the context of sacrifice that the mission of the congregation, their ministry, and their payment for the services and talents of their members became associated. Amata Miller says:

> Compensation of religious for their ministries in the church became inextricably linked in people's minds to their dedication and to their lifestyle. It was simply inconceivable that religious might share the need of other workers for higher wages and improved fringe benefits, much less pursue them when this pursuit became part of the nation's social agenda.[29]

Within this past context, when the American Catholic Church was characterized by necessarily frugal pastors and congregations composed of immigrant, mostly poor members, Catholic parishes in this country offered a minimal stipend to cover the needs of the religious working in their schools. This was supplemented with in-kind contributions: the convent building and its upkeep and furnishings, some food contributions, medical and dental services, the gifts of parents and parishioners at Christmas or special anniversaries.[30] Roland Faley defined this stipend as "basically a donation offered for voluntary services. This was seen as wholly consonant with the vowed life and at the same time providing vital assistance to a church which was itself poor and limited in resources."[31]

At this time religious congregations gave little thought to retirement needs. Vocations were numerous, elderly members were few, and there was great faith in a Provident God. Yet the sisters knew there were needs other than the parochial school. Miller continues:

> Few people, however, realized that religious, in addition to buying their food and clothing, paid the costs of their own education, of the care of sick members, and of the operation of Motherhouses. The sense of privacy among religious about internal congregational matters, and their dedication to unselfish service, contributed to the myth that religious were taken care of by someone else. . . . All of this gave credibility to the myth that religious congregations had no financial need and that the low levels of compensation were no problem.[32]

In the 1930s third party reimbursement for health care led congregations which ran hospitals to pay sisters at levels equivalent to their lay peers. In some cases, this also happened when religious taught or worked for colleges or universities. Miller notes that because of this, congregations which operate hospitals have healthier financial situations today than those which engaged primarily or solely in parochial school education. "It should be noted that differential compensation for religious has existed, but because of the concentration of religious in parochial and diocesan settings this has been the exception rather than the norm. Nonetheless uniform compensation for religious is still a prevailing mindset regardless of the real circumstances."[33]

The stipend form of compensation, supplemented with some in-kind benefits, has been the norm for religious in this country. It reflected the socio-economic standing of the members of the church, and the mission of religious to serve mostly poor, immigrant needs. The stipend system is now being questioned.

Challenges to the Stipend System

Most non-ordained religious in the U.S. today are paid by the stipend system. This system is different than procedures under which salaries are given to lay people and to priests. The stipend and benefits package given to diocesan priests and religious order priests who staff parishes is usually set by the diocesan bishop and has another salary scale. An analysis of some of the elements of the stipend system for vowed religious shows why there are legitimate reasons to suggest it does not adequately express Catholic social teaching on justice and a just wage. These elements are low wages, responsibility for congregational dependents, the vow of poverty, and choosing ministries.

The stipends have been held at levels too low both to meet current costs and to support the retirees for whom it was impossible to set aside reserves in the past. A survey of 139 dioceses in the United States by the Tri-Conference Retirement Project revealed that the average base cash compensation in 1987 (latest year available) was $8,772, with a range of $3,800 to $15,000.[34] By comparison, the average wage for lay church workers in Allegheny County (see Chapter Four) in 1989 was $11,909, with a range of $2,393 to $24,523. Of course, this does not include in-kind contributions of housing and transportation (in 1987, averages of $1,648 for housing and $1,630 for transportation for religious).

To compare this with figures supplied by the U.S. Department of Agriculture, in 1988 a single person on a "thrifty" budget would need $17,396 to satisfy ordinary household needs (Figure 18). If one presumes that most, if not all, religious would have a college education, then their cash compensation pales before the average income, $31,000, and average expenditures spent on ordinary household needs, $27,217, of a college graduate head of household with 1.9 dependents in the U.S. in 1988.[35] The *Just Wages* survey of church professionals in 1989 reveals a much higher median figure for cash compensation for religious, $14,996.[36] This is $6,224 more than the 1987 Tri-Conference survey average for cash compensation. Both are significantly under the single person thrifty budget figures for ordinary household needs.

The stipend schedule for women religious in the Diocese of Pittsburgh (Appendix Four, D.) for the fiscal year 1990-91 is higher that either the Tri-Conference average (for 1987) or the NCDD survey (for 1989). Religious women who are employed by a parish or the diocese and who do not live in a parish convent will receive a stipend of $15,620. Their congregations will also receive contributions for health insurance ($1,600), retirement ($1,425), and housing ($2,580). This is a total compensation package of $21,225. This figure is $3,829 above the thrifty budget for a single person. (It is also $9,316 above the average wage of all respondents to the Allegheny County parish workers survey, and $4,647 above the average wage of business managers, the highest average of any job title in the survey.)

The schedule for women religious in the Diocese of Pittsburgh is part of a three-year agreement. In the second and third year the stipends and benefits will rise approximately 8%. This percentage of increase is almost double the annual U.S. cost of living for each of the last five years. The 8% increase would seem to indicate that the bishop of Pittsburgh, who negotiates the agreement with the major superiors of congregations which have missions in the Diocese of Pittsburgh, is serious about improving the historically low stipends for women religious.

These low dollar amounts of the Tri-Conference and *Just Wages* surveys point to the question of whether the religious are given enough to provide for their own well being and basic needs. The Diocese of Pittsburgh stipend schedule for 1990-93 offers an example of where local church leaders are listening and responding to the concerns of religious congregations.

A second challenge to the stipend system is that it does not begin to address or assist the unfunded costs of providing health care for elderly and infirm members of religious congregations. Nor does it cover the general administrative costs supporting these members.

A usual presumption by the faithful is that the stipend is provided for the needs of the individual religious and that it is like a personal allowance. One seldom thinks of a member of a religious community having "dependents." Just as the right to a living wage states the support is for the worker and the worker's family, by analogy the compensation given to an individual member of a religious institute supports that worker and a portion of the community expenses. The demographics of the men and women religious show increasing numbers of retirees and elderly and decreasing numbers of active workers.

There is the further concern, long-standing in the magisterial teaching, that the just wage should assist in providing future benefits for the worker. Often this takes the form of participation in Social Security. How will the future needs of younger members of the religious communities be met? Faley says, "Some assurance must be present that the still active 'work force' will have basic provisions at the time of illness or retirement. The health care facilities that provided this care for sick or elderly religious [for free] in the past are no longer in a financial position to do so and moreover would not be able to meet the increasingly heavy demands presented today."[37]

Liberato and Schervich's study calculated for the purposes of comparison that religious had 1.8 dependents in their congregations.[38] There was no explanation for how this figure was arrived at. One way to begin to calculate the number of "dependents" is to assess certain facts. It is necessary to acknowledge that there is a wide range of financial and vocational health in religious congregations. Different congregations have varied needs. In the Living Wage Model proposed by the Tri-Conference Retirement Project report, *Promises to Keep*, it is suggested that each congregation use a common formula to determine each member's share of the current cost of support of elderly and infirm members and congregational services and activities. Each congregation would arrive at its own figure, based upon the state of its financial health, number of income earning members, revenues, and savings. This respects the needs of each institute and enables the earner to contribute a fair share toward overall community costs.

Whatever model of compensation used needs to take into consideration the "dependents" of each income earning religious.

A third challenge to the stipend system involves living out the vow of poverty. A basic assumption of every model of compensation for religious, including the stipend system, is that compensation belongs to the congregation. It does not belong to the individual. This is rooted in the religious understanding of a voluntary vow of poverty (PC, 13). This is also the basis for the tax exemption for any religious institute in the U.S. The charitable organization contributes "good works" and the government in response exempts the institute from taxes. It is not the level of compensation, nor the conformity of the compensation of one member of a religious institute with that of others in the same community, which is the basis of the exemption. The tax exemption is applied to the congregation, not the individual.

Each member of a religious institute is called to live "in the poverty of Christ . . . in fact and spirit." (PC, 13) This is not mere obedience to the superior. It is a freely chosen and personally engaged imitation of Christ, who called all to have their treasures in heaven. Each house or community shares its possessions so that freely embraced poverty is possible. In this sense, it is not enough for individual members to profess poverty. There needs to be a corporate witness as well, which avoids "every appearance of luxury, of excessive wealth, and accumulations." (PC, 13) Simplicity of life is to be carried out in view of the mission of the institute and the perceived understanding of luxury in the culture.

Some have argued that the more a religious institute moves toward financial independence, with the assistance of a just wage for its members, the further it moves from a spirit of dependence and trust in Providence. This is a worthwhile concern. The Vatican Council stated "to the degree that their rules and constitution permit, religious communities can rightly possess whatever is necessary for their temporal life and mission." (PC, 13) What is necessary, Faley says, is that

> every religious institute walks the narrow path between the
> Scylla of exaggerated financial concern and the Charybdis of
> penury and the inability to provide for its members.[39]

It is the duty of each religious superior to be responsible for the temporal needs of the community as well as alert to avoid the appearance of greed or wealth. The question of remuneration is and should remain distinct from concerns about the way the vow of poverty is lived. Whether or not a religious institute is living out its commitment to a simple life style is a matter of conscience for the whole community and each member individually. This is a separate issue and should not be confused with the issue of compensation.

The stipend system links the two in a way which does not reflect trust in the community as a whole to carry out its commitment to be a witness of poverty. Other systems of payment may reflect better the distinction between just compensation and the vow of poverty.

A fourth challenge to the stipend system is that the lack of a just wage deprives the congregation of the choice of allocating their financial subsidy as they feel called to do by the Gospel and the social teachings of the church. With fewer and fewer paid workers, communities have the implicit pressure of forcing their wage earning members to take the most lucrative jobs, in order that the superiors can balance the budget and care for the costs of the whole community. Some outsiders have wondered if such financial pressure has contributed to an erosion of selfless dedication and generosity, and the basic values of religious life.

Another aspect of choice is that in some instances (15% of those who responded to the Tri-Conference survey) the religious congregation is not consulted in the decision-making process of setting the stipend within a diocesan region. Catholic social teaching has stressed the value of participation of those who are affected by decisions in the decision making process. It seems clear that non-participative decisions are inconsistent with the current understanding of the the church as the people of God.

Portions of the stipend system, such as the in-kind provision for parish-provided convent residence and automobile, may express patterns of paternalism and mutual dependency which are not beneficial either to the religious or the particular ministries. In a few cases such in-kind contributions may communicate a sense of privileged status for religious in the church.

The issue of choice is not an end in itself. It is a recognition of the unique charism and generosity of each religious institute. The whole purpose of the just wage is to provide what is necessary for the community to survive and continue its service. A just wage (or substantial professional salary) paid to religious in one ministry or diocese often supports the continued presence of the same religious institute in another, poorer, portion of the Lord's vineyard. In this regard, there is always the freedom for religious communities to act out their vow of poverty by allowing certain members to work voluntarily for less than just compensation. This preserves congregational choice to serve the Gospel wherever the Spirit calls.

Summary

For the above reasons, therefore, the stipend system of compensation for religious has received justifiable criticism. Whatever models or combination of models are chosen have to respond to the concerns of low wages, the community dependents, the practice of the vow of poverty, and freedom for congregational choice of ministries and jobs. The Tri-Conference Retirement Project offers three possible models: Market Value, Living Wage, and Compressed Scale. Each of these models uses a system of administration to respond to the needs of religious today. These include addressing the historically lower wages paid to religious, the unfunded retirement liability and health care costs for retired members of congregations, the false dichotomy of receiving just compensation and practicing the vow of poverty, the dependents within the community each income-earning member of the community supports, and the opportunity for congregations to choose how they exercise the preferential option for the poor.

As bishops, pastors, religious superiors, and administrators grapple with the just wage for all workers, including religious, in the church, it is well for them to realize that no one expects perfect decisions from them. What is asked for is participation in decision making, acknowledgment for the past sacrifices given to the church, and respect for the human dignity of each person concerned.

The Virtue of Industriousness

Much of the forgoing reflection and analysis of the just wage in Catholic social teaching has focused on the theory and practice of structures. What does the church teach? How is or is not this teaching applied? What forms does this teaching have? How can it be improved? Crucial to structures are the ones in power--in this case, the employer. In church structures this person may be a bishop, pastor, principal, executive director, administrative secretary, rector, religious superior, or business manager. Structures are initiated, built, maintained--and ignored or destroyed--by people. Most often for the structures of employment the people in power are the employers. The explication of Catholic social teaching specifically relating to the just wage in this study intends to reach and instruct both employees and employers. But in the realities of power and its exercise, great burdens and great opportunities rest with the employer.

Yet the individual worker is not without responsibility. What does the individual worker do? Does she or he stand around waiting for a benevolent boss to ask for an opinion or to name the worker to a grievance committee? I think not. Our Christian religion teaches that there are many virtues which we can learn to cultivate and apply in the situation of our daily lives.

Among these certainly honesty, loyalty, integrity, patience, and charity apply to workers.

I would like to address one virtue which relates directly to the teaching on a living wage for a worker and his or her family. This is the virtue of industriousness.

Industriousness as a virtue is the Christian response to the question, why toil? The so-called "sensible" modern response is that one works to make money. This is the answer from utility. To make money one works. One makes more money by doing work judged to be valuable by the culture and society. It is but a short jump from judging the work a person does as important to judging the person by how important is his/her work. In this way of thinking the value of the person is set by the value of the work done.

John Paul II offers a different view. In *Laborem Exercens* he says "human work is a key, probably the essential key, to the whole social question." (LE, 3) Human work is valuable not just because it is useful. Human work is valuable because it is done by human beings. This is what John Paul means when he refers to the human being as the subject of work. "The sources of the dignity of work are to be sought primarily in the subjective dimension, not in the objective one." (LE, 6) The ethical value of work is in the fact that a human being, a free person, carries it out. Work expresses human dignity and has the possibility of increasing it.

Industrious work is virtuous because through work the human worker "becomes good as man . . . more a human being." (LE, 9) The industrious worker achieves a partial fulfillment of himself. The industrious worker expresses and increases human dignity.

Webster's defines "industrious" as "perseveringly active; marked by steady dependable energetic work; skillful; clever; zealous." Synonyms of industrious are hardworking, diligent, assiduous, productive, and unflagging. These words positively radiate energy. And that is one important aspect for the industrious worker. He or she is active. The industrious worker engages in productive toil, for useful purposes (e.g., completion of a project, making money, support of oneself and one's family) and as an expression of who he/she is. Engagement in the business of work means that the employee brings one's whole self to the endeavor: body, mind, and spirit; past experiences and present skills; mistakes, reflected and unreflected upon; ambition and hopes for the future.

It is an active and alert focus on the job which enables the worker to be productive. In this regard the worker reflects the creativity of the One Who Creates and the underappreciated positive value of creativity. Human beings are made in the image of God (Genesis 1:27). They carry on the creation of the world, within the limits of their own capabilities and sinfulness. They imitate the Creator in working (and in resting).

John Haughey says it this way:

We never cease to make ourselves according to the image we
have of ourselves. As people of faith we know we are to make
ourselves according to the image God gives us of who we are.
. . . Here is a Creator who creates, produces, works--in a word,
takes dominion. Here is a creature made in the image of this
God to whom God gives dominion over what God has made.
What could be clearer?[40]

The notion of dominion is a call for men and women, made in the
image of the energetic and resourceful God of Genesis, to pick up with their
productivity where God left off. Purposeful work gives meaning to our lives
and allows us to fulfill our image. Dominion is the opposite of alienation.
Dominion, Haughey says, "must mean bringing form to formlessness,
fecundity to waste, and content to a void." Industrious workers bring
meaning to their tasks, large or small. They refuse to acquiesce in the
feelings of powerlessness and the presence of chaos. Industrious workers
bring purpose to the abyss of alienation. "Dominion wins when work
becomes purposeful, when we take the measure of it, not it the measure of
us."[41]

Industrious work, like all human endeavors, is in some way social as
well as personal. John Paul II says industriousness must be linked to the
social order. Without such a link, industrious workers have been and can be
exploited, degraded, and oppressed. It is here that a just wage is joined to
the virtue of industriousness. A just wage affirms the dignity of the worker.
It offers the opportunity to take care of one's basic needs, and the possibility
to found a family. A just wage and industrious workers are parallel positive
moral responses in the social and personal orders. They both express and
support human dignity through work and toil.

Certainly, church workers have been industrious even without a just
wage. Comments from some of the respondents to the survey of Pittsburgh
Diocese church workers express their gratitude to be able to work for the
church and to be of assistance to the needy and to members of the church,
in spite of low wages, unjust decisions, and non-existent administrative
processes.

It has to be admitted, too, that some church workers are not
industrious. Some ecclesial employers are not industrious either. Often the
prevailing system in parishes has been that the pastor paid poorly, so the
employee worked poorly, and no one complained. A full appreciation of the
axioms which express a just wage forces pastors and employees to shake off
unspoken agreements or attitudes such as these.

Not all work is pleasurable and purposeful, regardless of the energy
applied. Toil is the word John Paul gives to the kind of work which "marks
the way of human life on earth and constitutes an announcement of death."

(LE, 27)   He sees this toil as an opportunity for workers to share in the toil--the suffering and death--of Christ, and so participate in the work of redemption. This happens not in some faraway, supernatural aerie, but in the ordinary activities of life.   Further, John Paul sees "a new good" springing from toil and from workers' participation in the saving Paschal Mystery of Christ.   This new good offers an inbreaking of the kingdom of God, an anticipation of that new life and fullness of justice wherein all love will be revealed (LE, 27).

The perseverance, zeal, and hard work of the industrious employee are what he or she brings to the work place. This is especially true for the paid worker in the church.   All Christians, and all Christian structures, are to model the service and self-sacrifice of the Master. When workers use their industry, energy, and talents to the fullest, the whole church structure can begin to move with joy and justice toward the fulfillment of what John Paul calls "the gospel of work."

Conclusion

The magisterial teaching on the right to a just wage is deeply rooted in Catholic tradition. It recognizes the fundamental quality of work in the lives of men and women, and how work allows people to support themselves.   Since Pope Leo XIII, who began what is considered the contemporary period of Catholic social teaching with his encyclical *Rerum Novarum* in 1891, the right to a just wage for the support of the worker and the worker's family has been explicitly upheld.   This right is one of a constellation of basic human rights which is due to each human person. The right to a just wage is rooted in the dignity of the human person.   Just remuneration can be conditioned by the contexts of the particular time and culture in which one lives, the financial situation of the business or organization which employs, and the needs of the common good. Nevertheless, the just wage is at least a minimum package of cash payment and certain socially necessary benefits which allows the worker and his/her family to live in reasonable comfort and with hope and security in the future.

Further examination of magisterial teaching in this century reveals that it is the explicit intention of the highest levels of Roman Catholic Church authority that administrators of church institutions, dioceses, and parishes pay a just wage as well. This applies to all men and women who are employed by the church, whether they are laborers or professionals, whether they be lay faithful, ordained clergy, or vowed religious.

A survey of the Catholic parishes in Allegheny County, Pennsylvania, shows that in many instances the wages paid to workers by the church do not meet the minimum standards of ecclesial teaching on the just wage. Much improvement is needed, in setting a fair wage scale with adequate and clearly agreed upon benefits, and with the establishment of signed contracts and mutually agreed upon evaluation and grievance procedures. The respondents to the survey were confused and in many cases did not know what benefits they were to receive for working for the church. A just wage demands that the conditions and benefits of employment be clearly explained and known by all employees. Analysis of wage scales for some professional groups employed by the church, and listings by the state and federal governments of annual surveys of wage rates, are both helpful for determining an approximate salary scale for each occupation. All employees need to participate in the formation of wage scales and negotiation of benefits.

In the concluding chapter are presented twelve axioms which define the complex factors that help to judge what a just wage is and how to implement it in ecclesial structures. There is the basic notion that the term "just wage" (and its synonyms living wage, family wage, just compensation, and equitable sustenance) refers to the full package of cash remuneration and benefits which is given to the employee by the employer in return for labor. There is no one universal just wage. Employers must use all the axioms which make up the just wage to determine what fulfills human dignity for the worker. A just wage is the minimum needed to permit the worker to receive all that is needed for the full and integral development of the human person. In this sense the just wage is a floor below which dignity is trampled upon and not given the means to be upheld.

A just wage is that which benefits not only the worker but also the worker's family. It is in this sense that a just wage is a family wage. In the ideal situation it allows only one wage earner to supply what is necessary for all the members of the family. The just wage is best set within an administrative system, which determines the salary scale, benefits package, responsibilities and duties of all parties, grievance procedures, and processes of evaluation and promotion. Setting such a scale includes the participation of employers, employees, and those whose funds pay for the ministries and their personnel costs. This is concluded with a signed agreement between employer and employee.

The just wage involves equal pay for equal work. The church, like all other employers, is not to discriminate. A hierarchy of wages is not ruled out for the purposes of recognizing greater responsibilities, as long as the range is set within a fair system, and the minimum represents a just wage. Yet for the church to show practical concern for the family of the worker, benefits are to be adjusted to family needs.

The context of the employer cannot be ignored. The employer's ability to pay, the market forces, and the common good all have to be taken into consideration. These contexts may occasion church leaders to seek greater fund-raising efforts and new appeals for support from the faithful, in order to ensure a just wage is paid to all workers.

From these axioms, and the magisterial and conciliar teaching on which they are based, it becomes clear that the just wage applies to all workers, including all workers employed by any structure or agency of the church. This is an arduous task, given the past and present record of the church as an employer. It is also a necessary task, which is rooted in the human dignity of each and every person, and the just structures which make upholding human dignity a reality.

In the preparation and writing of this book, the author has taken a great deal of kidding about just and unjust wages in the church. Beneath such humor, however, is a pessimism that the institutions and parishes of the church do not change and will not change. It can be, indeed must be, asked: Are the conclusions presented here feasible? Can they be put into practice in the real world by church authorities?

Are church institutions able to implement this official teaching of the magisterium? I believe the answer is yes. Greeley and McManus show how the giving patterns of American Catholics have gone down by half at the precise time when the average income of American Catholics is higher than it has ever been. Special collections for specific and worthwhile purposes, with widespread, high quality advertising, receive substantial sums. The annual national collection for the retirement needs of religious, and appeals for famine victims in Ethiopia or Somalia, earthquake victims in Armenia, and hurricane victims in Hawaii or South Florida, offer proof. One also can look at the occasional large bequests sought and received by some of the Catholic colleges, seminaries, and universities around the country.

At the same time, pastors know that most parishes are only supported by 30 to 40% of hard-core, regular contributors. These observations indicate ability to contribute. The money is there. The number of untapped potential donors is large. American Catholics in most middle and upper class neighborhoods and in many rural areas have funds to contribute to the continued ministry of the church through paid workers given a just wage. The common good calls for those parishes with greater sources of donated income to share with the poorer parishes or institutions.

The harder question is, will Catholic leaders and faithful implement the teaching on a just wage for all employees? Are leaders and people sufficiently motivated to do so? This has two elements. The first is education. You cannot put into practice what you do not know. This study is but one contribution among many recent reports and surveys to further knowledge and practical understanding of the just wage. Prime among these is the clarion call for just wages for all employees in *Economic Justice for All.*

The second element, and more difficult, is motivation. Can the papal, conciliar, and episcopal teachings motivate local church leaders to act for

economic justice in wages and benefits? Is the fear of being shown as less
just than some businesses or non-profit institutions, and thereby labeled
hypocritical, sufficient to move ecclesial leaders to establish salary scales,
promotion steps, grievance procedures, evaluation conferences? Do church
employers want to cultivate attitudes of stinginess and parsimony, or fairness
and generosity (Matthew 20:15).

Professional experts in fund-raising agree that only those men and
women who are convinced of the rightness of their cause receive positive
response to their begging. Administrators must want to implement just
remuneration before they ever attempt to "sell" this to the faithful, who will
pay for it.

It has been shown throughout that the justice in a just wage is almost
as dependent on an open and consultative process as it is on what salary and
which benefits a worker receives. Dialogue among managers and employers
is all important. Church administrators show concern for their employees
when they listen to their gripes and complaints. The respondents' comments
voiced anger and frustration over the inability of pastors to listen to their
grievances. The church workers were often very aware of their parish's
financial difficulties, which prevented immediate increases in wages or
benefits. What the parish employees were asking for was sympathetic
concern from their employers.

Good leaders and managers know listening is vital to gain respect for
authority and the confidence of their employees. Listening to their own
workers can lead to reframing the issue of wages from "mere" economics to
moral inquiry and shared problem solving.

Dialogue also acknowledges that employees within church systems
cannot remain silent about what they perceive as injustice. If they want to
see change happen, they have to express their criticisms and agree to
cooperate in seeking solutions. What *Lumen Gentium* said of lay faithful (in
a terribly sexist translation) can rightly be said also of church workers:

> Every layman should openly reveal to [pastors] his needs and
> desires with that freedom and confidence which befits a son of
> God and a brother in Christ. An individual layman, by reason
> of the knowledge, competence, or outstanding ability which he
> may enjoy, is permitted and *sometimes even obliged* to express
> his opinion on things which concern the good of the Church. .
> . . Let it always be done in truth, in courage, and in prudence,
> with reverence and charity toward those who by reason of their
> sacred office represent the person of Christ. (LG, 37; author's
> emphasis)

Both employers and employees have to take seriously their roles of speaking and listening in the process of dialogue.

It is my hope that this study of the just wage in church institutions not be seen only as bad news. After one reveals the nonexistent processes for participation and consultation and inadequate wages in the church, Christian hope calls for conversion, a movement from injustice to just practices. *"Indeed, the Church should be exemplary."* Self-criticism is also a door which opens a heretofore locked room, to allow in the light of truth, the fresh air of justice, and the sweeping away of all furnishings which deny basic human rights for workers and their families.

NOTES

1. David Hollenbach, "A Prophetic Church and the Catholic Sacramental Imagination," in John C. Haughey, ed., *The Faith That Does Justice: Examining the Christian Sources for Social Change* (New York: Paulist, 1977), 246.

2. Hollenbach, *Justice, Peace*, 33.

3. See GS, explanatory note; CP, 8-12; and EJA, 126-7;

4. The listing of axioms here is mine. However, I am indebted to the groupings of principles in Garland, *Compensation*, 15-20, and Liberato and Schervich, *Just Wages*, 39-40.

5. Liberato and Schervich, *Just Wages*, 40.

6. The Consumer Expenditure Survey data of the U.S. Bureau of Labor in 1990 determined that 1.4 persons shared in the income earning effort at the income level sufficient to meet ordinary needs. For further reflection on the right to a just wage in light of this statistic, see William P. Daly, "A Theoretical Framework for a Just Wage," *Church Personnel Issues* (November, 1992), 4-5.

7. See Garland, *Compensation*, 35-92, for a detailed description of the process of establishing such a system.

8. Integral to modern Catholic social thought is support for labor unions as an agency of economic participation and justice. For magisterial references, see RN, 48-57; MM, 15-22; GS, 68; OA, 14; and LE, 8. American episcopal support begins with James Cardinal Gibbons; corporate episcopal support begins with the 1919 *Program of Social Reconstruction*, 28, in Byers, *Justice in the Marketplace*, 378.

9. Excellent practical guidelines for non-professionals dealing with nonviolent conflict resolution are in two publications from the Harvard Negotiation Project: Roger Fisher and William Ury, *Getting to Yes: Negotiating Agreement Without Giving In* (New York: Penguin, 1981), and Roger Fisher and Scott Brown, *Getting Together: Building Relationships As We Negotiate* (New York: Penguin, 1988).

10. Liberato and Schervich, *Just Wages*, 39.

11. For a brief history of this concept, from the perspective of feminist activism, see Sara M. Evans and Barbara J. Nelson, *Wage Justice:*

Comparable Worth and the Paradox of Technocratic Reform (Chicago: University of Chicago Press, 1989), 16-41.

12. Quoted in ibid., 26.

13. Ibid., 27-30, 34-41.

14. GS, 25-6; FC, 23-4. Affirmative action in employment is a positive step to redress long-standing imbalances in minority representation. See the support of U.S. bishops in *Pastoral Statement on Race Relations and Poverty* (November 19, 1966), in Byers, *Justice in the Marketplace*, 465; *To Do the Work of Justice: A Plan of Action for the Catholic Community in the U.S.* (May 4, 1978), and *Brothers and Sisters to Us: A Pastoral Letter on Racism* (November 14, 1979), in J. Brian Benestad and Francis J. Butler, eds., *Quest for Justice: A Compendium of Statements of the United States Catholic Bishops on the Political and Social Order 1966-1980* (Washington: United States Catholic Conference, 1981), 204 and 383.

15. Garland, *Compensation*, 15.

16. Liberato and Schervich, *Just Wages*, 26-36; Garland, *Compensation*, 21-30; Amata Miller, *Promises to Keep: Compensation for Religious in the United States* (Washington: United States Catholic Conference, 1989), 23-6; and Philip J. Murnion, *New Parish Ministers: Laity and Religious on Parish Staffs* (New York: National Pastoral Life Center, 1992), 92-4.

17. See the position paper of the Chicago-based Business Executives for Economic Justice: Gregory F. Augustine Pierce, *On the Firing Line: The Manager's Perspective on the Issue of Terminations and Layoffs in the Light of Catholic Social Teaching* (Chicago: ACTA, 1990).

18. Andrew M. Greeley and William McManus, *Catholic Contributions: Sociology and Policy* (Chicago: Thomas More Press, 1987), 21-60.

19. Greeley and McManus, *Catholic Contributions*, 146.

20. Bishop McManus points out that his suggestion, if implemented and adjusted to inflation, would have given 5,000 Catholic school teachers employed during the 1990-91 school year a $4,000 raise, over their average salary of $14,000. William McManus, "Pay Them Well," *Momentum* 24 (1992): 26.

21. See Daly, "Theoretical Framework," 5-11.

22. Pierce, *On the Firing Line*, 20-2.

23. Charles E. Curran, "Catholic Social and Sexual Teaching: A Methodological Comparison," *Theology Today* 44 (1988): 425-40. See also his "The Changing Anthropological Bases of Catholic Social Ethics," in idem, *Directions in Catholic Social Ethics* (Notre Dame, IN: University of Notre Dame Press, 1985), 5-42.

24. See Sacred Congregation of Bishops, *Directory on the Ministry of Bishops*, 32-41 and 68-70; and Congregation for Catholic Education, *Guidelines for the Study and Teaching of the Church's Social Doctrine in the Formation of Priests* (Washington: United States Catholic Conference, 1988), 47-61.

25. Curran, "Methodology," 425.

26. Ibid., 438-9.

27. Miller, *Promises to Keep*, 1-4, 33-52.

28. Ibid., 13.

29. Ibid., 14.

30. As a child attending parochial school in the 1960s, I remember my mother giving each Sister who taught in my grade a Christmas gift of a set of initialed white handkerchiefs, with a five dollar bill enclosed. My father was often called upon to drive the Sisters to the doctor or to the motherhouse, because the convent did not have any vehicles.

31. Roland Faley, "The Financial Compensation of Religious," *Review for Religious* 49 (1990): 392.

32. Miller, *Promises to Keep*, 15.

33. Ibid., 16-7.

34. Ibid., 24.

35. Table 2, "Income and Expenditures by Education in the General Population," in Liberato and Schervich, *Just Wages*, 82

36. Table 12, "Median Salary for Full-Time Professionals by Area of Ministry, Gender, and Lay/Religious," in Liberato and Schervich, *Just Wages*, 87.

37. Faley, "Financial Compensation," 392.

38. Liberato and Schervich, *Just Wages*, 32.

39. Faley, "Financial Compensation," 393.

40. John C. Haughey, *Converting 9 to 5: A Spirituality of Daily Work* (New York: Paulist, 1989), 33.

41. Ibid., 34, 37.

APPENDIX ONE

LETTER TO PASTORS

October 4, 1989

Dear Father,

I need your help. A few minutes of your time can be of great benefit to me personally, and perhaps to the church.

I am in the process of writing a dissertation to complete the requirements of a Ph.D. degree in Roman Catholic systematic theology from Duquesne University. The dissertation is entitled, "Criteria for a Just Wage for Church Employees." One chapter of this dissertation is a "case study," a practical analysis, of the wages and benefits paid to workers by various church agencies. I am limiting my case study to clerical/office and maintenance workers. (I am excluding the categories of business manager, DRE, musician, and school teacher.)

Here's how you can assist me in this project. I would like to send a one page questionnaire to all part-time and full-time employees of your parish, who work in food service and facility service (for example, janitor, housekeeper, cook, cleaner, etc.) and in the office (secretary, typist, receptionist, bookkeeper, etc.). To do this I need their names and addresses. Would you please inform these employees that your are forwarding their names and addresses to me, and that I will be sending them a questionnaire regarding their wages and benefits?

All names and all information will be kept *strictly confidential*. The questionnaire will be anonymous. No worker, pastor, or parish will be identified by name in this case study, or in the dissertation. I am interested only in cumulative data.

Please take five minutes to list the names and addresses of your maintenance and clerical workers on the enclosed sheet. Mail it to me by October 30 in the stamped envelop. If you have any questions, or if you would like to receive a summary of the data, please give me a call at 261-2112 or 261-0110.

Thank you so much for your time and assistance. May the Lord bless you and your parishioners.

Sincerely,
Frank D. Almade
Parochial Vicar

LETTER TO WORKERS

October 30, 1989

Greetings in the Lord:

I need your help. Let me tell you about my project, and how you might give me valuable assistance.

I am a Pittsburgh diocesan priest, serving St. Mary's "at the Point" in Downtown Pittsburgh. I am also trying to write a dissertation, to complete the requirements for a Ph.D. degree in Roman Catholic systematic theology from Duquesne University. The title of my dissertation is "Criteria for a Just Wage for Church Employees." Part of my dissertation is a practical analysis of the wages and benefits of some church workers. I have chosen to focus on men and women who are employed by parishes, in the areas of food service, maintenance, and clerical/office work.

At my request, the pastor who employs you has given me your name, in strictest confidence. You can help me in my research by answering the questions in the one-page survey I have enclosed. Would you take ten minutes right now, and fill out the questionnaire?

All responses to this survey will be *anonymous*. I do *not* want you to identify yourself or your parish on the sheet of questions. All information will be kept *strictly confidential*. No worker, pastor, or parish will be identified by name in my research or in my dissertation. I am interested only in cumulative data.

When you are finished filling out the survey, please mail it to me in the stamped envelope I have provided by November 27. If you have any questions, or if you wish to receive a summary of the data, please feel free to call me at 261-2112 or 261-0110.

I am very grateful to you for your assistance. Thank you for your time and help. God's blessings on you and your loved ones.

Sincerely,
Frank D. Almade
Parochial Vicar

APPENDIX TWO

SURVEY OF LOCAL PARISH WORKERS

Please use a check mark, a circle, or fill in the blank, where appropriate, to answer each question.

1. Identification: Male__ Female__
    Age: 18-25__   26-40__   41-55__   56-70__   70+__

2. What job title best describes your position?__
    A. bookkeeper   E. janitor
    B. cook in rectory   F. receptionist
    C. food service worker in institution   G. secretary
    D. housekeeper   H. other__

3. How many years have you been in your current position?__

4. How many years have you worked for the church, in any paid position?__

5. How many hours make up your normal work week?__
    A. 1-10__   B. 11-20__   C. 21-30__   D. 31-40__   E. 41+__

6. What is your hourly rate, before taxes? $_____

7. Do you get paid for overtime? Yes__ No__
    If Yes, what is your hourly rate for overtime?__
    A. Same as hourly rate   B. 125% of hourly rate (time and a quarter)
    C. 150% of hourly rate (time and a half)
    D. Twice hourly rate (double time)   E. Other__

8. Does the parish pay for your health insurance? Yes__ No__
    If Yes, what is the name of your coverage?__
    A. BC/BS   B. Major Medical   C. HMO   D. PPO
    E. Keystone   F. Other__

9. How many days paid leave do your receive annually for:
    A. Vacation days__   B. Sick days__
    C. Personal days__   D. Parental leave__

10. Does the parish pay towards your pension (retirement)?
    Yes__ No__
    If Yes, what is the dollar amount annually?__
    If Yes, how many years does it take to become vested?__

11. Does the parish give you tuition assistance for your children who
    attend Catholic school? Yes__ No__
    Does the parish provide you with any educational benefits?
    Yes__ No__
    If Yes, for whom? Myself__ Family members__ How much?__

12. Does the parish contribute financially to child care for your children?
    Yes__ No__
    If Yes, what is the dollar amount?__

ALL INFORMATION IS STRICTLY CONFIDENTIAL

THANK YOU VERY MUCH FOR YOUR KIND ASSISTANCE. PLEASE
ENCLOSE THIS SURVEY IN THE STAMPED ENVELOPE PROVIDED,
AND MAIL BY NOVEMBER 27, 1989. GOD BLESS YOU!

Please use the back of this page for any additional comments you may wish
to make.

APPENDIX THREE

FIGURES AND TABLES

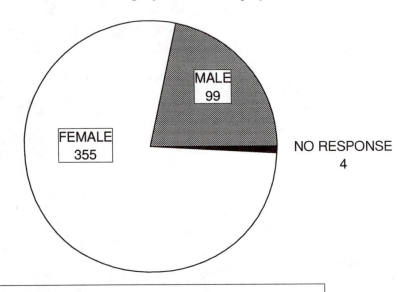

FEMALE
355

MALE
99

NO RESPONSE
4

FIGURE 1: RESPONDENTS BY SEX

Unless otherwise indicated, information in figures refers to
Allegheny County survey of Parish Workers, Fall 1989.

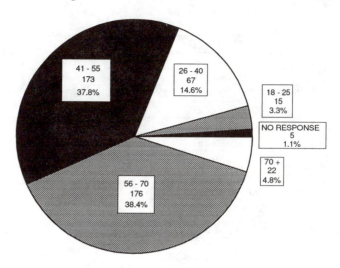

41 - 55
173
37.8%

26 - 40
67
14.6%

18 - 25
15
3.3%

NO RESPONSE
5
1.1%

70 +
22
4.8%

56 - 70
176
38.4%

FIGURE 2: RESPONDENTS BY AGE GROUP

JOB TITLE	NUMBER	PERCENT
BOOKKEEPER	11	2.4
COOK IN RECTORY	28	6.1
FOOD SERVICE WORKER	41	9.0
HOUSEKEEPER	68	14.8
JANITOR	111	24.2
RECEPTIONIST	15	3.3
SECRETARY	156	34.1
OTHER	7	1.5
GARDENER	1	0.2
GROUNDS KEEPER	1	0.2
SACRISTAN	6	1.3
TEACHER AIDE	1	0.2
BUSINESS MANAGER	3	0.7
OFFICE MANAGER	3	0.7
SOCIAL WORKER	1	0.2
PASTORAL ASSOCIATE	1	0.2
LAUNDRESS	4	0.9
TOTAL	458	100.0

FIGURE 3: JOB TITLE

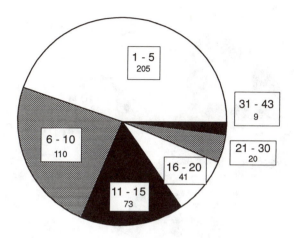

FIGURE 4: YEARS IN CURRENT JOB

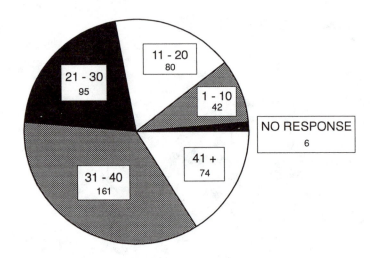

FIGURE 5: HOURS WORKED PER WEEK

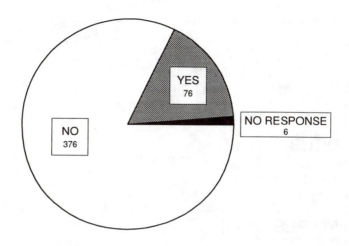

FIGURE 6: PAID FOR OVERTIME

	NUMBER	PERCENT
SAME AS HOURLY RATE	58	12.7
TIME AND A QUARTER	2	0.4
TIME AND A HALF	4	0.9
DOUBLE TIME	1	0.2
SALARIED	57	12.4
OTHER	10	2.2
NO RESPONSE	326	71.2
TOTAL	458	100.0

FIGURE 7: OVERTIME RATE

HOURLY RATE	NUMBER	PERCENT	ANNUAL RATE
$1.15 - 3.79	48	10.5	$2,392 - 7,883
$3.80 - 6.99	290	63.3	$7,904 - 14,539
$7.00 - 8.99	66	14.4	$14,560 - 18,699
$9.00 - 11.79	29	6.3	$18,720 - 24,523
NO RESPONSE	25	5.5	NO RESPONSE

FIGURE 8: RESPONDENTS IN WAGE GROUPS

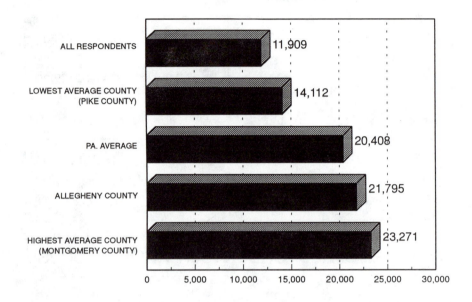

FIGURE 9: ANNUAL AVERAGE WAGES RESPONDENTS AND WORKING IN PENNYSLVANIA

Source: Annual Planning Information Report Pittsburgh PMSA, 1989

JOB TITLE	$1.15 - 3.79	$3.80 - 6.99	$7.00 - 8.99	$9.00 - 11.79
BOOKKEEPER	1	4	4	2
COOK IN RECTORY	7	17	1	0
FOOD SERVICE WORKER	5	31	3	0
HOUSEKEEPER	12	45	5	2
JANITOR	5	68	20	12
RECEPTIONIST	4	10	1	0
SECRETARY	8	105	29	11
OTHER	0	2	0	0
GARDENER	0	1	0	0
GROUNDS KEEPER	0	1	0	0
SACRISTAN	2	2	0	0
TEACHER AIDE	0	1	0	0
BUSINESS MANAGER	0	1	1	1
OFFICE MANAGER	2	0	0	1
SOCIAL WORKER	0	0	1	0
PASTORAL ASSOCIATE	0	0	1	0
LAUNDRESS	2	2	0	0
TOTAL	48	290	66	29

FIGURE 10: HOURLY WAGE GROUPING BY JOB TITLE

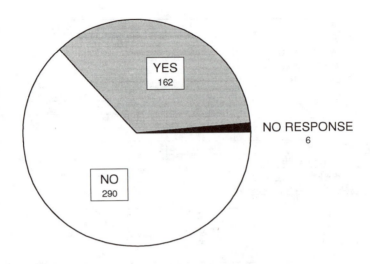

FIGURE 11: PAID HEALTH INSURANCE

YEARS EMPLOYED	NUMBER	PERCENT
1	12	2.6
3	1	0.2
5	38	8.3
9	2	0.4
10	120	26.2
14	1	0.2
20	2	0.4
NO RESPONSE	282	61.6
TOTAL	458	100.0

FIGURE 12: YEARS TO BECOME VESTED

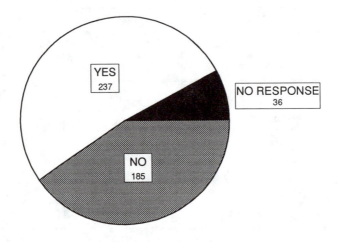

FIGURE 13: PENSION BENEFITS

# OF DAYS PERMITTED	VACATION LEAVE	SICK DAYS	PERSONAL DAYS	PARENTAL DAYS
1	2	0	0	0
2	2	0	7	0
3	5	3	3	0
4	5	0	4	0
5	36	17	6	0
6	3	4	1	0
7	11	0	1	0
8	3	0	1	0
9	3	0	0	0
10	109	13	3	0
12	5	6	0	0
13	1	0	0	0
14	24	0	0	0
15	36	1	0	0
20	11	0	0	0
21	7	0	0	0
31	0	0	0	1
AS NEEDED	6	53	29	1
PART TIME, NOT ANY	22	26	29	24
UNLIMITED	0	2	1	0
DO NOT KNOW	8	13	10	9
WILL OF PASTOR	0	1	0	0
NO RESPONSE	159	319	363	423
TOTAL	458	458	458	458

FIGURE 14: PAID DAYS OFF

Just Wages for Church Employees

JOB TITLE	RESPONDENTS		PITTSBURGH WORKERS		US WORKERS	
	HOURLY	ANNUAL	HOURLY	ANNUAL	HOURLY	ANNUAL
BOOKKEEPER	$6.92	$14,394	$ 8.00	$16,640	$7.95	$16,536
COOK IN RECTORY	4.72	9,818			5.40	11,232
FOOD SERVICE WORKER	4.82	10,026			4.77	9,922
HOUSEKEEPER	5.02	10,442			5.32	11,066
JANITOR	6.25	13,000			6.72	13,978
RECEPTIONIST	4.56	9,485	6.97	14,498	6.52	13,562
SECRETARY	6.11	12,709	10.02	20,842	8.20	17,056
OTHER	5.89	12,251				
GARDENER	5.00	10,400				
GROUNDS KEEPER	5.00	10,400				
SACRISTAN	4.25	8,840				
TEACHER AIDE	5.00	10,400				
BUSINESS MANAGER	7.97	16,578				
OFFICE MANAGER	5.16	10,733				
SOCIAL WORKER	7.00	14,560				
PASTORAL ASSOCIATE	7.80	16,224				
LAUNDRESS	4.07	8,466				

FIGURE 15: AVERAGE ANNUAL AND HOURLY RATES OF RESPONDENTS, PITTSBURGH WORKERS, and US WORKERS

Source: Pittsburgh PMSA Area Wage Survey, February 1990, Employment and Earnings, January 1990

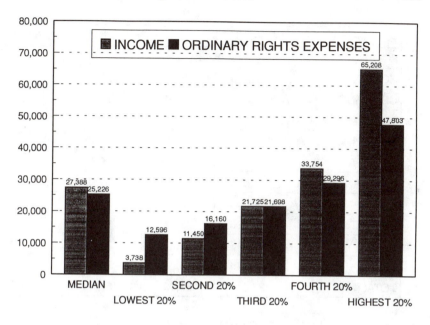

FIGURE 16: INCOME AND ORDINARY RIGHTS EXPENSES IN U.S.

Source: Bureau of Labor Statistics, Consumer Expenditure Reports, 1988, and NCDD National Project, Table 1.

ITEM	LOW-COST	THRIFTY	MODERATE	HIGH-COST
FOOD	$ 4,994	$ 6,374	$ 7,980	$ 9,626
HOUSING	7,299	9,316	11,664	14,068
CLOTHING	1,262	1,611	2,017	2,433
TRANSPORTATION	5,131	6,549	8,200	9,890
HEALTH CARE	851	1,086	1,359	1,640
RECREATION	1,454	1,856	2,324	2,803
INSURANCE - LIFE	1,070	1,366	1,710	2,063
INSURANCE - FICA	2,168	2,767	3,464	4,178
EDUCATION	796	1,016	1,272	1,534
CHARITY	1,043	1,331	1,666	2,010
TAXES	2,744	3,852	5,262	7,140
TOTAL	28,812	37,124	46,918	57,385

FIGURE 17: COST OF ORDINARY RIGHT FOR A FAMILY OF FOUR

Source: U.S. Department of Agriculture, 1988.

ITEM	SINGLE	COUPLE	FAMILY	CHILD
FOOD	$ 2,945	$ 5,412	$ 6,374	$1,230
HOUSING	4,304	7,910	9,316	1,741
CLOTHING	744	1,368	1,611	345
TRANSPORTATION	3,026	5,561	6,549	784
HEALTH CARE	502	922	1,086	365
RECREATION	858	1,576	1,856	772
INSURANCE - LIFE	631	1,160	1,366	
INSURANCE - FICA	1,278	2,349	2,767	
EDUCATION	469	862	1,016	172
CHARITY	615	1,130	1,331	
TAXES	2,023	4,015	3,852	
TOTAL	17,395	32,265	37,124	5,409

FIGURE 18: THRIFTY BUDGET FOR VARIOUS SIZE HOUSEHOLDS

Source: U.S. Department of Agriculture, 1988.

APPENDIX FOUR

DIOCESE OF PITTSBURGH SALARY GUIDELINES

Coordinators of Religious Education
(Bachelors Degree Required)

Years of Service	10 Month Contract	11 Month	12 Month
1	$12,500	$13,750	$15,000
2	13,000	14,300	15,600
3	13,520	14,872	16,224
4	13,926	15,319	16,711
5	14,343	15,777	17,212
6	14,918	16,410	17,902
7	15,456	17,124	18,680
8	16,344	17,978	19,613
9	17,755	19,530	21,613
10	18,505	20,355	22,206
11	19,442	21,386	23,330
12	20,228	22,251	24,274
13	20,758	22,834	24,910
14	21,322	23,454	25,586
15	22,263	24,489	26,716
16	22,825	25,107	27,390
17	23,391	25,730	28,069
18	24,139	26,553	28,967
19	24,891	27,380	29,869
20	25,713	28,284	30,856
21	26,380	29,018	31,656
22	27,634	30,397	33,161

(Revised April 20, 1990)

Directors of Religious Education
(Masters Degree Required)

Years of Service	10 Month Contract	11 Month	12 Month
1	$13,000	$14,300	$15,600
2	13,520	14,300	15,600
3	14,060	14,872	16,224
4	14,483	15,319	16,711
5	14,918	15,777	17,212
6	15,515	16,410	17,902
7	16,281	17,124	18,680
8	17,094	17,967	19,613
9	18,505	19,530	21,306
10	19,257	20,355	22,206
11	20,199	21,386	23,330
12	20,948	22,251	24,274
13	21,516	22,834	24,910
14	22,074	23,454	25,586
15	23,200	24,489	26,716
16	23,574	25,107	27,390
17	24,139	25,730	28,069
18	24,891	26,553	28,967
19	25,639	27,380	28,869
20	26,381	28,284	30,856
21	26,380	29,018	31,656
22	27,634	30,397	33,161

(Revised April 20, 1990)

Parish Music Ministers

Years of Full-time Experience	Liturgical Music Certificate	Bachelor of Music	Master of Music
0	$13,500	$16,500	$18,000
1	13,905	16,995	18,540
2	14,322	17,504	19,096
3	14,751	18,029	19,669
4	15,194	18,570	20,259
5	15,650	19,128	20,866
6	16,119	19,701	21,492

7	16,603	20,292	22,137
8	17,101	20,901	22,801
9	17,614	21,528	23,485
10	18,142	22,174	24,190
11	18,687	22,839	24,190
12	19,247	23,525	25,663
13	19,825	24,230	26,433
14	20,419	24,957	27,226
15	21,032	25,706	28,043

Note: All subsequent yearly levels increase by 3% per year.
Fees from funeral and wedding liturgies are in addition to salary.
(Revised July 1, 1990)

Schedule of Stipends and Benefits
for Religious Women

	10 Months	11 Months	12 Months
For Fiscal 1990-91			
Stipend	$10,496	$11,545	$12,595
Health	1,600	1,600	1,600
Retirement	1,425	1,425	1,425
TOTAL	$13,521	$14,570	$15,620
For Fiscal 1991-92			
Stipend	$11,060	$12,188	$13,315
Health	1,975	1,975	1,975
Retirement	1,580	1,580	1,580
TOTAL	$14,615	$15,743	$16,870
For Fiscal 1992-93			
Stipend	$11,668	$12,882	$14,095
Health	2.435	2,435	2,435
Retirement	1,770	1,770	1,770

TOTAL $15,873 $17,087 $18,300

Housing: When a parish/institution does not provide a convent or residence, each Religious shall receive the following monthly/annual housing stipend:

	Monthly	Annual
1990-91	$215	$2,580
1991-92	232	2,790
1992-93	252	3,024

When a Religious lives in a parish convent/residence but is employed outside of that parish, the Religious shall pay the parish a stipend equal to the amount listed above.

Religious who are retired and Religious who are in formation and are attending school full time shall be received without cost at any convent/residence.

Transportation: A vehicle shall be provided for the Religious. In the event that there are fewer than three Religious, the parish has the option of providing the following transportation allowance per person annually for transportation payable to the Congregation:

1990-91	$1,400
1991-92	1,500
1992-93	1,600

This provision refers to Religious working in a parish.

(Effective July 1, 1990 through June 30, 1993)

APPENDIX FIVE

WAGES OF SELECTED EMPLOYEES
OF MERCY HOSPITAL OF PITTSBURGH

Job Title	Minimum	Mid	Maximum
Secretary	$8.090	$9.506	$10.922
Receptionist	7.408	8.705	10.001
Housekeeping Aide	6.332	7.440	8.548
Food Service Worker	6.332	7.440	8.548

(as of October 15, 1990)

Approximate number of workers in each job classification: secretary (40), receptionist (5), housekeeping aide (120), and food service worker (120).

There are approximately 50 maintenance workers who are represented by the Operating Engineers Union. Their wage scales are not made public by Mercy Hospital or by their union.

BIBLIOGRAPHY

Magisterial Documents
(Listed Chronologically)

Leo XIII. Encyclical letter *Quod Apostolici Muneris*. December 28, 1878: *Acta Leonis* 1 (1878): 170-83.

_____. Encyclical letter *Quamquam Pluries*. August 15, 1889: *Acta Leonis* 9 (1889): 175-82.

_____. Encyclical letter *Sapientiae Christianae*. January 10, 1890: *Acta Leonis* 10 (1890): 10-41.

_____. Encyclical letter *Rerum Novarum*. May 15, 1891: *Acta Leonis* 11 (1891): 97-144.

_____. Address to French workers. September 19, 1891: *Acta Leonis* 11 (1891): 405-8.

_____. Encyclical letter *Graves de Communi Re*. January 18, 1901: *Acta Leonis* 21 (1901): 3-20.

Codex Iuris Canonici Pii X Pontificis Maximi iussu digestus Benedicti Papae XV authoritate promulgatus. Rome: Typis Polyglottis Vaticanis, 1917.

Pius XI. Encyclical letter *Casti Connubii*. December 31, 1930: *Acta Apostolicae Sedis* 22 (1930): 539-92.

_____. Encyclical letter *Quadragesimo Anno*. May 15, 1931: *A.A.S.* 23 (1931): 177-228.

_____. Encyclical letter *Non Abbiamo Bisogno*. June 29, 1931: *A.A.S.* 23 (1931): 285-312.

_____. Encyclical letter *Mit Brennender Sorge*. March 14, 1937: *A.A.S.* 29 (1937): 145-67.

_____. Encyclical letter *Divini Redemptoris*. March 19, 1937: *A.A.S.* 29 (1937): 65-106.00

Pius XII. Encyclical epistle *Sertum Laetitiae*. November 1, 1939: *A.A.S.* 31 (1939): 645-56

_____. Radio message. June 1, 1941: *A.A.S.* 33 (1941): 195-205.

_____. Christmas message. December 24, 1942: *A.A.S.* 35 (1943): 9-24.

_____. Address to Italian workers. June 13, 1943: *A.A.S.* 35 (1943): 171-79.

John XXIII. Encyclical letter *Mater et Magistra*. May 15, 1961: *A.A.S.* 53 (1961): 401-64.

_____. Encyclical letter *Pacem in Terris*. April 11, 1963: *A.A.S.* 55 (1963): 257-304.

Vatican Council II. Dogmatic Constitution on the Church *Lumen Gentium*. November 21, 1964: *A.A.S.* 57 (1965): 5-85.

_____. Decree on the Appropriate Renewal of Religious Life *Perfectae Caritatis*. October 28, 1965: *A.A.S.* 58 (1966): 702-12.

_____. Decree on the Apostolate of Lay People *Apostolicam Actuositatem*. November 18, 1965: *A.A.S.* 58 (1966): 837-64.

_____. Declaration on Religious Liberty *Dignitatis Humanae*. December 7, 1965: *A.A.S.* 58 (1966): 923-46.

_____. Decree on the Church's Missionary Activity *Ad Gentes*. December 7, 1965: *A.A.S.* 58 (1966): 947-90.

_____. Pastoral Constitution on the Church in the Modern World *Gaudium et Spes*. December 7, 1965: *A.A.S.* 58 (1966): 1025-1120.

Paul VI. Encyclical letter *Populorum Progressio*. March 26, 1967: *A.A.S.* 59 (1967): 257-99.

_____. Apostolic letter *Octogesima Adveniens*. May 14, 1971: *A.A.S.* 63 (1971): 401-41.

Synod of Bishops, Second General Assembly. *De Iustitia in Mundo*. November 30, 1971: *A.A.S.* 63 (1971): 923-43.

_____. *De Sacerdotio Ministeriali*. November 30, 1971: *A.A.S.* 63 (1971): 898-922.

Sacred Congregation of Bishops. *Directory on the Pastoral Ministry of Bishops*. February 22, 1973. Ottawa: Canadian Catholic Conference, 1974.

Paul VI. Apostolic exhortation *Evangelii Nuntiandi*. December 8, 1975: *A.A.S.* 68 (1976): 5-76.

John Paul II. Encyclical letter *Redemptor Hominis*. March 4, 1979: *A.A.S.* 71 (1979): 257-324.

_____. Address to the General Assembly of the United Nations. October 2, 1979: *A.A.S.* 71 (1979): 1143-60.

_____. Encyclical letter *Dives in Misericordia*. November 30, 1980: *A.A.S.* 72 (1980): 1177-1232.

_____. Encyclical letter *Laborem Exercens*. September 14, 1981: *A.A.S.* 73 (1981): 577-647

_____. Apostolic exhortation *Familiaris Consortio*. December 15, 1981: *A.A.S.* 74 (1982): 81-191.

_____. Apostolic constitution *Sacrae Disciplinae Leges*. January 25, 1983. *A.A.S.* 73 (1983): vii-xii.

Codex Iuris Canonici: Auctoritate Ioannis Pauli PP. II Promulgatus. Vatican: Libreria Editrice Vaticana, 1983. *A.A.S.* 73 (1983): 1-317.

Holy See. *Charter of the Rights of the Family*. October 22, 1983. Washington: United States Catholic Conference, 1983.

National Conference of Catholic Bishops. *The Challenge of Peace: God's Promise and our Response*. Washington: United States Catholic Conference, 1983.

Sacred Congregation for the Doctrine of the Faith. *Instruction on Certain Aspects of the "Theology of Liberation"*. August 6, 1984. Washington: United States Catholic Conference, 1984. *A.A.S.* 76 (1984): 876-909.

John Paul II. Apostolic exhortation *Reconciliatio et Paenitentia*. December 2, 1984: A.A.S. 77 (1985): 185-275.

Sacred Congregation for the Doctrine of the Faith. *Instruction on Christian Freedom and Liberation*. March 22, 1986. Washington: United States Catholic Conference, 1986. *A.A.S.* 79 (1987): 554-99.

National Conference of Catholic Bishops. *Economic Justice for All: Pastoral Letter on Catholic Social Teaching and the U.S. Economy*. Washington: United States Catholic Conference, 1986.

John Paul II. Encyclical letter *Sollicitudo Rei Socialis*. December 30, 1987: *A.A.S.* 80 (1988): 513-86.

_____. Apostolic letter *Mulieris Dignitatem*. August 15, 1988: *A.A.S.* 80 (1988): 1653-1729.

_____. Apostolic exhortation *Christifideles Laici*. December 30, 1988: *A.A.S.* 81 (1989): 393-521.

Congregation for Catholic Education. *Guidelines for the Study and Teaching of the Church's Social Doctrine in the Formation of Priests*. Washington: United States Catholic Conference, 1988.

Codex Iuris Canonici: Auctoritate Ioannis Pauli PP. II Promulgatus: Fontium Annotatione et Indice Analytico-alphabetico Actus. Vatican: Libreria Editrice Vaticana, 1989.

John Paul II. Encyclical letter *Centesimus Annus*. May 1, 1991: *A.A.S.* 83: 793-867.

Books

Abbo, John A. and Jerome D. Hannan. *The Sacred Canons: A Concise Presentation of the Current Disciplinary Norms of the Church*. Rev. ed. St. Louis: B. Herder, 1957.

Abbott, Walter M. and Joseph Gallagher, eds. *The Documents of Vatican II*. New York: America Press, 1966.

Andrade, Vicente. *La Enciclica "Rerum Novarum" y su Preparcion Historica. Trabajo y Salario desde los Santos Patres Hasta Leon XIII*. Bogota: 1941.

Antoncich, Ricardo. *Christians in the Face of Injustice: A Latin American Reading of Catholic Social Teaching.* Trans. by Matthew J. O'Connell. Maryknoll, NY: Orbis, 1980.

Aubert, Roger. *Le Pontificat de Pie IX, 1846-1878.* Paris: Bloud et Gay, 1952.

Avila, Charles. *Ownership: Early Christian Teaching.* Maryknoll, NY: Orbis, 1983.

Bardes, George Francis. *Catholic Moral Teaching on the Distribution of Profits in the Modern Corporation.* Studies in Sacred Theology (2nd. series) #61. Washington: Catholic University of America Press, 1951.

Baum, Gregory. *The Priority of Labor: A Commentary on "Laborem Exercens".* New York: Paulist, 1983.

_____. *Theology and Society.* New York: Paulist, 1987.

_____, ed. *Work and Religion.* New York: Seabury, 1980.

Belcher, David W. *Wage and Salary Administration.* Englewood Cliffs, NJ: Prentice-Hall, 1962.

Benestad, J. Brian. *The Pursuit of a Just Social Order: Policy Statements of the U.S. Catholic Bishops, 1966-80.* Washington: Ethics and Public Policy Center, 1982.

_____ and Francis J. Butler, eds. *Quest for Justice: A Compendium of Statements of the United States Catholic Bishops on the Political and Social Order 1966-1980.* Washington: United States Catholic Conference, 1981.

Bensman, Joseph. *Dollars and Sense: Ideology, Ethics and the Meaning of Work in Profit and Nonprofit Organizations.* New York: Macmillan, 1967.

Bock, Edward C. *Wilhelm von Ketteler, Bishop of Mainz: His Life, Times and Ideas.* Washington: University Press of America, 1977.

Bouscaren, T. Lincoln, Adam C. Ellis, and Francis K. North. *Canon Law: A Text and Commentary.* 4th Rev. ed. Milwaukee: Bruce, 1963.

Braybrooke, David. *Ethics in the World of Business.* Totowa, NJ: Rowman & Allanheld, 1983.

Broderick, Francis L. *Right Reverend New Dealer, John A. Ryan.* New York: Macmillan, 1963.

Brown, Ernest H. P. *The Inequality of Pay.* Berkley: University of California Press, 1977.

Byers, David M. ed. *Justice in the Marketplace: Collected Statements of the Vatican and U.S. Catholic Bishops on Economic Policy, 1891-1984.* Washington: United States Catholic Conference, 1984.

Calvez, Jean Yves. *The Social Thought of John XXIII.* London: Burns and Oates, 1964.

_____ and Jacques Perrin. *The Church and Social Justice: The Social Teaching of the Popes from Leo XIII to Pius XII, 1878-1958.* Trans. by J. R. Kirwin. Chicago: Henry Regnery, 1961.

Camp, Richard C. *The Papal Ideology of Social Reform: A Study in Historical Development 1878-1967.* Leiden: E.J. Brill, 1969.

Carlen, Claudia, ed. *The Papal Encyclicals 1743-1981.* 5 vols. Raleigh, NC: McGrath, 1981.

Cherlin, Andrew J., ed. *The Changing American Family and Public Policy.* Washington: Urban Institute Press, 1988.

Code of Canon Law, Latin-English Edition. Translated under the auspices of the Canon Law Society of America. Washington: Canon Law Society of America, 1983.

Coleman, John A. *An American Strategic Theology.* New York: Paulist, 1982.

Conferencia General del Episcopodo Latinoamericano. 2nd session. *The Church in the Present-Day Tranformation of Latin America in the Light of the Council.* 2 vols. Washington: USCC, 1968.

_____. 3rd session. *Evangelization at Present and in the Future of Latin America.* Washington: USCC, 1979.

Coriden, James, ed. *The Case for Freedom: Human Rights in the Church.* Washington: Corpus Books, 1969.

_____, Thomas J. Green, and Donald E. Heintschel, eds. *The Code of Canon Law: A Text and Commentary.* New York: Paulist, 1985.

Countryman, L. William. *The Rich Christian in the Church of the Early Empire: Contradictions and Accomodations.* New York: Edwin Mellen Press, 1980.

Cronin, John F. *Catholic Social Action.* Milwaukee: Bruce, 1948.

_____. *Catholic Social Principles: The Social Teaching of the Catholic Church Applied to American Economic Life.* Milwaukee: Bruce, 1950.

_____. *Social Principles and Economic Life.* Milwaukee: Bruce, 1959.

_____ and Harry W. Flannery. *The Church and the Workingman.* New York: Hawthorn Books, 1965.

Curran, Charles E. *Directions in Catholic Social Ethics.* Notre Dame, IN: University of Notre Dame Press, 1985.

_____ and Richard A. McCormick, eds. *Readings in Moral Theology No. 5: Official Catholic Social Teaching.* New York: Paulist, 1986.

Dorr, Donal. *Option for the Poor: A Hundred Years of Vatican Social Teaching.* Maryknoll, NY: Orbis, 1983.

Douglas, Paul H. *Wages and the Family.* Chicago: University of Chicago Press, 1927.

Douglass, R. Bruce, ed. *The Deeper Meaning of Economic Life: Critical Essays on the U.S. Catholic Bishops' Pastoral Letter on the Economy.* Washington: Georgetown University Press, 1986.

Ederer, Rupert J., trans. *The Social Teachings of Wilhelm Emmanuel von Ketteler.* Washington: University Press of America, 1981.

Evans, Robert A. and Alice Frazer Evans. *Human Rights: A Dialogue between the First and Third Worlds.* Maryknoll, NY: Orbis, 1983.

Evans, Sara M. and Barbara J. Nelson. *Wage Justice: Comparable Worth and the Paradox of Technocratic Reform.* Chicago: University of Chicago Press, 1989.

Ferree, William. *The Act of Social Justice.* Philosophical Series #72. Washington: Catholic University of America Press, 1942.

Fichter, Joseph H. *Roots of Change.* New York: D. Appleton Century, 1939.

Flynn, Frederick E. *Wealth and Money in the Economic Philosophy of St. Thomas.* Notre Dame, IN: University of Notre Dame Press, 1942.

Fogarty, Michael. *The Just Wage.* London: Herder & Herder, 1961.

_____. *Christian Democracy in Western Europe, 1820-1953.* London: Routledge & Kegan Paul, 1957.

Funk, Virgil C. *An NPM Workbook: Job Descriptions, Contracts, Salary.* Washington: National Association of Pastoral Musicians, 1989.

Gannon, Thomas M., ed. *The Catholic Challenge to the American Economy: Reflections on the U.S. Bishops' Pastoral Letter on Catholic Social Teaching and the U.S. Economy.* New York: Macmillan, 1987.

Garland, Barbara. *Compensation: A Manual for Administration of Church Systems.* Cincinnati: National Association of Church Personnel Administrators, 1987.

Gearty, Patrick W. *The Economic Thought of Msgr. John A. Ryan.* Washington: The Catholic University of America Press, 1953.

Gilson, Etienne. *Moral Values and the Moral Life: The Ethical Theory of St. Thomas Aquinas.* Trans. by Leo R. Ward. St. Louis: Shoe String Press, 1961.

_____, ed. *The Church Speaks to the Modern World: The Social Teachings of Leo XIII.* Garden City, NY: Doubleday & Co., 1954.

Giordani, Igino. *The Social Message of the Early Church Fathers.* Trans. by Alba Zizzamia. Patterson, NJ: St. Anthony Guild Press, 1944.

Grant, Robert M. *Early Christianity and Society.* San Francisco: Harper & Row, 1977.

Greeley, Andrew and William McManus. *Catholic Contributions: Sociology and Policy*. Chicago: Thomas More Press, 1987.

Gremillion, Joseph. *The Gospel of Justice and Peace*. Maryknoll, NY: Orbis, 1975.

Greinacher, Norbert and Inge Jens, eds. *Freiheitsrechte fur Christen? Warum die Kirche ein Grundgesetz braucht*. Munich: R. Piper, 1980.

Gudorf, Christine E. *Catholic Social Teaching on Liberation Themes*. Washington: University Press of America, 1981.

Hannan, Philip M. *The Canonical Concept of 'Congruo Sustentatio' for the Secular Clergy*. Canon Law Studies #302. Washington: Catholic University of America Press, 1950.

Haughey, John C. *Converting 9 to 5: A Spirituality of Daily Work*. New York: Crossroad, 1989.

_____, ed. *The Faith That Does Justice: Examining the Christian Sources for Social Change*. New York: Paulist, 1977.

_____. *The Holy Use of Money: Personal Finances in Light of Christian Faith*. Garden City, NY: Doubleday, 1986.

Healy, James. *The Just Wage 1750-1890: A Study of Moralists from St. Alphonsus to Leo XIII*. The Hague: Martinus Nijhoff, 1966.

Heisler, W.J. and John W. Houck, eds. *A Matter of Dignity: Inquiries into the Humanization of Work*. Notre Dame, IN: University of Notre Dame Press, 1977.

Henderson, Richard I. *Compensation Management: Rewarding Performance*. 3rd ed. Reston, VA: Reston Publishing, 1982.

Hengel, Martin. *Property and Riches in the Early Church: Aspects of a Social History of Early Christianity*. Trans. by John Bowden. Philadelphia: Fortress, 1974.

Hewlett, Sylvia Ann, Alice S. Ilchman and John J. Sweeney, eds. *Family and Work: Bridging the Gap*. Cambridge, MA: Ballinger Publishing, 1986.

Hogan, William E. *The Development of William Emmanuel von Ketteler's Interpretation of the Social Problem.* Washington: Catholic University of America Press, 1946.

Holland, Joe and Peter Henriot. *Social Analysis: Linking Faith and Justice.* Maryknoll, NY: Orbis, 1983.

Hollenbach, David. *Claims in Conflict: Retrieving and Renewing the Catholic Human Rights Tradition.* New York: Paulist, 1979.

_____. *Justice, Peace, and Human Rights: American Catholic Social Ethics in a Pluralistic Context.* New York: Crossroad, 1988.

Houck, John W. and Oliver F. Williams, eds. *Catholic Social Teaching and the U.S. Economy: Working Papers for a Bishops' Pastoral.* Washington: University Press of America, 1984.

_____, eds. *Co-Creation and Capitalism: John Paul II's "Laborem Exercens".* Washington: University Press of America, 1983.

_____. *Full Value: Cases in Christian Business Ethics.* San Francisco: Harper & Row, 1978.

_____, eds. *The Judeo-Christian Vision and the Modern Corporation.* Notre Dame, IN: University of Notre Dame Press, 1982.

Husslein, Joseph. *The Christian Social Manifesto.* Milwaukee: Bruce, 1931.

_____. *The Church and Social Problems.* New York: America Press, 1912.

_____. *Social Wellsprings: Fourteen Epochal Documents by Pope Leo XIII.* Milwaukee: Bruce, 1940.

_____. *The World Problem: Capital, Labor and the Church.* New York: P.J. Kenedy & Sons, 1919.

Jahoda, Marie. *Employment and Unemployment: A Social-Psychological Analysis.* Cambridge: Cambridge University Press, 1982.

Kaiser, Edwin G. *Theology of Work.* Westminster, MD: Newman Press, 1966.

Kammer, Fred. *Doing Faithjustice: An Introduction to Catholic Social*

Thought. New York: Paulist, 1991.

Larson, Martin A. *When Parochial Schools Close: A Study in Educational Financing*. Washington: R.B. Luce, 1972.

Latourelle, Rene, ed. *Vatican II: Assessment and Perspectives Twenty Five Years After*. New York: Paulist, 1988.

Lawler, Philip F. *How Bishops Decide: An American Catholic Case Study*. Washington: Ethics and Public Policy Center, 1986.

Leftwich, Richard H. and Ansel M. Sharp. *Economics of Social Issues*. 4th ed. Dallas: Business Publications, 1980.

Liberato, C. Michael and Philip H. Schervich. *National Project on Just Wages and Benefits for Lay and Religious Church Employees*. Washington: National Conference of Diocesan Directors of Religious Education, 1990.

Lilly, William S., ed. *Characteristics from the Writings of Henry Edward Cardinal Manning*. London: Burns and Oates, 1885.

Maguire, Daniel C. *A New American Justice: Ending the White Male Monopolies*. Garden City, NY: Doubleday & Co., 1980.

Maida, Adam, ed. *Issues in the Labor-Management Dialogue: Church Perspectives*. St. Louis: Catholic Health Association, 1982.

Manning, Henry Cardinal. *The Catholic Church and Labor*. London: Catholic Truth Society, 1908.

Masse, Benjamin L., ed. *The Church and Social Progress: Background Readings for Pope John's "Mater et Magistra"*. Milwaukee: Bruce, 1966.

McCormick, Richard A. *The Critical Calling: Reflections on Moral Dilemmas Since Vatican II*. Washington: Georgetown University Press, 1989.

McEntee, Georgiana. *The Social Catholic Movement in Great Britain*. New York: Macmillan, 1927.

Messner, Johannes. *Social Ethics*. Rev. ed. Trans. by J.J. Doherty. St.

Louis: B. Herder, 1965.

Metlake, George. *Christian Social Reform: Program Outlined by its Pioneer William Emmanuel Baron von Ketteler.* Philadelphia: Dolphin Press, 1923.

Michel, Virgil. *Christian Social Reconstruction: Some Fundamentals of "Quadragesimo Anno".* Milwaukee: Bruce, 1937.

Miller, Amata. *Promises to Keep: Compensation for Religious in the United States.* Washington: United States Catholic Conference, 1989.

Miller, David. *Social Justice.* Oxford: Clarendon Press, 1976.

Misner, Paul. *Social Catholicism in Europe: From the Onset of Industrialization to the First World War.* New York: Crossroad, 1991.

Muller, Alois and Norbert Greinacher, eds. *The Church and the Rights of Man.* New York: Seabury, 1979.

National Association of Church Personnel Administrators. *Just Treatment for Those Who Work for the Church.* Cincinnati: National Association of Church Personnel Administrators, 1986.

_____. *Pathfinder for Compensation Systems: A NAPCA Working Paper.* Cincinnati: National Association of Church Personnel Administrators, 1990.

Naughton, Michael. *The Good Stewards: Practical Applications of the Papal Social Vision of Work.* Lanham, MD: University Press of America, 1992.

Neumann, Johannes. *Menschenrechte: Auch in der Kirche?* Zurich: Benziger, 1976.

1992 Church Compensation Report: Nationwide Comparison of Pay and Benefits for Full- and Part-Time Church Employees. Carol Stream, IL: Christianity Today, Inc., 1991.

Novak, Michael. *Freedom with Justice: Catholic Social Thought and Liberal Institutions.* San Francisco: Harper & Row, 1984.

_____. *Free Persons and the Common Good.* Lanham, MD: Madison

Books, 1989.

_____. *The Spirit of Democratic Capitalism.* New York: Simon & Schuster, 1982.

_____. *Toward a Theology of the Corporation.* Washington: American Enterprise Institute for Public Policy Research, 1981.

_____. *Will It Liberate? Questions about Liberation Theology.* New York: Paulist, 1986.

O'Brien, David J. and Thomas A. Shannon, eds. *Renewing the Earth: Catholic Documents on Peace, Justice and Liberation.* Garden City, NY: Doubleday & Co., 1977.

O'Brien, Kenneth R. *The Nature of Support of Diocesan Priests in the United States of America.* Canon Law Studies #286. Washington: Catholic University of America Press, 1949.

Overberg, Kenneth R. *An Inconsistent Ethic? Teaching of the American Catholic Bishops.* Lanham, MD: University Press of America, 1980.

Patten, Thomas H., Jr. *Pay: Employee Compensation and Incentive Plans.* New York: Free Press, 1977.

Pierce, Gregory F. Augustine, ed. *Of Human Hands: A Reader in the Spirituality of Work.* Minneapolis: Augsburg, 1991.

_____, ed. *On the Firing Line: The Manager's Perspective on the Issue of Terminations and Layoffs in the Light of Catholic Social Teaching.* Chicago: ACTA, 1990.

Pohier, Jacques and Dietmar Mieth, eds. *Unemployment and the Right to Work.* New York: Seabury, 1982.

Quade, Quentin L., ed. *The Pope and Revolution: John Paul II Confronts Liberation Theology.* Washington: Ethics and Public Policy Center, 1982.

Rahner, Karl. *Theological Investigations.* Vol. 2, Man in the Church. Trans. by Karl-H. Kruger. Baltimore: Helicon Press, 1963

Ramsey, Boniface. *Beginning to Read the Fathers.* New York: Paulist,

1985.

Rasmussen, Douglas and James Sterba. *The Catholic Bishops and the Economy: A Debate.* New Brunswick, NJ: Transaction Books, 1987.

Reissner, Edward. *Canonical Employer-Employee Relationship: Canon 1524.* Canon Law Studies # 427. Washington: Catholic University of America Press, 1964.

Ritter, Emil. *Die katholisch soziale Bewegung Deutschlands im neunzehnten Jahrhundert und der Volksverein.* Cologne: J.P. Bachem, 1954.

Rocha, Manuel. *Les Origines de "Quadragesimo Anno": Travail et Salaire A Travers La Scolastique.* Paris: Desclee, 1933.

Rottenberg, Simon, ed. *The Economics of Legal Minimum Wages.* Washington: American Enterprise Institute, 1981.

Royal, Robert, ed. *Challenge and Response: Critiques of the Catholic Bishops' Draft Letter on the U.S. Economy.* Washington: Ethics and Public Policy Center, 1985.

Ryan, John A. *Distributive Justice: The Right and Wrong of Our Present Distribution of Wealth.* 3rd ed. New York: Macmillan, 1920.

_____. *A Living Wage: Its Ethical and Economic Aspects.* New York: Macmillan, 1906.

_____. *Social Reconstruction.* New York: Macmillan, 1920.

_____. *The Church and Socialism, and Other Essays.* Washington: University Press, 1919.

_____ and Joseph Husslein. *The Church and Labor.* New York: Macmillan, 1920.

Saxton, Stanley L., Patricia Voydanoff, and Angela Ann Zukowski, eds. *The Changing Family: Views from Theology and the Social Sciences in the Light of the Apostolic Exhortation "Familiaris Consortio".* Chicago: Loyola University Press, 1984.

Schindler, Thomas F. *Ethics: The Social Dimension.* Wilmington, DE: Michael Glazier, 1989.

Shields, Leo W. *The History and Meaning of the Term Social Justice.* Notre Dame, IN: University of Notre Dame Press, 1941.

Schuck, Michael J. *That They Be One: The Social Teaching of the Papal Encyclicals 1740-1989.* Washington: Georgetown University Press, 1991.

Sibson, Robert E. *Compensation.* New York: American Management Association, 1974.

Smith, Sharon P. *Equal Pay in the Public Sector: Fact or Fantasy.* Princeton, NJ: Industrial Relations Sector, Princeton University, 1977.

Steidl-Meier, Paul. *Social Justice Ministry: Foundations and Concern.* New York: Le Jacq Publishing, 1984.

Strain, Charles R., ed. *Prophetic Visions and Economic Realities: Protestants, Jews, and Catholics Confront the Bishops' Letter on the Economy.* Grand Rapids, MI: William B. Eerdmans Publishing Company, 1989.

Sullivan, Patrick J. *U.S. Catholic Institutions and Labor Unions 1960-1980.* Lanham, MD: University Press of America, 1985.

Thomas Aquinas. *Summa Theologiae.* Trans. by Marcus Lefebure. Vol. 38, Blackfriars Edition. London: Eyre & Spottiswoode, 1975.

Toward the Future: Catholic Social Thought and the U.S. Economy. New York: Lay Commission on Catholic Social Teaching and the U.S. Economy, 1984.

von Nell-Breuning, Oswald. *Reorganization of Social Economy: The Social Encyclicals Developed and Explained.* Trans. by Bernard Dempsey. New York: Bruce, 1936.

Vorgrimler, Herbert, ed. *Commentary on the Documents of Vatican II.* 5 vols. New York: Herder and Herder, 1969.

United States Catholic Conference Ad Hoc Committee on Implementation of the Pastoral Letter on the U.S. Economy. *Research and Planning Resource for Diocesan Leaders: Wages and Benefits Booklet.* Washington: United States Catholic Conference, 1989.

Williams, Oliver F. and John W. Houck, eds. *The Common Good and U.S. Capitalism*. Lanham, MD: University Press of America, 1987.

Woelfel, La Salle, ed. *Catholic Thought in Business and Economics*. 2 vol. Austin, TX: St. Edward's University Press, 1961.

Wogaman, J. Philip. *The Great Economic Debate: An Ethical Analysis*. Philadelphia: Westminster, Press, 1977.

Wojtyla, Karol. *Sources of Renewal: The Implementation of the Second Vatican Council*. Trans. by P.S. Falla. San Francisco: Harper & Row, 1980.

Wood, Simon P., trans. *Clement of Alexandria: Christ the Educator*. New York: Fathers of the Church, Inc., 1954.

Woywood, Stanislaus. *The New Canon Law: A Commentary and Summary of the New Code of Canon Law*. New York: Joseph F. Wagner, 1918.

_____ and Callistus Smith. *A Practical Commentary on the Code of Canon Law*. 2 vols. New York: Joseph F. Wagner, 1952.

Yzermans, Vincent A., ed. *The Major Addresses of Pope Pius XII*. 2 vols. St. Paul, MN: North Central Publishing Co., 1961.

Articles

Baum, Gregory. "The Impact of Marxism on the Thought of John Paul II," *Thought* 62 (1987): 26-38.

Benestad, J. Brian. "The Catholic Concept of Social Justice: A Historical Perspective," *Communio* 11 (1984): 364-81.

_____. "The Political Vision of John Paul II: Justice through Faith and Culture," *Communio* 8 (1981): 3-19.

Blakely, Paul J. "The Marriage Encyclical and Wages," *America* 44 (1931): 384-386.

Bonifield, William C. and Edgar Mills. "The Clergy Labor Markets and Wage Determination," *Journal of Scientific Study of Religion* 19 (1980): 146-158.

Bookser-Feister, John. "The Struggle for Workplace Justice," *The Other Side* 21 (1985): 46-49.

Calvez, Jean-Yves. "The Church and the Economy," *Chicago Studies* 25 (1986): 177-88.

Curran, Charles E. "Catholic Social and Sexual Teaching: A Methodological Comparison," *Theology Today* 44 (1988): 425-40.

Daly, William P. "A Theoretical Framework for a Just Wage," *Church Personnel Issues* (November 1992): 1-11.

Dorr, Donal. "John XXIII and Options for the Poor," *Irish Theological Quarterly* 47 (1980): 247-271.

Faley, Roland J. "The Financial Compensation of Religious," *Review for Religious* 49 (1990): 391-6.

Fogarty, Michael P. "The Catholic Theory of the Family Living Wage," *Review of Social Economy* 15 (1957): 91-103.

_____. "The Philosophy of Fringes," *Review of Social Economy* 16 (1958): 119-138.

Fonseca, Aloysius. "Reflections on the Encyclical Letter *Sollicitudo Rei Socialis*," *Gregorianum* 70 (1989): 5-24.

Glover, Veronica. "Justice for Teachers," *Momentum* 10 (October 1979): 14-17.

Greathouse, Gordon. "First Look at Religion and Labor from the 1920s to the 1960s," *Radical Religion* 4 (1978): 3-51.

Grosschmid, Geza B. "Pesch's Concept of the Living Wage in *Quadragesimo Anno*," *Review of Social Economy* 12 (1954): 147-155.

Guerin, Joseph R. "The Just Wage and the Two Earner Family," *International Journal of Social Economics* 16 (1989): 5-8.

Hanson, Bertil L. "Just Wage in America," *Christian Century* 93 (1976): 1169-74.

Higgins, George G. "Bargaining Rights of Catholic School Teachers,"

Origins 9 (1979): 177-81.

_____. "Economic Crisis and the Rights of Labor," *Origins* 10 (1980): 183-84.

_____. "Unions and Catholic Institutions," *America* 142 (1980): 54-56.

Hinze, Christine Firer. "Bridge Discourse on Wage Justice: Roman Catholic and Feminist Perspectives on the Family Living Wage," *Annual of the Society of Christian Ethics* (1991): 109-132.

Hoffman, Nicholas von. "Papal Economics," *The New Republic* (November 4, 1981): 18-21.

Hollenbach, David. "John Courtney Murray's Unfinished Agenda," *Theological Studies* 40 (1979): 700-15.

Joros, Helmut. "The Object of the Theology of Work," *Communio* 11 (1984): 136-144.

Kelly, B. "Towards a Theology of Work," *Irish Theological Quarterly* 36 (1969): 315-26.

Kelly, John J. "The Silence about Subsidiarity," *America* 145 (1981): 382-83.

LaMagdeleine, Donald R. "Expanding a Dual Labor Market Approach to Catholic Church Work: Comment on Wittberg," *Review of Religious Research* 30 (1989): 291-294.

_____. "U.S. Catholic Church-Related Jobs as Dual Labor Markets: A Speculative Inquiry," *Review of Religious Research* 27 (1986): 315-327.

Langan, Thomas. "The Changing Nature of Work in the World System." *Communio* 11 (1984): 120-135.

Levin, Michael. "Comparable Worth: The Feminist Road to Socialism," *Commentary* 78 (1984): 13-19.

Lo, Ping-Cheung. "Are There Economic Rights?" *Thomist* 52 (1988): 703-717.

Lynch, Thomas J. "Labor Unions in Catholic Institutions," *Origins* 10 (1980): 363-65.

McManus, William E. "Pay Them Well," *Momentum* 23 (1992): 24-26.

O'Grady, John F. "The Biblical Doctrine of Work," *Chicago Studies* 28 (1989): 65-78.

Paulhus, Normand J. "Uses and Misuses of the term 'Social Justice' in the Roman Catholic Tradition," *Journal of Religious Ethics* 15 (1987): 261-82.

"Paying Workers What They're Worth," [editorial] *Christianity and Crisis* 45 (1985): 243-44.

Philadelphia Pastors Committee. "Philadelphia Pastors Committee on Teachers' Rights and Responsibility," *Origins* 7 (1978): 561-66.

Provost, James H. "Ecclesial Rights." *Proceedings of the 44th Annual Convention of the Canon Law Society of America* (October 1982): 41-62.

Reicher, Robert. "Collective Bargaining and Catholic Schools," *The NCEA Bulletin* 64 (1967): 3-10.

Roos, Lothar. "On a Theology and Ethics of Work," *Communio* 11 (1984): 100-119.

Ryan, John A. "Cardinal Mermillod and the Union of Fribourg," *America* 45 (1931): 200-201.

_____. "Just Wages and 'Rerum Novarum'," *America* 45 (1931): 105-106.

Sandoz, A. "La Notion de Juste Prix," *Revue Thomiste* 45 (1939): 285-309.

Steinkamp, Kathleen. "The Search for Equitable Compensation for Religion Teaching in Catholic Schools," *Momentum* (1985).

Sullivan, Patrick. "The Churches and the Unions," *America* 140 (1979): 473-4.

_____ and Charles E. Craypo. "Workers' Rights in Catholic Institutions," *America* 144 (1983):

Trubac, Edward. "Competitive Salaries and Community Needs," *Sisters Today* (1977).

United States Catholic Conference. "Teachers' Unions in Catholic Schools," *Origins* 7 (1977): 225-30.

_____. "The Government and Catholic School Teachers," *Origins* 8 (1978): 214-18.

"Wages and Religion," *Christian Century* 102 (1985): 464-65.

Williamson, Clark M. "Notes on a Theology of Work," *Encounter* 37 (1976): 294-307.

Wittberg, Patricia. "The Dual Labor Market in the Catholic Church: Expanding a Speculative Inquiry," *Review of Religious Research* 30 (1989): 291-294.

Woodward, Judith L. "Is the Church Playing Fair as an Employer?" *Engage/Social Action* 4 (1976): 49-53.

Unpublished Dissertations

Berkley, Harlan Roy. *Economic Justice in Pluralistic Society: Study in Christian Social Ethics.* Ph.D., Vanderbilt University, 1978.

Callahan, John D. *The Catholic Attitude Toward a Familial Living Wage.* S.T.D., Catholic University of America, 1936.

Donlon, James I. *The Human Rights of Priests to Equitable Sustenance and Mobility: An Evaluation of Canon Law from the 'CIC' to the Proposed Revision of the Code of Canon Law.* Canon Law Studies #510. J.C.D., Catholic University of America, 1984.

Elsbernd, Mary. *Papal Statements on Rights: A Historical Contextual Study of Encyclical Teaching from Pius VI to Pius XI (1791-1939).* S.T.D., Catholic University of Louvain, 1985.

Fessola, Anthony George. *Justice and Ownership: A Procedural Theory of Entitlement.* Ph.D., Columbia University, 1978.

Hoffman, Eric Edward. *Justice in Theory and Practice.* Ph.D., University of Pennsylvania, 1978.

Ihne, Robert Wayne. *A Critique of Three Recent Attempts to Delimit the Boundaries of Distributive Justice Within the Moral Domain.* Ph.D., Columbia University, 1978.

Leonard, Joan de Lourdes. *Catholic Attitudes Toward American Labor, 1884-1919.* M.A., Catholic University of America, 1940.

McCabe, Clarence. *The Background of "Rerum Novarum".* M.A., Catholic University of America, 1941.

Murphy, Orlando Mari. *Il Lavoro e il Salario nella Teologia Morale del XVII. e XVIII secolo.* S.T.D., Gregorianium Pontifical University, 1962.

Nagelback, Michael Andrew. *Justice and Medical Care.* Ph.D., University of Illinois at Chicago Circle, 1978.

O'Grady, John. *A Legal Minimum Wage.* S.T.D., Catholic University of America, 1915.

Roohan, James Edmund. *American Catholics and the Social Question: 1865-1900.* Ph.D., Yale University, 1952.

Smith, Rosemary. *The Right of Lay Employees to Form Labor Unions.* J.C.L., Catholic University of America, 1981.

Von Magnus, Eric. *Theories of Economic Justice: Utilitarians and Rawls.* Ph.D., Syracuse University, 1978.